Series Editors:
Dario Castiglione (University of Exeter) and
Vincent Hoffmann-Martinot (Sciences Po Bordeaux)

widen the market, narrow the competition

banker interests and the making of a european capital market

Daniel Mügge

© Daniel Mügge 2010

First published by the ECPR Press in 2010

The ECPR Press is the publishing imprint of the European Consortium for Political Research (ECPR), a scholarly association, which supports and encourages the training, research and cross-national cooperation of political scientists in institutions throughout Europe and beyond. The ECPR's Central Services are located at the University of Essex, Wivenhoe Park, Colchester, CO4 3SQ, UK

All rights reserved. No part of this book may be reprinted or reproduced or utilised in any form or by any electronic, mechanical, or other means, now known or hereafter invented, including photocopying and recording, or in any information storage or retrieval system, without permission in writing from the publishers.

Typeset by the ECPR Press
Printed and bound by Lightning Source

British Library Cataloguing in Publication Data
A catalogue record for this book is available from the British Library

Paperback ISBN: 978-1-9073010-8-7

www.ecprnet.eu/ecprpress

To Liza, my love and academic partner in crime

Merchants and master manufacturers are, in this order, the two classes of people who commonly employ the largest capitals, and who by their wealth draw to themselves the greatest share of the public consideration. As during their whole lives they are engaged in plans and projects, they have frequently more acuteness of understanding than the greater part of country gentlemen. [T]heir thoughts, however, are commonly exercised rather about the interest of their own particular branch of business, than about that of the society [..]. Their superiority over the country gentleman is not so much in their knowledge of the public interest, as in their having a better knowledge of their own interest than he has of his. It is by this superior knowledge of their own interest that they have frequently imposed upon his generosity, and persuaded him to give up both his own interest and that of the public, from a very simple but honest conviction that their interest, and not his, was the interest of the public. The interest of the dealers, however, in any particular branch of trade or manufactures, is always in some respects different from, and even opposite to, that of the public. To widen the market and to narrow the competition, is always the interest of the dealers. [..] The proposal of any new law or regulation of commerce which comes from this order ought always to be listened to with great precaution, and ought never to be adopted till after having been long and carefully examined, not only with the most scrupulous, but with the most suspicious attention.

Adam Smith, 1776
The Wealth of Nations, Chapter XI

acknowledgements

In early September 2009 the European Consortium for Political Research first informed me of its decision to award my dissertation the Jean Blondel prize of that year. Needless to say, I felt honoured and grateful. My indebtedness to the ECPR Press multiplied when its team managed to turn a significantly revised version of the manuscript into this book in less than a year. That said, they only finalised a project that had been in the making for years, and for which thanks are owed to a wide range of colleagues and friends.

Geoffrey Underhill first introduced me to money and finance as political artefacts. More than anyone else's, his view on political economy has impregnated my own. Far beyond being just one domain of inquiry among others in the social sciences, it is a way of seeing and understanding social reality. The immodesty that speaks from this vision has always appealed to me, because in spite of the unavoidably circumscribed scope of concrete research projects, it imposes few limits on intellectual curiosity.

Brian Burgoon's part in this project goes beyond invaluable academic advice, offered without reserve. In spite of my undoubted failings measured by this standard, his admonition to strive for arguments that are no less than crystal clear has served as a guiding light ever since I grasped its centrality for scholarship. From him I learned that faith in one's own academic convictions need not, indeed should not preclude a sincere curiosity for those views that differ, no matter how fundamentally.

Both of them are now my colleagues at the Amsterdam Institute for Social Science Research (formerly ASSR) at the University of Amsterdam (UvA). Others there equally deserve thanks. Arne Niemann provided precious criticism from an EU integration-perspective. Years earlier, present-day colleagues Jeffrey Harrod and Otto Holman put me on the political economy track in the first place, combining scholarly prowess with normative convictions: whether we like it or not, political science is just that—a political science, and not just the science of politics. The most recent, but not least important, to my UvA environment has been Bart Stellinga, whose research assistance was crucial to updating the material in this book.

The International Political Economy club at the ASSR brought together young, enthusiastic scholars from both Amsterdam universities whose dedication to each others work has been a constant source of inspiration. This sense of purpose emerged most clearly from my countless discussions with James Perry, invariably over a beer in one of Amsterdam's many cosy cafés.

The ASSR hosted me and my project for more than four years. I have always experienced the generosity with which it has funded my intellectual curiosity as a great privilege for which I remain deeply thankful, not least to its staff, particularly Hans Sonneveld and José Komen.

External support has allowed me to venture beyond the Netherlands. First and foremost, this has come through the GARNET Network of Excellence, financed by the EU's 6th Framework Programme and managed by Eleni Tsingou with her seemingly inexhaustible goodwill. Also the Economic and Social Research Council of the UK, the Studienstiftung des deutschen Volkes and the Deutscher Akademischer Austauschdienst have contributed to my studies and research in ways for which I remain more than grateful.

When I interviewed policymakers, bankers and financial experts for this project, I invariably promised them confidentiality in return for the generosity with which they shared their insights and knowledge. This pledge keeps me from thanking them here in person. Nevertheless, the more than 50 interviewees in London, Paris, Berlin, Brussels, Frankfurt, Zurich and The Hague who took time and energy to answer my questions have provided a crucial component of this research. Beyond that, they have granted me a glimpse of a world that I find as fascinating today as I found it almost a decade years ago – however much the climate in investment banking has changed.

Thanks are also reserved for Jörn-Carsten Gottwald. Having done research in the same area as I, he freely shared his contacts and insights. Most importantly, he provided me with the manuscript of his unpublished German – , which proved a valuable resource for this book.

Takeo David Hymans deserves a special place among my long-time companions. He edited the original manuscript from beginning to end in record time, nevertheless not compromising his own quality standards.

Inevitably, my deepest thanks go to my family. The hallmark of the manifold contributions Mechthild and Wilhelm Mügge have made to this project is that it expects neither reward nor thanks. That may be for the better, because no amount of gratitude can measure up against my indebtedness to them.

That is even more true for Liza. Thanking her for all her patience, advice and comfort easily seems like taking stock at the end of a completed project – even though it is but one small step in the building our common future.

Finally, Kolja and Romy have challenged me to give this project a place in the 'real world' – both in my own life but also with respect to the society in which they will grow up. For better or worse, the financial crisis of the last years have re-politicised financial regulation and exposed just how much is at stake in this field. If by the time my children will be able to read this book, it still contains what they consider valuable lessons, it will have been time and energy well spent.

Amsterdam
April 2010

contents

List of Figures and Tables	viii
Chapter One: Introduction	1
Established Approaches and their Limits	3
The Argument: Banker Interests in EU Capital Markets	7
Chapter Two: Competition Politics and Supranational Integration	13
European Integration	13
Financial Market Liberalisation and Regulation	18
Private and Public Actors in Regulatory Policy	22
The Competition Politics Approach	25
The Core Features of the Approach	29
Chapter Three: The Domestic Roots of Regulatory Reform	31
European Capital Markets at the End of the 1980s	32
Regulatory Reform in German Managed Capitalism	35
Regulatory Reform in French State-led Capitalism	40
Regulatory Reform in British Market Capitalism	44
European State-market Condominiums in Comparison	49
Chapter Four: Negotiating the Single Market	51
Financial Services in the Single Market Project	52
Negotiating a European Market in Investment Services	58
Competitive Fault Lines and Intergovernmental Politics	67
Chapter Five: The 1990s' Capital Market Revolution in Europe	69
Measuring Change in EU Investment Banking Markets	70
Market Concentration as a Source of Economic and Political Power	72
The Rise of Capital Markets and Investment Banking in Europe	74
Explaining Internationalisation	80
European Bourses: From Members-only Clubs to Profit-Seeking Firms	88
Chapter Six: The Re-launch of Financial Market Integration	93
Shifting Industry Preferences in the 1990s	94
The Emergence of EU-level Lobbying	98
EU Action and Industry-Commission Contacts Ahead of the FSAP	102
The FSAP, the ISD and the Forum Groups	106
Chapter Seven: The Emergence of Supranational Governance	109
Supranational Cooperation before Lamfalussy	110

Launching Institutional Change	111
Negotiating Lamfalussy	113
Supranational Governance in Practice	120
Industry Interests and Institutional Reform	122
Chapter Eight: Renegotiating the ISD in the Supranational Constellation	125
European Lobbying Transformed	126
Lamfalussy in Action: Renegotiating the ISD	133
Clearing and Settlement: the Persistence of National Competition Politics	139
The supranational constellation in EU capital market governance	141
Chapter Nine: Conclusion	143
Banker Interests in EU Capital Market Integration	143
EU Capital Market Governance and The Crisis	148
Governing Finance in the Interest of All?	151
Appendices	155
Overview of the International Expansion of European Banks	155
References	159
List of Interviews	176
Index	179

LIST OF FIGURES AND TABLES

Figures

Figure 2.1: Actors and the political economy environment they confront and shape	25
Figure 2.2: A schematic depiction of EU financial market structuration	28
Figure 3.1: Financial structures in 1991	32
Figure 3.2: Economic relevance of financial sectors in 1985	34
Figure 5.1: The stock market boom	74
Figure 5.2: Germany: financial structure	76
Figure 5.3: France: financial structure	76
Figure 5.4: UK: financial structure	76
Figure 5.5: Securitisation of large commercial bank business	82
Figure 5.6: Comparing large commercial banks with banks in general, Germany	82

Tables

Table 3.1: Financial systems and their embeddedness compared	50
Table 6.1: Hypothetical policy preferences of firms	95

chapter one | introduction

ABN AMRO is a boring bank. The national champion of Dutch financial services serves mostly domestic customers in the Netherlands. Its investment banking outlet in the City of London has the feel of a forlorn trading outpost on a far-away shore. Profits are mediocre, executive remuneration meagre by Wall Street or City standards. ABN AMRO today looks much like it did when it was created in 1990 out of a merger of two mid-sized Dutch banks. A time-traveller jumping from 1990 to 2010 could be forgiven for concluding that she had skipped two decades of stasis and continuity.

How wrong she would be. In the mid-2000s, ABN AMRO had managed to free itself from the shackles of stale, traditional banking. It had built an international banking empire, reaching from Brazil to East Asia. Its market capitalisation had sky-rocketed. Real profits no longer came from faithful savers in the Dutch hinterland, but from round-the-clock traders in London's financial district. The Dutch bank had transmogrified into a modern, glittering investment bank and was at the vanguard of the financial services revolution sweeping the globe. But this transformation was not to last. After 2007 ABN AMRO, and many of its peers, fell from grace, in the process flooring the global economy. Only with unheard-of, and arguably reckless, fiscal deficits did governments prevent financial annihilation at the eleventh hour.

This book is not about ABN AMRO itself. It is about the financial industry in Europe as a whole. But the fate of the Dutch bank illustrates as well as any other the roller coaster of ambition, hope, expansion, hubris and eventual failure that characterised the financial industry in Europe over the two decades between 1990 and 2010. Since the meltdown of the financial sector, much ink has been spilt about unsustainable and outright toxic business models (e.g. Augar 2009) and the questionable practices of individual firms. These accounts, however, generally ignore the fact that banking did not transform in a vacuum. What banks do, where they do it, and how profitably, largely depends on the rules they must follow. Pan-European financial empires could never have been built if financial rules had not been stretched, bended, amended or simply abolished since 1990. The evolution of European banking is a story of financial governance as much as one of corporate strategies.

One aspect of this financial governance – the fragmentation of rules across the Continent – was a particular hurdle to the growth and internationalisation of European banks. In a world of split-second, computer-driven banking and investment, regulatory disparities between jurisdictions were the ultimate barrier to truly transnational finance empires; a single European rule set was a *sine qua non* for the consequent overhaul of banking. And as became clear quite quickly, no unified European rulebook could emerge without centralised policy-making and administration. By this logic, the transformation of banking exemplified by ABN AMRO hinged on the 'uploading' of political powers to Brussels. The supranational governance of financial markets was indispensable for the transformation of European finance: without it, banks would have largely remained stuck in their national markets.

It is the story of this 'uploading' of powers to Brussels that is recounted by this book. The novelty of supranational governance lies in its supplanting of national rule-making, thereby calling into question the viability of national varieties of capitalism and the socio-economic compromises these traditionally sustained. National financial market policies were always formulated within international contexts, just as domestic financial markets were embedded in global ones. But until roughly a decade ago, financial market governance could, without misrepresenting reality, be divided into domestic and international components – a domestic policy process and national laws on the one hand, and international bargaining and agreements on the other. Back then, domestic and international politics fit the image of two-level games (Putnam 1988), with governments translating the results of domestic deliberation into international negotiations.

The inclusion of investment services in the single market programme (to be completed in 1992) did little to change the structure of the two-level game. Member state negotiations over a single European capital market were acrimonious (Steil 1993; Brown 1997; Underhill 1997). By 1992 no rules had been agreed, let alone implemented. The deal that was eventually struck defied the spirit of the single market programme. Officially, financial firms were granted the freedom to operate throughout the European Union (EU) under home-country rules. Ideally, a German bank should have been able to buy Belgian stocks on the Paris bourse for a Portuguese customer through its London branch, all using German rules. But the small print of the 1993 Investment Services Directive (ISD) told a different story: governments could still require foreign firms to observe local conduct of business rules. In contrast to traditional banking and insurance, where significant regulatory strides towards a single market were taken around 1990, capital markets remained the prerogative of member states. A bank doing business in all twelve member states still battled with twelve different rule books.

A decade and a half later, there is no longer a neat division between the domestic and international levels in the governance of European capital markets. Few facets of capital markets today remain untouched by EU rules. In 2004 the patchy ISD was replaced by the all-encompassing Market in Financial Instruments Directive (MiFID), containing detailed rules on most aspects of capital markets, thus effectively harmonising regulation across the continent. The liberty of national authorities to impose local rules on foreign operators has disappeared. The institutions governing capital markets have also been overhauled. In 2001 member states installed two new EU committees to strengthen supranational governance. One of these, the Committee of European Securities Regulators, has since become a core player in EU capital market politics, even if officially its role has mostly been advisory. National parliaments have borne the brunt of this reshuffling of power; in effect, they have been relegated to rubber-stamping policy handed down to them from Brussels.

While global economic developments clearly contributed to regional integration and the reform of national models of capitalism (Glyn 2006), globalisation by itself did not spell the end of national diversity or pre-determine regional integration (Schmidt 2002). The supranationalisation and harmonisation of capital market governance was a question of political choice, not of economic necessity. The main question this book seeks to answer is what explains this choice.

This book's analysis of two decades of EU capital market politics can be distilled into four core claims. First, the politics of capital market integration was dominated by a small group of political insiders: the changing political preferences of financial firms were ultimately responsible for the scope and timing of integration. Second, firms' political preferences were inspired by the impact of regulation on the terms of competition between them, rather than, for example, immediate profits. Ultimately, a firm's fate depends on whether it can keep up with its competitors; it is this consideration that informs corporate lobbying as to how and by whom the financial sector is to be governed. Third, supranational integration can only be understood by examining both how agents create structures (collectively binding rules, political institutions and markets), and how these structures simultaneously shape agents' preferences. Even if this argument is widely accepted theoretically, this book provides a rare empirical illustration. Finally, such 'structuration' yields a political economy dynamic wherein outcomes remain open-ended and are fraught with unintended consequences and contradictions. The financial crisis and the implosion of what was to be the golden age of European investment banking is only the starkest illustration of this point.

ESTABLISHED APPROACHES AND THEIR LIMITS

The aim of this book is to understand why power over capital markets has shifted from national capitals to Brussels and why governments have chosen to open up financial markets and harmonise regulation with other countries. In our search for answers, we might expect two strands of academic literature to offer particular insight: studies of European integration and studies of financial market governance.

Theorists of European integration have sought to understand why and under what conditions political authority is relocated to higher levels of political aggregation – why, in other words, governments choose to 'pool' their sovereignty (Keohane and Hoffman 1991) and delegate authority to supranational bodies, thereby creating multi-level structures of governance (see Rosamond 2000, Hooghe and Marks 2001, Wiener and Diez 2004). Two questions have proven especially contentious: first, can integration theory say anything systematic about the conditions under which governments find integration desirable? And second, how does past integration affect future integration?

The most common answer to the first question – one that is shared with much regime theory (Krasner 1983, Hasenclever *et al.* 1997) – is that governments integrate policy-making when they face common problems that can be solved more efficiently or effectively through a bundling of forces (Scharpf 1997b, 1999). But it remains unclear where and how problems are defined. Neofunctionalist approaches (drawing on Haas 1958 as well as Schmitter 1970) often suggest that nation states simply face them and have clear ideas about desirable solutions (Niemann 2006 is an exception). In many policy areas, however, both the nature of common 'problems' and desirable 'solutions' are far from obvious (Adler 1991, Hall 1993). In a field as complex as the governance of capital markets, government preferences are not simply given; their origins need explaining. Scholars who focus on the 'problem-solving capacity' of supranational governance also seldom specify *whose* concerns are actually addressed through integration and why some issues (and not others) are considered important. Certainly in the economic sphere, different social groups are likely to have different, if not conflicting, interests. The precise process of how national governments aggregate domestic preferences remains unclear.

In addition, regional integration – especially in an organisation as complex as the European Union – is prone to producing unintended effects (Pierson 1996). Institutional outcomes do not necessarily reflect the interests of those actors who effected institutional change in the first place (Pierson 2000b). This makes it impossible to identify political input into supranational institutions and divine the core agents behind such input from the effects the new institutions generate. We require an approach that traces the actual political process that brought about integration, thereby identifying core actors and the specific contexts and compromises that shaped regulatory and institutional outcomes.

In line with neofunctionalist reasoning (e.g. Schmitter 1970), past integration may lead domestic actors to develop transnational identities, potentially based on their material interests. Such actors may then push national governments towards further integration – transnational business associations would be a case in point (Cowles 2001). As Feld wrote in 1970:

> [a]nother by-product [of previous integration] is the gradual emergence of an expanding, relatively young, Europe oriented business elite as the result of the subtle political socialization process operative in the coordinating mechanisms of collaborating entities. [...] [T]hey may be in time influential, through cross-communication with other elites, in soliciting support by the member governments for harmonization measures and for the community system in general. (Feld 1970: 237)

Feld and his intellectual successors, however, did not sufficiently specify when such a business elite would push in this direction, and, even more importantly, why governments would heed its call.

In sum, theories of European integration have tended to underspecify either the motivations behind supranational governance or the actual processes through which diffuse social preferences are translated into institutional change. At the same time, they have not offered a general theory explaining when past integration generates further integration. These shortcomings are not necessarily material defects. But they do invite deeper empirical examination of the actual political process propelling integration, as well as exploration of other sources of theoretical guidance to understand fully the dynamics of this process.

The second stream of relevant scholarship centres on financial governance. Actors with a stake in substantive rules (financial market regulation in this case) can be expected to take an active interest in procedural rules (policy-making institutions) as the latter preconfigure the former (Milner and Keohane 1996: 4). The logic of this argument extends to multi-level governance, pointing to the link between the supranationalisation of rule-making procedures and financial market opening itself. The question is what inspired member states to opt for collective market liberalisation in the late 1990s when only years earlier they had undermined Commission efforts to move capital market rules in the same direction.

Market liberalisation has not been exclusive to the European Union. As Pauly already found in the late 1980s:

> [i]f relevant [financial market] policies are grouped and compared along a theoretical spectrum ranging from closure and discrimination to openness and nondiscrimination, by the 1980s most states of the OECD moved decisively in the latter direction. (Pauly 1988: 5)

Since then, financial liberalisation has continued apace (Williamson and Mahar 1998), as have efforts by scholars to explain it (e.g. Quinn and Inclan 1997, Simmons 2001, Simmons and Elkins 2004). The Europeanisation of capital market governance, however, is not easily squared with the common approach of the scholarship. Almost all studies of financial liberalisation, including those dealing with European cases, conceive of market liberalisation as a unilateral, national-level affair (see, however, Singer 2004, Bach and Newman 2007, Posner 2009a). This country-level focus of many studies narrows the range of eligible explanations to interactions between domestic and 'systemic' factors such as technological change or capital mobility. Few studies seriously consider plurilateral or multilateral negotiation as sources of liberalisation and thus ignore a central channel through which governments 'make markets'.

Yet financial market opening is often conditional upon the actions of other governments, as shown by examples from the Pacific region and the World Trade Organisation (WTO) (Pauly 1988, Underhill 1993, Sauvé and Gillespie 2000). This is even more the case in the EU, where almost all market opening has been negotiated and reciprocal. Much of the existing scholarship is thus doubly limited by disregarding international negotiations and bargaining as a source of market opening, as well as the possibility of governments building supranational institutions to address policy concerns as an alternative to unilateral policy change.

With these caveats in mind, what driving forces behind financial liberalisation have scholars identified that may help explain the supranationalisation of EU capital market governance? Roughly, five answers emerge from the literature: capital mobility, technological innovation, regulatory capture, government-led adaptation, and competition between domestic firms. All arguments are attractive but also have their weaknesses.

Arguments about capital mobility as a driving force have two flaws. First, capital mobility itself is never properly accounted for. Rather than being exogenous, capital mobility is the result of various policy measures that facilitate the movement of capital across borders. In effect, such arguments explain public policy outcomes (the opening of financial markets) with earlier public policy outcomes (introducing capital mobility) without ever examining in detail the underlying political processes and compromises involved. Such approaches furthermore remain insensitive to the structuration of the political economy: market structures may influence government policy, but government policy also clearly affects market structures. It is far from obvious that one ontologically precedes the other.

The technology argument has similar flaws. Undoubtedly, technology matters greatly to financial markets as we know them today (Lee 1998). Yet technology does not simply push market developments in one direction or the other. Why is the efficiency-enhancing potential of technology exploited in some instances but not in others? Technology makes market restructuring *possible,* but it does not in itself explain why it happens in one case but not in another. In addition, most information technology in financial markets is proprietary. It is a tool box that market participants use to attain their goals. This makes it a weak explanation for market changes to which public policy might 'adapt'. Indeed, governments themselves can use regulation to limit the application of technology. For example, European stock exchanges were traditionally not allowed to place trading screens in other countries, even though this had long been possible. System-level properties, such as capital mobility or technological progress, as sources of policy change thus have little meaning without examining why actors introduce or obstruct them. They offer little to the explanation as to why governments might favour supranationalisation and cross-border integration over national governance and control.

From a normative perspective, the regulation of domestic financial markets provides public goods (see Vittas 1992, Herring and Litan 1995, Goodhart *et al.* 1998). Even a cursory reading of the evidence, however, suggests that regulatory politics involves more than debate over the optimal production of public goods. Empirically, regulation is rarely a question of the state reining in market excess. Regulation is, instead, jointly produced by public and private actors, while regulatory policy reflects diverse societal interests (Braithwaite and Drahos 2000, Clarke 2000). Sceptics argue that this makes 'regulatory capture' possible. Building on Stigler's (1971) classic account, regulation in this perspective is contested primarily between producers and consumers. The latter systematically lose out to the former, as Stigler argues that producers have a high stake in regulation and make more determined efforts to influence policy. Due to their smaller numbers, producers can also organise more easily. The combination of these two reasons tilts regulation in their favour. In securities markets, however, the line between consumers and producers is fuzzy at best. Many large financial conglomerates fulfil a range of functions: they act as investment vehicles, analysts, have stakes in clearing houses and securities exchanges, arrange initial public offerings, etc. They are simultaneously consumer and producer, often in overlapping products. The only consumers that truly deserve the label are retail customers. Stigler's theory predicts, probably correctly, that they regularly lose out in market regulation. But this says little about the effect of regulatory politics on the more complicated categories. More worryingly, it is not easily squared with market opening: if producers were still in charge, why would they want to invite foreign competition?

Vogel's insight (1996) that 'freer markets' tend to need 'more rules' has compounded the problem. Effective market liberalisation takes more than just deregulation. From liberalisation's emphasis on *enforcing* competition in domestic markets, Vogel concludes that governments must have had more room for manoeuvre than theorists of regulatory capture grant them. In his view, governments update regulatory systems to keep up with changing environments. Still, the question remains why governments, allegedly in charge, would choose to harmonise rules and surrender national autonomy in financial market policy-making.

Finally, Sobel (1994) has argued that conflicts over regulatory reform are not fought out between the producers and consumers of financial services (as stated by Stigler), nor between banks and international investors (Laurence 2001), nor between governments and national financial industries (Vogel 1996). Instead, the domestic producers of financial services struggle over regulation to either protect their own turf (in the case of market incumbents) or to invade that of others (in the case of market challengers). Sobel's approach, however, is not easily applied to countries that traditionally have no division between banking and capital markets (for example Germany or, to a lesser degree, France).

More importantly, it cannot accommodate the supranationalisation of policy-making and the emergence of multi-level forms of governance. Depending on the dynamic hypothesised to lie behind liberalisation, such supranationalisation could play very different roles: is it a bulwark against the corrosive effects of global economic pressures, for example regulatory competition? Is it a vehicle for governments to optimally update their regulatory systems? If so, why would they harmonise policy and surrender autonomy? As pointed out earlier, EU member states in the early 1990s were loath to do either; in many policy fields, this remains the case. Why, then, the shift towards supranational policy-making?

THE ARGUMENT: BANKER INTERESTS IN EU CAPITAL MARKETS

This book argues that the supranationalisation of EU capital market governance can best be explained by the shifting preferences of and alliances between a small group of private actors – banks and investment banks active in capital markets – and their public sector interlocutors. The political preferences of these private actors were formed in response to the expected impact of regulatory and institutional change on their competitive positions. Firms' preferences shifted in favour of European integration as their market environment changed; whereas many had previously preferred regulatory protectionism, they began to perceive competitive advantages in transnational market integration. This market transformation was itself the result of the regulatory changes that private-public coalitions had pushed through since the mid-1980s.

The 'competition politics' that lies at the heart of the supranationalisation of EU capital market governance – firms using their political power to manage competition through regulation – are an instance of social structuration (Giddens 1984) where actors collectively and interactively shape the environment that they confront. This process extends to the political institutions where regulation is made:

agents try to influence the institutions, anticipating their effects on rule-making.

How does competition politics account for the supranationalisation of capital market governance in the EU? Firms care about regulation because it structures the competitive environment, that is, it sets the terms of competition between them. Regulation shapes markets, and economic agents have diverse preferences in this regard. Around 1990 continental European banks were focused largely on their domestic markets. Only the American investment banks conducting their business from London had significant European operations and clear ambitions to expand them. Weighing the benefits of effective cross-border integration (market access abroad) against its costs (heightened competition in home markets), most continental firms preferred a protectionist regime over true market opening. Nationally idiosyncratic rules and national discretion were thus left intact.

Deteriorating profit margins in the credit business, a global stock market boom and growing, if limited, international market openness triggered a strategic reorientation among many large banks in Europe in the 1990s. Many of these banks developed European, if not global, ambitions, and they discovered capital markets as a source of profits in their own right. The banks' preferences shifted in favour of EU market integration and reduced transaction costs for cross-border operations, and hence in favour of rule harmonisation and increased supranational governance.

How could such a small group of firms command such influence over capital market governance? Banks' regulatory preferences only matter to the extent that they are successful in translating them into public policy. The institutional power (Barnett and Duvall 2005) that enables banks to effect this translation derives from their central position in national economies. The state and society at large have an interest in well-functioning and stable financial systems, and, for better or worse, this includes thriving banks which constitute the core of financial systems. States are much more likely to listen to the business concerns of banks than to those of firms in other sectors. This access to policy-making is a generalisable power resource that banks can use for a wide range of purposes.

This book does not argue that governments – or the European Commission, for that matter – were puppets of the financial industry. It does argue, however, that as one among many stakeholders in capital market policy, banks have had power resources at their disposal that have given their interests disproportionate weight in policy-making. Bankers have been the central private actors in the public-private alliances that first obstructed and later pushed for market integration by political means.

Banks of various national origins active in EU capital markets have not always held similar preferences. Indeed, their conflicting interests largely explain the restrictive regime that emerged in the early 1990s. But during that decade, a consensus in favour of cross-border market access emerged among the top banks as well as the large bourses. With more than 90 per cent of the EU capital market business concentrated in the hands of less than two dozen firms, agreement among them constituted a de facto industry consensus. Through their privileged access to government policy, this consensus informed government opinion to a degree that would have been unthinkable in most other sectors.

Financial firms trumped other stakeholders in Brussels as well. As they developed pro-integration preferences, they discovered the European Commission, and later the European Parliament (EP), to be natural allies. Neither of these organisations needed to be convinced of the desirability of further integration. Firms nevertheless lobbied heavily, both individually and through organisations such as the European Banking Federation and the London Investment Banking Association. The Commission created consultation committees with industry leaders to find out where, in their view, the single market 'worked' and where it did not. Equally important, banks' political weight in domestic politics made them sought-after political allies for the Commission; without the banks' agreement, progress in capital market integration was all but impossible. Industry lobbied both for the abolition of cross-border barriers and for more technocratic, supranational governance in Brussels and national capitals alike.

The under-representation of other societal stakeholders was the flip-side of this intensive industry input. As the European industry consolidated on the back of market integration and a new European 'Champions League' of investment banks emerged, small banks from around the EU with little voice in negotiations, either individually or through business associations, were the most visible losers. But other financial market stakeholders were also (surprisingly) absent: non-financial corporations that issue securities, institutional investors such as pension funds, and of course retail consumers. Most importantly, the disproportionate role of policy community insiders squeezed out the interests of the broader public – a point driven home by the ruinous impact of the credit crisis on economic growth and employment in Europe.

Agreement on collective rules and transnational regulatory harmonisation is facilitated by centralised decision-making. Large banks' preference for market integration thus informed their support for supranational governance. Over time, supranational governance decreases the political power of actors who oppose market integration: smaller firms with protectionist inclinations have difficulty legitimising their positions in supranational forums and have to rely on national governments to represent their interests. In addition, the EU lobbying arena – as compared to the domestic one – is tilted even more in favour of large businesses: collective action problems among thousands of small firms and the enormous resources necessary to navigate the Brussels institutional labyrinth play into the hands of large firms. Taken together, these factors make the economic beneficiaries of integration the natural supporters of supranational governance.

The European Commission's role has been one of a catalyst. As a focal point for supporters of capital market integration, its policy initiatives have provided the political space for integration to proceed. Skilful manoeuvring has also allowed the Commission to inject some of its own priorities into policy. However, without the support of the European financial industry, the Commission's efforts would have led nowhere. They would have been stymied, as they were in capital market negotiations around 1990 and in many other policy fields since then. The visibility of the Commission's role in capital market policy has belied its political dependence on the most powerful constituency in capital markets: the banks.

Taken together, this means that competition among firms *within* European capital markets has been key to the way the governance *of* these markets has developed. The dynamic at the heart of this book is thus one of market structuration: actors, both public and private, aim to change market structures in the light of their preferences, while these preferences in turn bear the strong imprint of past changes in market rules, political institutions and actors' economic environments. Both regulation and policy-making institutions, then, can be understood as tools in the market-structuring project that public and private actors pursue. As actors use political power to advance their economic interests and economic power to advance their political interests, an equilibrium can emerge in which a 'fit' develops between market structures, market rules and political institutions. The resulting ensemble is what Underhill (2001, see also Underhill and Zhang 2005) has called a 'state-market condominium'. The stability of this ensemble is often seen as the norm and forms the intellectual point of departure for analysis in comparative political economy (Hall and Soskice 2001b), studies of the state (Krasner 1984, Cerny 1990), economic sociology (Fligstein 2001) and critical approaches to political economy focusing on hegemony (Cox 1996).

This book traces the shift from one such constellation – markets fragmented across national borders, nationally idiosyncratic rules and governance, combined with international negotiations to manage externalities – to transnationally integrated markets and rule-making. The following chapters will refer to these two ideal-types as the international and the supranational constellations, respectively. Market transnationalisation and supranational governance developed in tandem. The purposeful agency of market participants translated developments in one area into change in the other. Two caveats apply, however: the link connecting market structures and the institutions that govern them is not unidirectional, and it is not deterministic.

The relationship between market transnationalisation and supranational governance involves political struggle and agency, and therefore it has not always been straightforward. Actors have made strategic mistakes and miscalculations. For example, many mid-sized banks supported capital market integration, believing they could profit from it. In the end, most of them, including for example Dresdner Bank, Commerzbank and Crédit Lyonnais, abandoned their cross-border ambitions. But market integration had in the meantime become a fact. Public actors also miscalculated: in the late 1990s, the German and French governments saw Frankfurt and Paris as serious competitors to London as an international financial centre, which helps explain their support for integration at the time. Such dreams turned out to be unrealistic, but market integration had already been signed up to.

The most striking example, however, was the demutualisation of European bourses. As members and owners of the stock exchanges, banks turned them into independent, profit-seeking firms during the 1990s and unwittingly created their fiercest competitors for share trading a decade later. When the Investment Services Directive was renegotiated in the early 2000s, stock exchanges formed the most vocal and effective opposition to banks' wishes for a liberal trading regime. The eventual outcome of those negotiations, the 2004 Markets in Financial Instruments Directive, bore the clear imprint of the competitive preferences of bourses – a group of actors that had not even existed as independent firms a decade earlier. Unintended consequences and the unpredictability of market evolution and political processes have thus played their part in creating the current arrangements. They underline how bottom-up agency has to be studied in conjunction with mechanisms operating at the macro-level.

To do justice to both influences, this book's analysis and argumentation builds on several strategies. The perspective advanced here, it is claimed, explains supranationalisation better than alternative approaches such as theories that build on conceptions of national interest, the public good or the pressures emanating from financial globalisation. 'Congruence methods' (George and Bennett 2005: 181) compare the empirical evidence against the predictions of (rival) theories. Even though this study (taken as a whole) focuses on a single case, there is ample variation across different units of analysis that matter at crucial junctures of the causal mechanism. Most obviously, the outcomes of two rounds of negotiations – around 1990 and around 2000 – differ markedly. Variation in national political institutions, market structures and industry interests – notably between the three countries discussed in detail, Germany, France and the United Kingdom – explain their different positions on market integration. Finally, there is variation between firms: large firms with international operations have different interests from small, domestic ones, while the preferences of universal banks on given issues differ from those of securities houses and stock exchanges.

Both the time-frame covered by this book and the theoretical approach which underlies it have called for a variety of sources. A great deal of scholarly research had already been done on the period up to the mid-1990s, while EU financial politics has been well-covered in the specialised financial press and niche publications such as *The Banker*, *Euromoney*, *European Banker* and the *Financial Regulation Report*, which provide a level of detail that academic publications rarely achieve. Needless to say, public documents were equally crucial to piecing together two decades of EU capital market politics. In addition, even though statistical data on European investment banking is too thin on the ground to allow advanced quantitative analysis, it has been indispensable for tracing trends in the sector over time and in comparing countries and firms.

Finally, and perhaps most importantly, this book draws on more than fifty indepth interviews with a wide variety of insiders in EU capital market politics. The interviews were conducted in Brussels, London, Frankfurt, Paris, Bonn, Berlin and The Hague (see overview in the appendix). Respondents included Commission representatives, Members of the European Parliament (MEPs), the EU embassies of central member states, the Committee of European Securities Regulators

(CESR), the most important lobbying organisations,[1] public officials in France, Germany and the UK, lobbyists of individual (investment) banks and exchanges, and a member of the Lamfalussy Committee. Many of the issues discussed were politically sensitive. To allow respondents to be frank and forthcoming with information, the interviews were generally conducted under Chatham House Rules: content can be quoted, but only in a way that does not reveal the identity of the respondent. Because the capital markets policy community is small – its core comprises no more than 150 people who generally know each other – respondents' concrete identities remain opaque in most citations.

Most of the interviews were conducted in 2005/06, when capital markets in Europe and beyond were still roaring and when the sustainability of the boom was rarely questioned. To many respondents it was self-evident that EU capital markets were destined to follow the trail that had been blazed by the USA. Whether for private gain or for the public good, many of them became agents of the overhaul of EU financial markets, conveniently forgetting that the transformation they were witnessing was of their own making. They created the regulatory and institutional preconditions for the wholesale transformation of the European financial industry, exposing it to transatlantic competition that EU firms could only withstand by engaging in similarly risky practices as their US counterparts. It was not to last. By 2008, the brave new world of turbocharged EU finance lay in shatters. With hindsight, the European Champions League of investment banks had sown the seeds of its own demise.

---

1. These included the London Investment Banking Association, the European Banking Federation, the European Savings Banks Group, the International Capital Market Association, Association Française des Entreprises d'Investissement, the Future and Options Association, the British Bankers Association, the Bundesverband deutscher Banken, the Federation of European Securities Exchanges, the European Securitisation Forum, the Investment Management Association and Association of Private Client Investment Managers and Stockbrokers.

chapter two | competition politics and supranational integration

At the heart of this book stands a question that has been fundamental to, if not defining for, political economy as an academic field: what is the relationship between the domains nowadays denoted as 'the economy' and 'politics' (Underhill 2000)? Many scholars have pointed to the tenuousness of the distinction (see Chavagneux 2001), which only gained currency in the twentieth century (Mitchell 2002: 80, cf. Krätke and Underhill 2006, Milonakis and Fine 2008). Avoiding the artificial economics-politics distinction, the issue is one of the mutual constitution of market structures and patterns of governance (Cerny 1990, Strange 1988, Underhill 2006).

This chapter has two aims. Extending the sketch in the introduction, it critically reviews the two strands of theorising that are most relevant to the case at hand — theories of European integration, financial liberalisation and deregulation. These theories fail to properly analyse the agency of a small group of well-connected private and public actors, which is the crucial link between changing market structures and transformations in governance patterns. The significance here, it is argued, lies in the political and economic stakes these actors have in how political institutions and regulatory regimes structure inter-firm competition and thereby market access. As regulatory and institutional preferences are in turn inspired by the market environment that actors confront, we see in action a process of 'structuration' (e.g. Giddens 1984, Wendt 1987). Over time, changes in either market structures or patterns of governance can only be understood with an eye to this larger whole.

In the second part of this chapter an analytical approach is constructed to explain the supranationalisation of capital market governance based on these insights – an approach I term 'competition politics'. While scholars of International Political Economy (Cerny 2000, Hobson and Ramesh 2002, Underhill 2006) and European integration (Christiansen and Jørgensen 1999, Niemann 2006) have repeatedly advocated taking structuration seriously, its empirical application to date has been rare. The approach developed in this chapter is a step to bridge this gap.

EUROPEAN INTEGRATION

With the emergence of supranational governance in EU capital markets as the empirical anchor of this book, theories of European integration are a natural place to begin our exploration. Ever since Haas' seminal monograph *The Uniting of Europe* (1958), states' willingness to integrate policy-making and potentially transfer authority to the supranational level has been a subject of academic debate (Lindberg 1963, Hoffmann 1966, Schmitter 1969, 1970; for overviews, see Rosamond 2000, Wiener and Diez 2004).

One popular approach was formulated as liberal intergovernmentalism (Moravcsik 1991, 1993, 1998). It argued that regional integration was in essence comparable to the building of international regimes traditionally studied in International Relations (Krasner 1983, Haggard and Simmons 1987, Hasenclever *et al.* 1997). In a nutshell, regional integration served national interests. Moravcsik's own contribution to this strand of thinking was his emphasis on the domestic sources of government preferences (Moravcsik 1997, cf. Weiss 2003), which, together with international institutions' potential for providing collective goods, explained observable patterns of governance (cf. Keohane 1988, Scharpf 1997a).

Two kinds of criticisms have been levelled against liberal intergovernmentalism: that it misrepresents the functioning of existing supranational institutions, and that it misunderstands the process that leads to their emergence (on the distinction, cf. Jachtenfuchs 2001). Many scholars of multi-level governance have argued that regional integration has compromised the sovereignty of EU member states more than is compatible with Moravcsik's depiction of European politics as a purely intergovernmental affair (Marks *et al.* 1996, Risse-Kappen 1996, Kohler-Koch and Eising 1999, Hooghe and Marks 2001, Peters and Pierre 2001). The degree to which supranational bodies such as the European Court of Justice and the European Commission have escaped direct government control makes it implausible to think of them solely as agents of member states (cf. Pollack 1997), while the development of supranational bodies has also encouraged informal political institutions to transcend nation-states (e.g. Cowles *et al.* 2001). In short, the world of 'two-level games' (Putnam 1988) – to which liberal intergovernmentalism is indebted – is an inappropriate representation of both formal and informal flows of political authority in the European Union.

The second charge against liberal intergovernmentalism is that it has little to say about regional integration as a systematic *process*. It has failed to theorise the conditions under which past regime formation could feed back into 'domestic interests', either through the redefinition of individual actors' interests or their identities, and thus unleash a dynamic of its own. While the early neofunctionalist integration theorists had tried to do just that, they were unsuccessful in the eyes of Ernst Haas, who is widely credited as the founding father of the field. As West European governments failed to cooperate in the face of the economic crisis of the 1970s, Haas declared that regional integration theory was obsolete.

With the re-launch of European integration since the mid-1980s (Tsoukalis 1997, Dinan 1999), theorising based on neofunctionalism has enjoyed a revival (Sandholtz and Stone Sweet 1998, Niemann 2006). Even Haas revised his earlier, negative judgement in the preface to the 2004 edition of *The Uniting of Europe*. Neofunctionalism, however, has often been misunderstood and caricatured, thanks to its common association with apolitical automatism in the evolution of political institutions, which clashes with more political readings of EU history (e.g. van Apeldoorn 2002). It is therefore worthwhile to revisit some of its central tenets. Schmitter's (2005) summaries of Haas' original propositions largely overlap with his own theory of regional integration (Schmitter 1970). The four most relevant ones are discussed below; they are complemented by related, often more recent, insights from EU integration and governance studies.

First, "*[s]tates* are not the exclusive and may no longer be the predominant actors in the regional/international system." (Schmitter 2005: 259, emphasis in original) States – understood here as national state governments – may be the most visible actors but this facade may only mask a temporary equilibrium of different social groups, for example classes. In addition, non-state actors can oppose or promote integration independently of government action. In his original formulation of integration theory, Schmitter pointed out that change in the constellation of actors over time can itself be the result of previous integration:

> The most important transformation in the structure of the model during these stages occurs in the nature of national actors. Up to this point they have been treated as units with a single integrative or disintegrative strategy during any crisis. Now they begin to appear as *differentiated* actors, as a plurality of negotiating units (classes, status groups, sub-regions, *clientelas*, bureaucratic agencies, ideological clusters, etc.). [..] These "subnational" fragmented actors [..] will begin to form stable "transnational coalitions" of support and opposition to particular measures. The policy vector now becomes the product of alliances that cut across national boundaries [..]. National governmental actors may continue to play the preponderant role in the concatenation of strategies, but they can be circumscribed, if not circumvented, by coalitions of other governmental actors with subnational groups and regional *técnicos*. (Schmitter 1970: 864, emphasis in original)

It is widely acknowledged that the most important non-state actors directly participating in EU policy-making are firms and business associations (Feld 1970, Cowles 1995, van Apeldoorn 2002). Over the past decade, business lobbying in Brussels has grown exponentially (van Schendelen 2006, Greenwood 2003, cf. Coen 2007) while business actors increasingly organise transnationally (Coen 1998, for financial services, see Grossman 2004, cf. Quaglia 2008). Supranational actors have actively created opportunities for the direct participation of such societal actors – what Schmidt (2004) has called 'government with the people' – through consultation procedures, expert committees, etc. For the purpose of analysis, there is no ex ante reason to focus exclusively on (unified) public actors, either at the national or supranational level.

Second, "*[d]ecisions* about integration are normally taken with very imperfect knowledge of their consequences and frequently under the pressure of deadlines or impending crises." (Schmitter 2005: 259, emphasis in original) Actors therefore frequently miscalculate the results of their own political efforts. Knowledge, both as a product of political processes and a resource to influence these processes, has attracted increased attention within EU integration studies since the second half of the 1990s (Risse 2004). Fusing the ideas that genuine deliberation at the EU level is both more democratic and that it produces better policy than hard-nosed strategic bargaining, scholars have searched for the conditions under which such deliberation can emerge (Joerges and Neyer 1997, Neyer 2003, cf. Schmalz-Bruns 1999). For example, high issue complexity, the shared 'life world' of a policy community's members and a low degree of politicisation all promote communicative action (Niemann 2004, cf. Risse 2000). The composition of the policy community itself can, of course, be highly political by excluding important stakeholders; communication between insiders may actually reflect the institutionalised limits of their discussion. Consensus reached through communicative action may still be the result of an unrecognised intellectual hegemony (Hay and Rosamond 2002, McNamara 2002), while the complexity of an issue area such as banking may force policy-makers to rely on experts (McKenzie and Khalidi 1996) and expose them to self-interested manipulation. Whatever the strength of these 'knowledge' effects in practice, they call for close empirical attention to the process of rule making and supranational integration, beyond imputing 'rational' interests into actors.

Third, "[s]ince *actors* in the integration process cannot be confined to [actors at the national level], a theory of it should also explicitly include a role for supranational persons, secretariats and associations." (Schmitter 2005: 260, emphasis in original) Departing from the realist/liberal intergovernmentalist proposition that member states are in control of EU integration (Moravcsik 1993, 1998), scholars have explored ways in which supranational EU bodies – especially the Commission – may themselves influence the integration process, as well as exploring the reasons why member states would allow such an erosion of their sovereignty (e.g. Marks *et al.* 1996, Pollack 1997, Hooghe and Marks 2001, for financial markets see e.g. Posner 2009b). One branch of this debate, mirroring discussions among institutionalist scholars more generally (Hall and Taylor 1996), has questioned what sort of control principals retain over the supranational agents they have created (cf. Jupille and Caporaso 1999, Pollack 2004). Whereas rational institutionalists have argued that institutions, by and large, can still be understood as the instruments of those who established them (Scharpf 1997a, 2001), historical institutionalists have pointed to ways in which the agents eventually outgrow the intentions of their creators (Pierson 2000a, 2000b, cf. Jervis 1997).

It is hardly disputed that both the European Court of Justice and the Commission enjoy room for manoeuvre (Pierson 1996, Pollack 1998). In a review of Nordlinger's *On the Autonomy of the Democratic State* (1981), Krasner lists the ways in which state actors (they are equally applicable to supranational actors such as the Commission) can exercise independent influence on policy:

> [they] may initiate policy and provide access for particular societal groups [and] reinforce a weak level of convergence [of social preferences] by manipulating information, inflating the success of ongoing programs, setting agendas, appealing to widely shared symbols, playing upon deference to official expertise, and deflecting potential opposition. (Krasner 1984: 231)

That much is widely accepted in contemporary European studies. What is much less clear, and hence also a question for this book to answer, is how supranational actors' room for manoeuvre relates to other contextual factors. Gottwald (2005), for example, argues that the supranationalisation of capital market governance is largely attributable to the agency of the Commission. However, he does not specify how the visible actions of the Commission may have depended on the much less visible economic and political environment in which it operates. Similarly, Posner (2009b) has shown how the Commission was crucial to setting up EASDAQ, the European version of the American NASDAQ stock market. But again, it remains unclear how much this (eventually unsuccessful) initiative relied on contingent environmental factors. As this book shows, two initiatives to integrate European markets for investment services produced strikingly different results, even though the Commission was supportive of integration in both cases. An explanation for integration will therefore have to be sought elsewhere.

Finally, "*[i]nterests*, rather than common ideals or identity, are the driving force behind the integration process [..]." (Schmitter 2005: 259, emphasis in original) The interests of actors can change in the course of the integration process, often in light of the (potentially unequal) distribution of its benefits.

The idea that actors' pro-integration inclinations can be both the *source* and the *result* of actual integration is central to neofunctionalism as a *theory*. To see interests as the driving force behind integration is not particularly controversial (see, however, Neyer 2003; Niemann 2006: 24), especially if interests are not seen as objectively given and integration is understood as a mix of creating joint gains ('problem-solving' in Scharpf's language) and conflicts over the distribution of these gains ('distributive bargaining', Scharpf 2001, cf. Garrett 1992). What is controversial, however, is whose interests actually count in the supranationalisation of governance.

Critical approaches to EU integration, for example, see conflicting class interests at the heart of European integration (e.g. van Apeldoorn 2002, Bieling 2003, Cafruny and Ryner 2007). Supranational governance is seen as a result of and mechanism for the transnational integration of capitalist relations of production. By emphasising the functionality of supranational governance for a particular set of societal interests, the analysis dovetails with neofunctionalism. At the same time, the approach leaves little room for the independent effects of either political or economic institutions, and therefore offers insufficient theoretical guidance to the actual political process by which collective actors translate their economic interests into institutional change.

Supranationalists also see the interests of particular social groups behind integration. For example, Stone Sweet and Sandholtz argue that:

> supranational governance serves the interests of (i) those individuals, groups, and firms who transact across borders, and (ii) those who are advantaged by European rules, and disadvantaged by national rules, in specific policy domains. (Stone Sweet and Sandholtz 1998: 4)

In contrast to critical theorists, they are relatively agnostic about the societal alliances that may promote or oppose integration:

> Some elite groups (leadership of political parties, industry associations, and labour federations) begin to recognize that problems of substantial interest cannot be solved at the national level. These groups push for the transfer of policy competence to a supranational body, finding each other and establishing cross-national coalitions along the way. If the problem is important enough

and pro-integration elites are able to mount sufficient political leverage, governments establish supranational institutions. (Stone Sweet and Sandholtz 1998: 5)

While this argument is plausible, it cannot account for two crucial ingredients of the dynamic it describes: just what are the 'problems of substantial interest' that motivate these elite groups to push for supranational integration? And equally importantly, why can some groups 'mount sufficient political leverage' to implement their vision on supranational integration while others cannot? Even though neofunctionalism and its theoretical offspring posit a generally positive relationship between supranational integration and the cross-border integration of social and economic space, they underspecify the concrete actors and processes that act as 'transmission belts' between the two. Sandholtz (1993) himself has pointed out that different theories were needed to explain and connect integration dynamics and domestic preference formation, so this lacuna is not a material defect of neofunctionalism and related theories. But these gaps do point towards the need to examine political economy dynamics in the policy field in question to fully understand the emergence and functioning of supranational governance.

FINANCIAL MARKET LIBERALISATION AND REGULATION

The supranationalisation of EU capital market governance has had the cross-border integration of financial markets as its professed goal. Such market-opening has not been limited to the European Union, and given the global trend towards financial liberalisation until the credit crisis (Williamson and Mahar 1998), many scholars have first looked to the international level for the forces underlying it. In particular, they have drawn inspiration from debates in International Political Economy that have identified capital mobility as the driver behind globalisation and domestic change in general (affirmatively Gill and Law 1989, Andrews 1994, Pauly 1995, Keohane and Milner 1996, Garrett 1998, sceptically Swank 2002, Mosley 2003, for an overview see Berger 2000).

Laurence (2001) has combined this insight with the notion of regulatory competition (Esty and Geradin 2001, McCahery and Geradin 2004 for a critical assessment), which builds on Tiebout's original contribution about patterns of local taxation and expenditures. Tiebout (1956) argued that if citizens were free to settle in any of a number of municipalities, they would choose the one offering the 'optimal' mix of costs (taxes) and benefits (desirable municipal expenditures). To attract mobile citizens from elsewhere or prevent emigration, municipalities would adapt their taxation and expenditure regime to match citizens' preferences (cf. D. Vogel 1995, Lazer 2001).

Laurence (2001) has interpreted past waves of financial market liberalisation in this vein. In his eyes, inter-jurisdictional capital mobility has allowed investors to break the previous, often cartel-like grip of local financial services producers on national markets and regulatory regimes. In the face of capital mobility, governments opened national markets and invited foreign competition, much to the chagrin of domestic financial firms, whom Laurence has seen as the primary losers of financial liberalisation.

The empirical record is not easily squared with this argument. Studies of regulatory competition in financial services have generated mixed evidence (Hertig 2001, Jackson and Pan 2001, Trachtman 2001). Major variations in the timing of liberalisation remain unexplained. Most importantly, rather than being losers of financial integration, large investment banks continued to post record profits as markets were opened (cf. Augar 2005).

The core failure of Laurence's argument lies in its disregard for the actual process that translates abstract macro-forces (capital mobility) into policy change. Of internationalisation's four 'pathways of influence' on domestic politics, he suggests that one is crucial: the 'threat of exit' of mobile asset holders. Yet it remains unclear how these threats matter to policy-makers, especially given these asset holders' lack of embeddedness in the actual policy process. The most concrete suggestion Laurence makes is that domestic banks, who *are* well-established in national policy communities and allegedly worry about their business, 'lobby policy-makers on behalf of mobile-asset consumers whose business the service providers want to keep or win' (Laurence 2001: 193). Here the argument falters: if large banks have been beneficiaries of market opening – as empirical evidence strongly suggests – it is much more plausible that their lobbying was self-interested rather than kowtowing to mobile investors. The regulatory competition dynamic that forces change on unwilling banks and governments becomes unconvincing as the source of market-opening.

Indeed, it is misleading to construe capital mobility as an exogenous force. Helleiner (1994) has shown how central financial market developments over the recent decades have been the result of conscious public policy rather than outside forces (cf. Abdelal 2007). Rather than being able to explain financial market opening with capital mobility, the puzzle lies in the political choice of governments to introduce capital mobility in the first place.

Models of regulatory competition also generally ignore that governments not only compete with each other but can also cooperate (McCahery and Geradin 2004). To the extent that regulatory competition is seen as undesirable, governments can establish regimes to uphold higher standards (Krasner 1983, Hasenclever *et al.* 1997). Indeed, states have cooperated to agree on common rules in a number of financial domains (Porter 1993, Underhill 1993, Porter 2005: 31). Regardless of whether such regimes spring more from a desire to produce collective goods cooperatively or from distributive struggles (Kapstein 1992, Oatley and Nabors 1998, Singer 2004), market opening can be the result of multilateral bargaining as much as of unilateral adaptation (Simmons 2001).

Among EU member states, governments have chosen a mix of both strategies. Most financial market opening in the 1980s was unilateral (see Cerny 1989 for France, Moran 1991 for the UK, Story 1997, Lütz 2000 for Germany). Agreeing EU-wide rules, in contrast, is by definition a multilateral affair. Here liberalisation is an instance of negotiated market opening – something that most comparative studies (prominently S. Vogel 1996) cannot accommodate because they model liberalisation as a domestic political adaptation to changes in the global environment (cf. Keohane and Milner 1996). Regardless of whether market opening is a unilateral or multilateral affair, these shortcomings call for a much more in-depth appraisal of the actual policy processes and the actors who lobby, draft policy proposals and bargain to effect eventual outcomes.

This also applies to the second popular 'top-down' explanation of financial market change: technological progress (overviews of such arguments can be found in Cybo-Ottone *et al.* 2000, Lee 2002). This line of argument is particularly common in the business literature (e.g. Holland *et al.* 1998, Walter and Smith 2000, Smith and Walter 2003): technology undermines the boundaries between national financial markets and at the same time generates economies of scale that increase the welfare gains associated with market integration.

There is no doubt that technological innovation has changed the face of financial markets. But arguments that attribute causal power to it have clear weaknesses (Sobel 1999: 8). Technology is an instrument that purposeful actors use to attain their own ends (e.g. Henwood 1997: 137, Partnoy 2002), even if success is never assured (Goldstein 1995). In this sense, it is no more than a means towards an end that emerges from a dynamic distinct from technological progress – be it the struggle between capital and labour, between different firms, between firms and governments, or between debtors and creditors.

Technological progress by itself cannot explain why existing innovations are applied in some cases and not in others. For example, why do institutional investors still have to pay intermediaries to trade shares for them when they could communicate directly with exchanges (Mahoney 2002)? What has motivated governments to obstruct the use of technology, for example the setting up of remote trading screens (Mügge 2006)? In short, technology is an insufficient explanation for financial change without an account of the motivations of those who regulate its application and, indeed, financial markets as a whole.

Normative theories of financial regulation draw on neo-classical economic thinking to explain the necessity of such regulation as well as the desirability of clear limits to state intervention in 'markets'. In this view, market failures stemming from systemic risk, 'moral hazard' and 'adverse selection' (Akerlof 1970) serve as the central justification for otherwise illegitimate state interference in the marketplace (Herring and Litan 1995, Goodhart *et al.* 1998). Governments provide collective goods: they increase the safety of the financial system as a whole, increase the allocative efficiency of financial markets through the alleviation of information asymmetries, and thereby boost overall welfare (Gertler 1988).

Yet even before the credit crisis, when such views still stood prominently, they left regulation underdetermined (Laurence 2001: 30). For example, governments can design stringent rules to prevent individual bank failures – an approach likely to entail limits to competition, driving up costs for consumers. Alternatively, governments can provide a general safety net for institutions that fail and leave them exposed to more competition, which is likely to lower costs but also to increase the chance of future failure. Normative theories thus fail to explain specific policy decisions as well as the more general undersupply of effective rules to subordinate finance to the public interest.

Stigler's theory of 'regulatory capture' addresses this gap, arguing that regulation routinely falls prey to self-interested manipulation by both regulators and the regulated (Stigler 1971). Regulation not only provides collective goods, but entails costs and benefits that are distributed unevenly throughout society. Independent of its alleged goals, regulation is contested between social groups aiming to secure benefits for themselves and shift costs onto others:

> [The] problem of regulation is the problem of discovering when and why an industry (or other group of like-minded people) is able to use the state for its purposes, or is singled out by the state to be used for alien purposes. (Stigler 1971: 4)

Stigler envisioned four kinds of 'favours' that industries desire from governments: money (through direct or indirect subsidies), controls on market entry, limits on the availability of substitutes for their own products combined with an encouragement of the consumption of complements, and price controls. Over time, he argued, government officials were likely to build their own 'constituencies' with whom they entertain reciprocally beneficial relationships. Stigler's vision of what policy-makers received in return for granting privileged access to policy-making remained narrow, however:

> The industry which seeks regulation must be prepared to pay with the two things a [political] party needs: votes and resources. (Stigler 1971: 12)

Conceiving of 'politics' in terms of elections and using the US political system as the base for his arguments, Stigler concluded that in the struggle over the costs of regulation, producers would regularly win out over consumers. Producers are relatively small in number but have high individual stakes in their field of regulation. Individually, they are willing to invest significantly in tilting policy in their favour. The costs of competition-restricting regulation, in contrast, are spread over a large group of consumers, whose individual burden from a specific measure is relatively small. Individual producers thus have a higher incentive to lobby regulators than do individual consumers. Second, also owing to the difference in numbers, producers find it easier than consumers to organise and mobilise collectively (cf. Olson 1965). Third, in industries with significant employment, producers might be able to mobilise the votes of their employees based on the extension of political favours. These three factors taken together, Stigler argued, would systematically advantage producers and tilt regulation in their favour.

Stigler's image of regulatory capture has a number of shortcomings however. First, though it is plausible that consumers generally lose out from regulatory capture, it is not clear that domestic producers are the only societal actors vying for influence on regulatory policy or, for that matter, that they do so as a united front. Producers are, after all, rivals. Sobel (1994) has used an approach that focuses on competition *between* providers of financial services to explain reform trajectories within British, Japanese and US capital markets in the 1970s and 1980s. He concluded that market liberalisation resulted from domestic struggles over market domination; international pressure was secondary. In all three cases, commercial banks had been excluded from the lucrative capital market business. When for idiosyncratic and exogenous reasons they faced problems of profitability related to market saturation, they challenged the market position of the securities houses and brokers – the market incumbents – by lobbying for market opening. In all three cases, commercial banks were successful. Kroszner and Strahan (1999, 2000) have found similar dynamics behind the abolition of inter-state branching restrictions in the USA.

However, Sobel's perspective shares a second shortcoming with Stigler's approach. Neither can easily account for the opening of national markets to foreign competitors. In both cases, it is argued that national policy insiders dominate regulatory policy-making. If this is true, why would they allow foreign firms in? Finally, Stigler operated with a highly simplified model of politics, one that saw public and private actors connected by money, votes and regulatory favours. This model, however, grossly misrepresents the way regulatory policy functions in practice. In order to examine this in more detail, we need to put policy processes and the actual functioning of the state under the analytical magnifying glass.

PRIVATE AND PUBLIC ACTORS IN REGULATORY POLICY

In the pluralist view that underlies Stigler's model, to borrow Krasner's words,

> [t]he government is seen as a cash register that totals up and then averages the preferences and political power of societal actors. (Krasner 1984: 227)

As Krasner himself points out, this is an inadequate description of the American state, let alone of more corporatist ones, for at least two reasons: political institutions have independent effects, and the state can be a powerful actor in its own right.

What has come to be known as historical institutionalism underlines that political institutions are neither reducible to societal forces at any given moment, as functionalist, rational-choice institutionalism has suggested, nor, for that matter, to the intentions of their originators (Skocpol 1985, Pierson 2000b). Institutions are hard to change ('sticky' in the jargon), and by benefiting some societal groups more than others, create their own constituencies which invest in their reproduction (Pierson 2000a). Path dependency is the result.

As Hall and Taylor (1996) point out, both sides of this debate have a point: on the one hand, when actors establish institutions, they are likely to have clear intentions. Though path dependencies can clearly be identified in political-economic research, paths shift and can be broken, often for reasons that remain poorly integrated into historical institutionalist models (Deeg 2001, Crouch and Farrell 2004). On the other hand, whether these institutions then deliver the results hoped for by the initiating actors depends on factors that must be established empirically.

Political institutions, above all, matter for regulatory politics because they structure societal groups' access to policy-making (Pierre and Peters 2002). Empirically, policy communities that cover specific issue areas are relatively circumscribed and their institutions function to keep outsiders out. Political institutions thus give members of policy communities what Barnett and Duvall (2005) call 'institutional power' – power that can be used for a broad variety of ends not necessarily related to the reasons for the existence of the institution.

Banks' institutional power derives from the key roles they play within national economies (e.g. Zysman 1983, Crouch and Streek 1997, Allen and Gale 2000). Germany's coordinated market economy was linked to a corporatist political system that enabled the positive coordination of economic policies (Schmitter 1979, Jayasuriya 2001). France's state-led economy was mirrored in highly centralised structures with the state, and in the case of financial markets, particularly at their apex, the Trésor, the directorate of the finance ministry responsible for financial markets (Loriaux 1991, Schmidt 1996, Lalone 2005). Lack of coordination between economic policy fields in Britain after the Thatcher revolution translated into weak political institutions to connect the government with economic associations, be they trade unions or business groups. These patterns, originally embedded in national varieties of capitalism, also emerge in the governance of securities markets (Coleman 1996).

In his analysis of financial market regulation, Vogel (1996) identified 'national varieties of capitalism' as key factors in the different trajectories taken by financial liberalisation, including the three countries most relevant to this book: the UK, Germany and France. He concludes that all three faced similar external pressures for adaptation but that their responses were path dependent: the UK, as a liberal economy, further opened its markets whereas Germany and France 'strategically reinforced' their governments' steering roles in their markets. That said, Vogel does not clarify whether path dependency is best understood as an adaptation of dysfunctional economic institutions or the result of an institutional legacy that empowers specific actors.

The former view draws on institutional complementarities within national varieties of capitalism (Hall and Soskice 2001b). Due to the co-evolution of economic institutions, it is argued, financial markets have come to 'fit' their economic environments. These institutional complementarities have often generated positive externalities and have thus increased overall welfare. State actors with a stake in overall economic performance should favour reproducing advantageous national regulatory regimes or adapting them to those changes in the global environment that compromise their optimality (on such 'adaptive pressures', see Schmidt 2002, Glyn 2006, for a critical view see Hay and Rosamond 2002).

Yet comparative political economists still debate whether this is a valid depiction of national varieties of capitalism and the factors decisive in their convergence or continued diversity (e.g. Cerny 1997, Amable 2000, Lane 2000, Radice 2000, Deeg 2001, Yamamura and Streeck 2003, Morgan and Kubo 2005). With the evidence inconclusive, it remains a question for empirical research to determine how varieties of capitalism matter to trajectories of financial market opening.

As is the case with other institutions, the role of knowledge in policy-making is a double-edged sword. It has independent effects, for example by structuring access and pre-selecting policy solutions (Haas 1992, Hall 1993, Zito 2001). In highly complex policy fields, actors with expertise and a clear sense of their own interests are likely to be at an advantage over less well-informed actors with only vague preferences. On the other hand, actors can purposefully generate and manipulate knowledge for their own ends. How the 'independent' effects of knowledge compare to its instrumentalisation by purposeful actors can thus differ from case to case and is therefore again a question for empirical research.

Comparative studies of financial market policy-making (e.g. Moran 1991, Coleman 1996, Josselin 1997, Lütz 2002) show that central banks, finance ministries, regulatory agencies and the regulated themselves often form the inner circle of policy communities. The policy communities matter to political outcomes because they

> limit participation in the policy process, [..] define the roles of actors, [..] define which issues will be included and excluded from the policy agenda, [through] the rules of the game [..] shape the behaviour of actors, [..] privilege certain interests, not only by according them access but also by favouring their preferred policy outcomes [and] substitute private government for public accountability. (Rhodes 1997: 10)

In contrast, the wider public, other stakeholders and national parliaments are normally at the fringes of financial market policy-making. These studies also shatter the idea that regulation is a tug-of-war between the regulators and the regulated (cf. Clarke 2000). Historically, what is nowadays considered regulation has been mostly effected by guilds (for an overview cf. Braithwaite and Drahos 2000). Rather than opposing each other, private and public actors have formed 'advocacy coalitions' (Sabatier 1988, Sabatier and Jenkins-Smith 1999) that jointly pursue shared policy objectives. Given the conceptual and historical blurring of the public-private divide, '[in] this world the language of regulatory capture is largely devoid of meaning' (Hancher and Moran 1989: 276) – notwithstanding Stigler's valuable insights about the impact of particularistic interests on regulation.

> If regulation is to be located, then, we may say that it exists on a political space between law and society, a space inhabited by the state, private interest groups and regulatory agencies, some public, some private, some mixed. (Clarke 2000: 21)

If this blurring of the line between the public and private is taken seriously, theories of institutional change or market opening based on a stark public-private distinction will invariably fall short. Private and public actors form coalitions both to shape markets in their own interest and to craft political institutions that help them attain their goals and solidify their grip on public policy. In the long-term process of this mutual constitution, little remains fixed: the responsibilities of 'public' and 'private' actors in policy-making change, as do the levels of aggregation at which they come together. It is in this sense that the state – the crystallisation of the political economy struggles unfolding in society – can be understood as '*the* problem of international political economy' (Underhill 2006: 16, emphasis in original, cf. Cerny 1990).

THE COMPETITION POLITICS APPROACH

Most of the theories discussed thus far have described different parts of the political economy elephant, to borrow Puchala's (1972) phrase. But they insufficiently appreciate the mutual constitution of patterns of governance, market structures and market rules – with purposeful actors as the nexus between them (see Figure 2.1). The final part of this chapter proposes a framework to study financial market governance that addresses this shortcoming. The different theories discussed earlier all have their merits; the processes they describe all contribute to real-world political economy outcomes. They can, however, be fruitfully synthesised to describe one integrated, larger dynamic: competition politics.

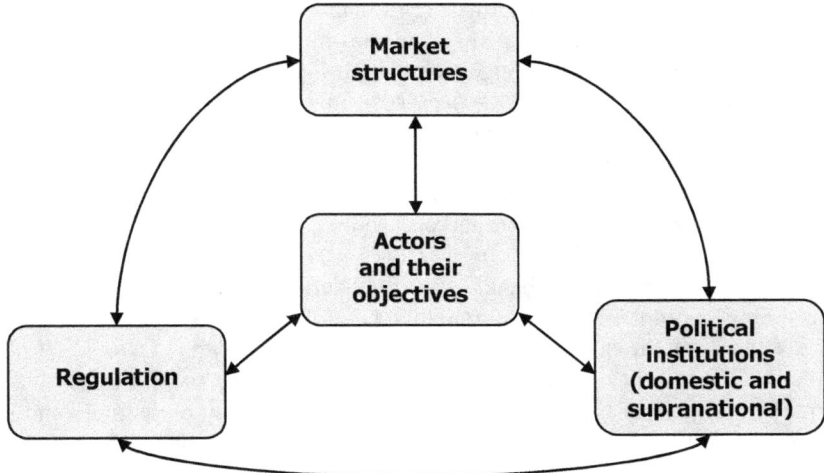

Figure 2.1: Actors and the political economy environment they confront and shape

Regulation structures the behaviour of economic agents and thereby markets. Indeed, market sectors dealing in intangibles such as investment services are effectively 'regulation-defined' (Vietor 1987). But what ends does regulation serve? In the passage that prefaces this book, Adam Smith argued that producers in particular sectors oppose efficiency-enhancing competition:

> [the] interest of the dealers [..] in any particular branch of trade of manufactures, is always in some respects different from, and even opposite to, that of the public. To widen the market and narrow the competition, is always in the interest of the dealers [..]. (Smith 1937 [1776]: 250)

How important are these producer interests for financial market regulation? As a number of studies of domestic regulatory reform have found, they can be considerable (Sobel 1994, Kroszner and Strahan 1999, 2000, Vitols 2004, for an overview, see Hardy 2006). To sustain prices for their products and thus their profits, producers use regulation, not so much against consumers, but against each other. Fligstein has argued that in an economic-sociological perspective, the primary function of regulation is to prevent ruinous competition (Fligstein and Mara-Drita 1996, Fligstein 2001). From the perspective of firms, keeping competitors out and thereby securing rents and organisational survival are core aspects of regulatory regimes (for a similar argument from a firm's perspective, see Shaffer 1995).

For market incumbents and their (potential) challengers, the central quality of regulation is that *it sets the terms of competition* (Underhill 2003: 765, see also Underhill 1998): it determines who is allowed to compete in which market segment under what conditions. In wholesale financial markets, regulation plays a much larger role in reproducing prevailing market structures than in other sectors where factors such as ownership of scare resources, inherited product differentiations (potentially bolstered by patents), and hard-to-change customer relationships form larger impediments to change. Regulation is one of the main obstacles for large players commanding both the necessary financial resources and reputations to establish themselves in new markets or segments. To use Stigler's language, 'capturing' financial market regulators – or preventing their capture by others – becomes an integral part of companies' business strategies. Struggles over regulation are struggles over shaping markets – how different segments and fields of economic activity are delineated.

This does not mean that banks' strategies derive neatly from their environments. Studies of their strategy-formulation have shown that no single theory can capture the different environmental, institutional and firm-level factors that play a role (Milbourn *et al.* 1999, Flier 2003, Froud *et al.* 2006). As political strategies normally derive from business objectives, both firms' policy preferences and the vigour with which they pursue them do not always reflect their 'objective' situation in the market place. Disruptive events are often necessary to break organisational and cognitive inertia. It is therefore difficult to predict when environmental change will translate into a review of strategy. But as Flier's study (2003) shows, once the review takes place, environmental and institutional factors play an important role in determining the direction of change (cf. Hillman and Hitt 1999).

Over time, firms adapt to their market environments; those that come to dominate a market segment owing to the rules governing the segment will become the natural constituency in favour of their reproduction (cf. Fligstein 2001). But how are these preferences inserted into the actual policy process? In the case of banks, their central role within national economies creates privileged access to public actors. Financial firms jointly create regulation with regulators and cooperate with governments in selling the latter's debt; they are, in short, an integral part of the apparatus through which most governments directly or indirectly implement economic policy. This makes banks insiders in the relevant policy communities.

The institutional power deriving from banks' membership in these policy communities, in turn, allows them to further consolidate their market position by regulatory means; at the least, preferential access to political resources forms a de facto insurance against unwelcome market intrusion by firms outside the group of market incumbents – both domestic and foreign. The relationship, then, is reciprocal:

market incumbency generates the political resources to reproduce itself.

Of course this depiction of state-market dynamics vastly overstates market stability. In past decades, the trend has clearly been in the direction of market opening, not only in financial markets but across a wide range of economic sectors. How can such liberalisation be squared with an emphasis on firms' own control over the terms of competition? The answer lies in the negotiated character of much market opening, whether through the World Trade Organisation, regional trade agreements, bilateral agreements or agreement on common standards (Abbott and Snidal 2001, Mattli and Büthe 2003).

The fact that regulatory change with market-opening effects is often negotiated gives it a quality akin to trade politics (cf. Busch 2001). When market-opening is reciprocal, the most competitive firms in all jurisdictions stand to gain, commonly at the expense of smaller, domestically-oriented players (cf. Krugman 1986). Cross-border market integration through regulatory means may therefore become salient once market incumbents have reached domestic limits to growth and identified cross-border expansion as their way ahead (Milner and Yoffie 1989). Because the price to pay, that is increased competition 'at home', is disproportionately borne by smaller firms, coalitions in support of opening may emerge in all the jurisdictions involved. The European Round Table of Industrialists, a vocal supporter of the single market project in the late 1980s, has been repeatedly analysed in this vein (Sandholtz and Zysman 1989, Cowles 1995, van Apeldoorn 2002).

In this context, supranational institutions matter because they affect the ease with which cross-border market-opening can be attained. This much is undisputed even among liberal intergovernmentalists (Moravcsik 1993). Supranational institutions lower transaction and monitoring costs and solve collective action problems (cf. Scharpf 1997a). The process of agreeing on a common rule-set has such potential for distributive bargaining that some degree of centralised authority can greatly enhance efficiency in finding workable compromises.

This is not the only reason firms interested in market integration push for supranational governance. Because supranational bodies themselves enjoy room for manoeuvre in policy-making, they provide opportunities for actors with a stake in supranational governance to build alliances with what are, in this respect, their natural allies. Indeed, as policy-making is transferred from the national to the supranational level, the influence of pro-integration actors rises whereas that of its opponents, who still rely on national governments, decreases. The installation of supranational bodies is therefore more than just adding an extra layer of governance that otherwise leaves patterns of governance unaltered. It is the formalisation of political authority at a level of aggregation that matches the interests and market structures subject to these institutions. It is, in short, a transnationalisation of the state in the face of altered competitive dynamics in the market place.

This feedback between patterns of governance and market structures gives structuration its momentum. Market structures inspire actors to reproduce political institutions or work towards their transformation depending on the impact that rules made through these institutions have on the competitive landscape. Changes in the competitive landscape, in turn, affect both the economic might of firms – including their (potential) status as market incumbents – and the political resources they command at different levels of governance. The overall model is shown in Figure 2.2.

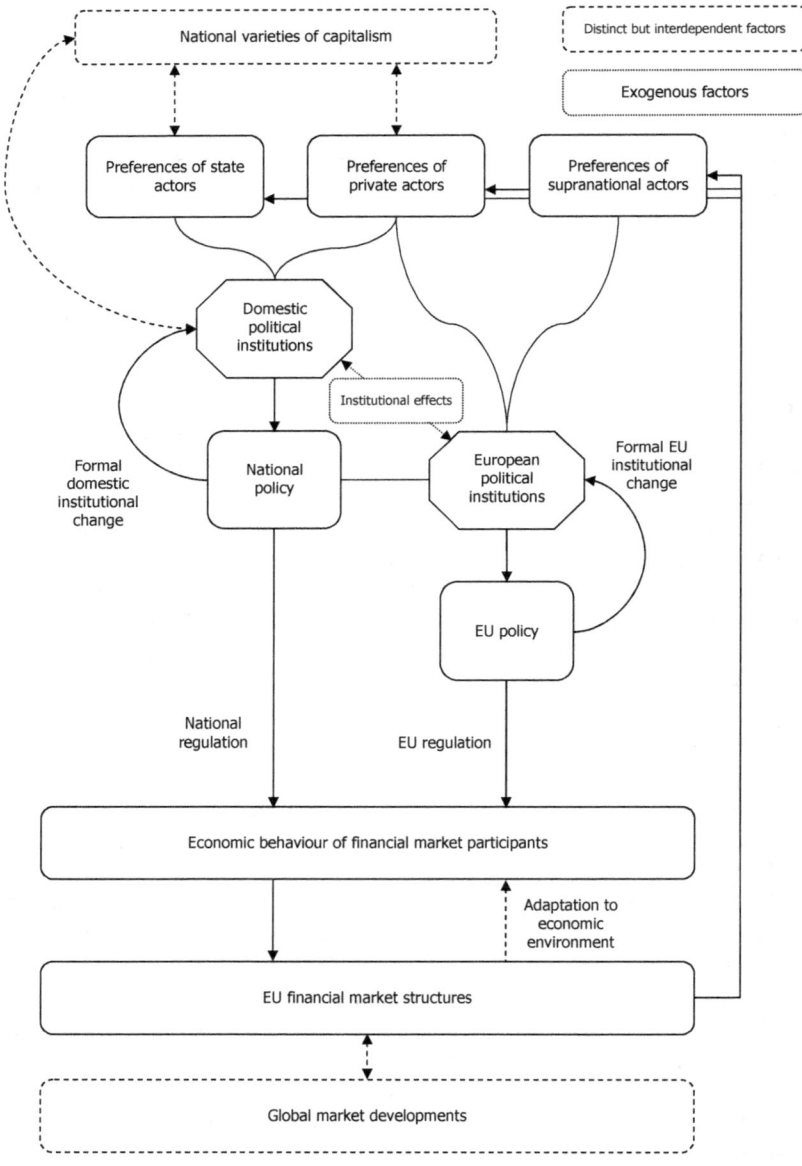

Figure 2.2: A schematic depiction of EU financial market structuration

Because structuration is not ruled by a single dynamic (cf. Cerny 2006), equilibriums between structures and agents' places in them are likely to be temporary. Even the 'fit' between the nation-state and the global economy of embedded liberalism (Ruggie 1982) was more transitory than is often suggested (Frieden 1991, Cerny 1995). The Bretton Woods system, the pinnacle of this order in financial markets, was fully operational for no more than a decade before countervailing forces and underlying tensions inspired the USA to initiate its demise in the late 1960s (Eichengreen 1998). As change in political institutions is typically relatively abrupt, the co-evolution of the two can nevertheless be conceptualised as one of 'punctuated equilibriums' (True *et al.* 1999, cf. Krasner 1984, Crouch and Farrell 2004). With a new set of political institutions created at the supranational level, it may be that at least for the time being, patterns of governance have settled into a stable state converging around the bodies of the European Union. To what degree the financial crisis erupting in 2007 will inspire agents to upset this institutional arrangement in more than fleeting ways will only become clear once the dust settles in the years to come.

Even though the supranationalisation of governance is the explanandum of this study, it is seen as one side of the transformation of what Underhill (2003, see also Underhill and Zhang 2005, Underhill 2007) has called the 'state-market condominium'. Figure 2.2 is a flow-model of structuration dynamics for capital market governance. Actors' preferences, filtered by political institutions, are turned into regulatory policy, which affects economic behaviour and thus overall market structures. Changes in this economic environment can, in turn, affect actors' preferences. As Figure 2.2 shows, two factors are denoted as 'distinct but interdependent'. In practice, the distinction between factors that are endogenous and exogenous to a dynamic is less clear cut than the dichotomy suggests (cf. Jervis 1997). Global market developments are not separate from EU trends, especially in capital markets, where London has challenged New York as the most important global financial centre (Corporation of London 2005, McKinsey 2007). European financial markets are not footnotes to global finance; they are central to it. As has been elaborated above, varieties of capitalism can inform actors' preferences and leave their imprint on domestic and eventually cross-border political institutions, even as comparative political economists debate the degree to which they have fallen prey to economic globalisation and the transformation of financial markets.

THE CORE FEATURES OF THE APPROACH

The competition politics framework that this chapter has elaborated aims to connect abstract notions of structuration in political economy with concrete insights from a broad range of theoretical literatures, including those dealing with European integration, financial liberalisation and regulation, policy-making, the emergence and functioning of political institutions and national varieties of capitalism. In addition to showing how theories from these fields can be synthesised, the competition politics approach generates four specific contributions to our understanding of political economy to which we return throughout the book.

First, the governance of financial markets – both in terms of substantive regulation and governing institutions – is the product of an elitist form of private interest politics. It is true that private actors have to forge successful alliances with public actors to achieve their aims. But as this chapter has argued, financial market incumbents typically command sufficient institutional power to do so. This emphasis on insider politics contradicts both the idea that financial market governance was guided by an overarching collective interest or that it was the outcome of a political struggle among broad coalitions.

Second, such private interest politics generate a dynamic that I call 'competition politics'. Firms' regulatory preferences are primarily informed by their desire to control and manage the competitive landscape within which they operate, rather than for example profit maximisation. Socio-economic approaches have emphasised the stability in market structures that can result from regulation as an instrument for restraining competition (Fligstein 2001). The approach advocated here, in contrast, sees competition politics both as an instrument for the reproduction of existing market structures *and* as a force behind cross-border governance and market integration, both across borders and between market segments (cf. Gadinis 2008).

Third, this dynamic defies simplistic categorisations that see either structural forces at work or a small group of agents designing market structures at will. Rather, competition politics is an instance of market structuration: actors simultaneously use both economic and political resources to affect the market structures they confront in line with their preferences. At the same time, actors' policy preferences and the resources they command to further them are influenced by the political and economic market structures within which agents operate. Changes over time in the political institutions that govern markets, including supranational integration, thus need to be analysed with an eye for both how agents' preferences shape structures (collectively binding rules, political institutions and markets) *and* how these structures inspire and constrain agents.

Fourth, the resulting stance on supranational integration emphasises actors' material interests and the transnational political-economic context in which they are embedded; at the same time, it highlights that the open-endedness of the interaction between market structures and patterns of governance is central to competition politics. This weighting of material interests challenges approaches that see free-floating identities, the supranational loyalties of bureaucrats, the independent effects of institutions or the more efficient provision of public policy as the driving forces behind supranational integration. The approach is transnational in scope because both the competitive dynamics at play and the patterns of political association and exercise of power defy the liberal intergovernmentalist notion that member states and their governments are the core actors in EU integration. It is open-ended because the attendant complexities, uncertainties and unintended consequences infuse supranational integration with more vagaries and internal contradictions than transnational historical materialists allow. Indeed, it is precisely this non-linearity of supranational integration that motivates the empirical tracing of supranational capital market governance back to its origins in the mid-1980s – the point at which the following chapter will pick up the historical thread.

chapter three | the domestic roots of regulatory reform

Scholars of financial markets often portray the 1980s as the decade when finance went global and markets were deregulated (e.g. Strange 1998, Smith and Walter 2003). Financial regulation was already in flux when the opening of capital markets first appeared on the EU agenda in the second half of the 1980s.[2] In a way, the EU seemed to be jumping onto a moving train.

This wave of domestic market opening has important consequences for analysing EU capital market integration. Most obviously, it may be that EU-level developments were epiphenomenal to domestic regulatory reforms. From this perspective, core changes took place at the national level while EU politics were only a side-show to the main story. The pattern of EU negotiations and regulation, however, does not support this view. The European regime that member states agreed in the early 1990s contained many protectionist clauses. In important respects, it was not an extension of national market liberalisation, but contained elements pointing in the opposite direction. How can these two trends be squared?

When viewed through the lens of competition politics, the tension between national market liberalisation and protectionist rules at the European level disappears. Both bear the imprint of the strategic considerations of financial market incumbents. While the subsequent chapters support this claim for EU-level politics, this chapter focuses on liberalisation at the national level. In doing so, it addresses the apparent tension between an explanation of EU politics stressing strategic agency on the one hand and national changes supposedly driven by global market structures on the other. The chapter's reappraisal of the 'decade of deregulation' shows how the two complement rather than contradict one another.

The question of whether regulatory reforms are best understood as de-regulation, the simple abolition of rules, or re-regulation, the creation of new rules, possibly to substitute old ones (cf. Cerny 1994, Vogel 1996) will be side-stepped. The debate only makes sense when re-regulation is equated with state control over markets and de-regulation with its loss. As the previous chapter argued, such a state-market dichotomy oversimplifies regulatory politics and ignores how public and private actors are often political partners. It is thus hardly surprising that financial market reforms have included both de-regulation and re-regulation and a mix of market opening and protectionism.

This chapter is important for the book's overall argument in two ways. First, it shows that EU capital market integration did not unfold against a backdrop of universal financial liberalisation driven by global market forces. Rather, the backdrop

---

2. In the 1990s, the European Community (EC) was incorporated in the European Union (EU), the label commonly used since then. For the sake of consistency, 'EU' will also be used for time periods when strictly speaking, 'EC' would be correct.

was one of regulatory reforms heavily influenced by the strategic re-orientations of national financial champions. While domestic reforms reveal national policy-making dynamics, a comparison of the UK, France and Germany shows the influence of domestic political institutions and different market structures on policy output. Second, the analysis exposes the institutional power of financial market incumbents. In this way, the chapter lays bare the domestic side of the international constellation through which national financial industries and 'their' governments jointly governed capital markets in Europe at the time.

EUROPEAN CAPITAL MARKETS AT THE END OF THE 1980s

A comparison of European financial systems and structures at the end of the 1980s shows the UK in an exceptional position (Walter and Smith 1989, Gardener and Molyneux 1990). In line with most other European countries, the French and the German financial systems were dominated by bank credit and debt securities, with stock markets playing a secondary role. In the UK, the picture was reversed. In 1985, French stock market capitalisation stood at a mere 13 per cent of GDP, compared to 24 per cent in West Germany and 60 per cent in the UK (Graham 1987b). This pattern was to continue into the early 1990s (Figure 3.1).

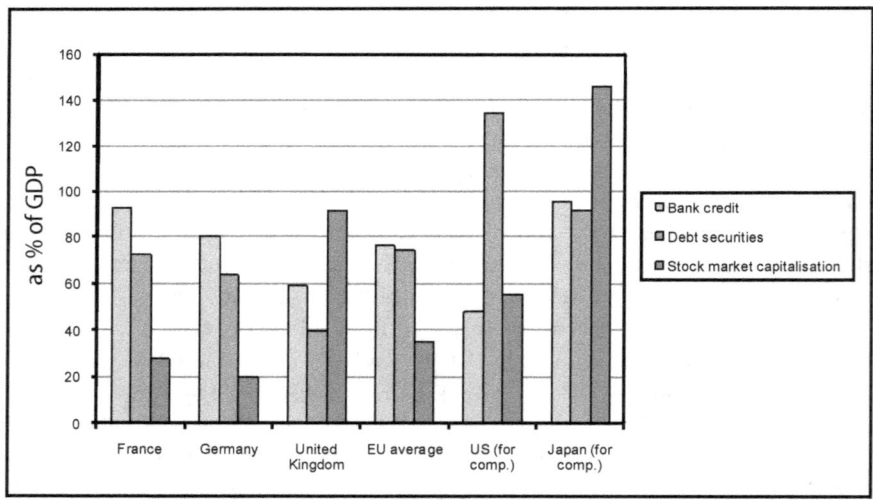

Source: European Commission 2003

Figure 3.1: Financial structures in 1991

Elsewhere in the EU, markets for non-government securities were dwarfed by credit markets; only the Benelux countries formed something of an exception. Even Italy, the fourth-largest EU economy at the time, had no significant market for non-government securities (Colvill 1995). For most European countries, this meant that their financial institutions and market places had few prospects of ever becoming internationally important. Within European securities markets, the

Swiss were the only ones in the same league as Germany, France and the UK – and Switzerland remained outside the EU.

The prominence of capital markets in the UK put the City in a leading position in Europe. In 1992, it boasted 44.1 per cent of the EU's stock market capitalisation, more than Frankfurt, Paris and Amsterdam combined. Around the same time, 43 per cent of London's equity turnover was in foreign shares; on the continent, the figure was negligible. Over 95 per cent of EU foreign equity turnover went through the City, with German shares accounting for roughly 25 per cent and French ones for half of that (Steil 1993: 3).

The City was also prominent in other ways. To establish the global reputations of firms in the securities business, *Euromoney* polled financial institutions in 1990 and 1991 and asked them to name their favourite firm. US institutions came out on top with 1,803 votes followed by the UK with 1,213. In contrast, Germany (175) and France (112) fared dismally (Sobel 1994: 132). The firms' reputations matched that of their home markets. Quantitative studies comparing European financial centres have invariably found London on top, with Frankfurt and Paris on the second tier, often alongside Zurich (Bindemann 1999: 24).

More interesting are the reasons that respondents in Bindemann's study gave for London's dominance in Europe (Ibid.: 28). Commissions, i.e. the price for trading, were not among the top ten of the twenty-three options presented. Investment firms cared little about locally specific operational costs (ranked twenty out of twenty-three) and considered fiscal regulation, which affects prices through taxes like stamp duty, the least important of all. Instead, respondents valued the human resources offered by London, the diversity and size of its markets, the diversity of its financial products, the presence of international banks, and its transaction volumes as the leading five criteria. Regulation came in sixth place. These findings challenge the notion of financial centres competing via the costs of their services – central for example in Laurence's work (2001). Rather, it confirms Sobel's finding that regulatory reforms show little statistical connection to price developments.

The relevance of the financial sector in national economies differed markedly (Figure 3.2): for employment, the UK was roughly in line with the Community average (3.7 per cent compared to 2.9 per cent). Financial services' share of national GDP, however, was more than double that of Germany, and almost triple that of France. The sophistication of London's capital markets and the concentration of international business in the City caused compensation levels to be significantly higher in the UK than in Germany or France, even though employment levels were roughly similar. In Britain, finance was, and still is, a major economic sector in its own right (cf. *The Economist* 1988).

Equity markets in Germany and France not only differed in size from those in the UK, they also played different roles in their respective economies (cf. Walter and Smith 1989: 68–93). As a first rough-and-ready distinction, British markets functioned to generate returns for investors and as markets for corporate control. On the continent, they were mainly vehicles for industrial policy, direct in the case of France, mediated by commercial banks in Germany. Accordingly, acquisitions of listed companies opposed by the target were a rarity in continental

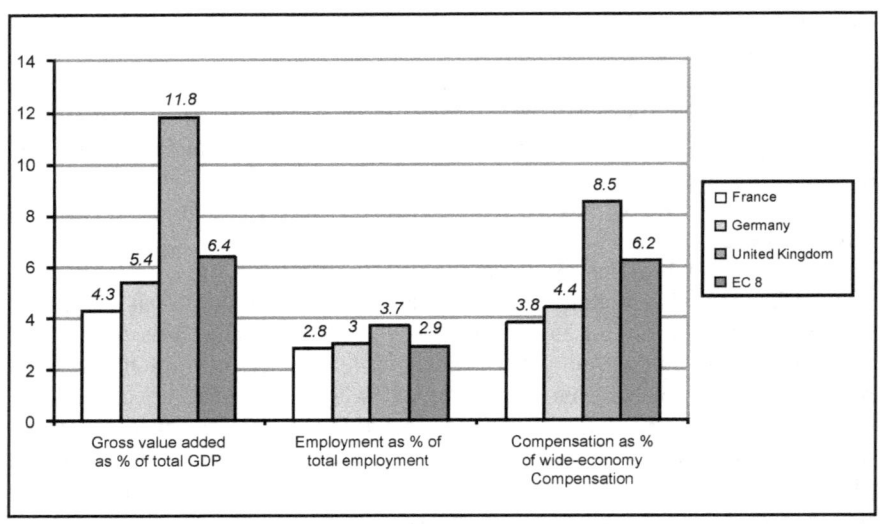

Source: Gardner and Molyneux 1990: 13

Figure 3.2: Economic relevance of financial sectors in 1985

Europe. Between 1983 and 1988 (inclusive), a mere three transactions were completed there, with a total value of $539m (Walter and Smith 1989: 60). In the UK, in contrast, twenty-five such transactions were completed, with a total value of almost $20bn.

Capital markets in the three countries were entrenched in and supported by detailed regulation. A comparison of withholding taxes is instructive: in 1988, Germany had a 25 per cent tax on dividends but none for bond interest payments. It was the mirror opposite in the UK, with dividends untaxed but a 25 per cent tax on gilt interest payments. The German regime thus encouraged firms to retain earnings and reinvest them. It discouraged holding equity for immediate reward (and thereby depressed equity prices) but encouraged bond holding instead. The opposite was true in the UK. In France, the dividing line ran between resident and foreign holders of securities: residents paid no tax on either bond interest or dividends; foreigners had to pay up to 50 per cent for the former and 25 per cent for the latter. The flexible interest withholding tax for bonds is a classic example of French interventionism, trying to fine-tune foreign investment in domestic debt. The dividend tax discouraged foreign equity ownership and was meant to keep business 'in the family'.

The credit markets dominating the French and German financial systems were controlled by national firms – a pattern typical of continental Europe at the time, with the exception of Belgium. In 1988, foreign banks accounted for 13.5 per cent of assets in France and no more than 1.8 per cent of assets in Germany (Gardener and Molyneux 1990: 21). In the UK, foreign-owned banks accounted for more than half of the total. This pattern is all the more remarkable when seen against measures of the formal openness of financial systems, which contradict stereotypical typologies (Grilli 1989). Germany, rather than being in a cluster with other 'coordinated market economies', was ranked by Williamson and Mahar (1998) as the financially most liberal country in the early 1970s out of the thirty-four they studied, more liberal than the UK or the USA. Already before the wave of 'deregulation', the authors detected little overt state intervention. Existing limits to competition rather emerged out of the behaviour of private actors, for example through self-regulation.

The German example shows how the suppression of competition can work in subtle ways. Foreign financial institutions were in principle allowed to have seats on Frankfurt's stock exchange from 1982 – almost half a decade earlier than on the London Stock Exchange (LSE) and nearly a decade before the full opening of French markets (Walter 1988: 14). But members of the German exchanges needed banking licences, which automatically excluded most foreign brokers. The tight relationships that corporate clients enjoyed with their Hausbanks meant that in spite of the formal openness of German banking, foreigners made few inroads. As already mentioned, the share of foreign banks' assets in 1988 stood at a negligible 1.8 per cent.

The overall picture is one of market fragmentation along national borders and significant differences in financial structures that reflect national varieties of capitalism. These national market places were complemented by the Euromarkets, centred in London, where currencies and securities were traded 'offshore' without technically entering the UK's financial system. These markets grew until the late 1970s but had little impact on domestic markets for financial services. As the coming sections show, this was to change in the 1980s.

REGULATORY REFORM IN GERMAN MANAGED CAPITALISM

For Schmidt (2002), Germany is the archetypal example of 'managed capitalism', which she contrasts with market capitalism (for example the UK) and state-led capitalism (France). The typology is reminiscent of Zysman's (1983: 91), who distinguished between the tripartite-negotiated, the company-led and the state-led models of economic adjustment.

The managed character of German capitalism was evident in its financial system. German banks were instrumental in the implementation of the Bundesbank's monetary policy as well as the industrial policy of national and regional governments. As has often been noted, such positive coordination (Jayasuriya 2001) of financial market policy with other policy domains generated tight policy communities that bridged the public-private divide (e.g. Coleman 1996). In securities markets, banks were given leeway to set market rules (Lütz 2002).

German industry had traditionally relied on credit rather than equity financing. Firms thus developed tight links with 'their' banks – the so-called Hausbanks (Allen and Gale 2000). Stock markets functioned as mechanisms to allocate corporate control – not through the market, but through negotiations between banks, unions and enterprises. Exposure to corporate fortunes through sizeable loans was complemented by shareholdings. These equity stakes placed bank representatives on supervisory boards and granted access to inside knowledge and decision-making. In addition, cross-shareholdings tamed potential inter-firm rivalries and thereby limited corporations' exposure to competition. German markets for corporate equity were thus more of an appendix to the economy than its central battleground. As late as 1990, only 14 per cent of German shares were in foreign hands (Story 1997: 254).

The legal provisions underpinning this system included high capital gains taxes to encourage long-term cross-shareholdings as well as flexibility in accounting for the depreciation of assets to limit companies' need for quick capital. High corporate taxes further promoted the retention of profits rather than their distribution. Holding equity with an eye for attractive dividends played only a secondary role in Germany. Conversely, the absence of rules on what elsewhere was considered insider trading deterred involvement by foreign firms. Deutschland AG – as the web of German cross-shareholdings became known – thrived on personal connections and informal information channels. This placed outsiders at a disadvantage and made Germany relatively unattractive in spite of its impressive economic performance and formal openness to foreign banks. Transparency and the concept of insider trading were so unpopular in Frankfurt that Germany stymied EU attempts to introduce binding rules in the early 1980s (McCahery 1997, Interview 020506).

Nevertheless, reform of the system, which had not seen any legal changes since the late 1960s (Franke 2000: 71), began in 1984. Deeg (2001: 21) concurs with Vitols, who found that

> [i]n Germany reform has been driven for the most part by the large banks, who desire to create a "home base" supportive of global player investment banks on the US model. (Vitols 2003: 18)

With German corporations increasingly relying on their own reserves to finance investment (Story and Walter 1997: 174) and margins in the lending business declining (Overbeck and D'Alessio 1997: 92), banks began searching for new sources of revenue in the early 1980s.

> Unable to find enough growth potential in lending and retail banking, they needed to develop fee-based sources of income. Some of this could come from offering services such as consulting to firms, but the big banks quickly determined that their best opportunities lay in financial activities related to capital markets, most importantly underwriting and trading. (Deeg 2001: 23)

Towards this end, capital markets needed to be updated and old restrictions on innovative (and lucrative) financial products lifted. It was in this spirit that the 'Frankfurt coalition' – with large Frankfurt banks at its helm – initiated reforms in the mid-1980s (Lütz 2002: 235).

The first element of these reforms concerned the admission of new financial instruments, for example floating rate notes and zero coupon bonds, and the updating of market structures to create a fully-fledged capital market infrastructure. In principle, the Bundesbank was eager to boost Frankfurt as a financial centre. But it entertained second thoughts when innovations began interfering with its own tasks (Evans 1992). For example, the Bundesbank at first resisted calls to introduce Certificates of Deposit (CDs). CDs functioned much like time deposits for lenders, but were tradeable. The Bundesbank had used banks' reserve requirements against time deposits as its preferred instrument to expand or contract credit. But it found that CDs did not fall under reserve requirements (Carr 1985c), and so if they were to replace term deposits, the Bundesbank would lose one of its favoured instruments. When it finally did admit CDs, the Bundesbank introduced reserve requirements for them as well (Carr 1985b), though it eventually compensated national banks by lowering the levels required. In another example, the Bundesbank took until 1990 to approve German banks' underwriting of debt in foreign currencies raised by German corporations (Wall Street Journal 1990). Hitherto this had not been allowed in Frankfurt; the business had been left to London.

These episodes show how the coordinated character of regulatory policy-making slowed reforms in Germany. This was in contrast to France and the UK, where state domination and greater distance between the state and business, respectively, permitted more rapid change. At the same time, disputes in Germany were usually resolved to the satisfaction of business. When the big banks told the finance ministry that specific rules were hampering the development of capital markets and sending business to foreign firms, their concerns were normally heeded. For example, banks in early 1989 were irate over the introduction of withholding taxes for foreign owners of German securities (Simonian 1988a, 1989a). They protested loudly and the tax was soon abolished.

The coordination of policy between large banks and state institutions was even more evident in the selective market opening to foreign banks. In spite of official market openness, many barriers remained, often hidden in arcane rules. In 1986, after consultation with German banks and the Bundesbank, the government invited foreign banks to participate in the Federal Bond Consortium through which the government placed its debt on the market (Carr 1986). The aim was not so much to let foreigners in, but to increase demand for German government securities, thereby driving down financing costs. Almost a third of the new players came from Japan, easing access to that country's huge savings pool. However, with foreign players' share fixed at 20 per cent of the total, there remained clear limits to competition. Foreign firms were not to challenge domestic dominance of the market.

The fixed share for foreign players was only lifted when Germany faced greater financing needs in the wake of reunification. Now the placing power of foreign players became highly important. The Bundesbank introduced a partial auctioning of bonds in 1990, meaning a loosening of fixed quotas (Campbell 1990). The top tier of German banking, however, did not relinquish this lucrative business without compensation. Deutsche Bank's growing international ambitions (Brady 1992) had been frustrated for years by its inability to get a foot into the American primary government bond market. Now that the Bundesbank was about to grant more freedoms to foreign institutions, the New York Federal Reserve reciprocated by granting Deutsche Bank 'primary dealer' status (Harverson and Campbell 1990). Liberalisation here was not a unilateral affair; it took place on a mutual basis. The main losers, particularly in Germany, were the smaller players such as the cooperatives, which for years had been complaining about the size of their allotments of government debt and received nothing in return for falling commissions.

The issue of reciprocity had come up in other liberalising measures, belying the idea that liberalisation was a matter of adapting to 'global pressures'. In 1985, for example, the Bundesbank had allowed foreign firms to lead-manage foreign issues of DM-denominated bonds in Frankfurt (Davies 1985).[3] This was to bolster Frankfurt's standing as a financial centre against the City's Euromarkets where Deutschmarks were readily available. Foreign corporations in need of German currency would in all likelihood approach their national banks first. To attract them to Frankfurt, they had to be allowed to lead-manage the issues and take the associated fees. German banks already had such rights in most important countries with the exception of Japan. Thus when the Bundesbank met with foreign banks in Frankfurt, the Japanese firms were informed that they, in effect, would be excluded from the new privileges until Japanese authorities made concessions to German banks (Carr 1985a). Liberalisation did not hurt the large German players as they continued to dominate the Frankfurt market. Rather than introducing stiff competition, one senior US banker likened foreign lead managers in Frankfurt to 'gnats buzzing around German heads' (Carr 1985d).

The biggest innovation of all was the Deutsche Terminbörse (DTB), a futures and options exchange opened in 1990 (Campbell and Hargreaves 1990). As with many German reforms, it came relatively late, the City's LIFFE had been opened in 1982, France's MATIF in 1986 and the Swiss OFFEX in 1988. Again, it was to be run and controlled by insiders in the German financial system. German banks were worried that unless Germany established its own exchange, foreign competitors would start offering products referring to German securities, for example equity options and bond futures (Simonian 1987). They also feared that cash markets could follow derivatives trading. The top firms – Deutsche Bank, Dresdner Bank, Commerzbank and Deutsche Girozentrale – thus set up a committee to study the matter. It soon found legal obstacles, including laws that banned futures trading dating from the 1930s.

Dresdner's chairman, as the head of the German Federation of Private Bankers, then sent the government an official wish list outlining the necessary regulatory changes. Hesitations notwithstanding, the government complied; one year later, most of the required legal changes were in force while the banks themselves worked out the details (Simonian 1988b). In the meantime, LIFFE had indeed announced the trading of Bund futures. All efforts, including those of the finance ministry itself, now concentrated on keeping business in the German family (Fisher 1988, Interview 020506). Deutsche Bank, in waiting for the DTB to become operational, went as far as renouncing LIFFE's contract to hedge its Bund exposures. The DTB venture proved successful over the following year, and by the mid-1990s, LIFFE's Bund contract had lost much of its significance.

---

3. A foreign issue in this case refers to selling bonds of non-German corporations denominated in Deutschmarks to a German audience.

One of the problems the DTB encountered was symptomatic of German finance at the time: the launch of the electronic exchange was followed by the question of trading screens in other countries (Lütz 2002: 237). Foreign authorities, however, were concerned about the lack of a proper regulatory framework in Germany. For the DTB to thrive, many now concluded, German regulatory and supervisory structures had to be updated. The banks had had similar experiences in other areas after realising in the second half of the 1980s that they needed foreign investors to fuel the German capital market business. The demand for (new) shares from the German public was likely to remain limited – in the 1980s, households invested no more than 1.6 per cent of their wealth in stocks (Story and Walter 1997: 173). Eventual reforms to introduce transparency were thus not inspired by global structural pressures and a heightened competition for capital. Banks had a *commercial* interest in developing capital markets, and given the lack of a domestic customer base, had to attract foreign investors (cf. Saunderson 1992).

The reform of national bourses had a similar rationale. Compared to the USA and the UK, securities markets were plainly underdeveloped – in effect the playground of a handful of large banks. Trading was done more over the phone than during the short opening hours of the eight regional stock exchanges. This fragmentation – eight bourses for equity stock that stood at a mere 30 per cent of GDP, with the majority of shares not for sale – had been consciously bolstered by the large banks (Lütz 2003b). Blue chip shares were distributed over four markets – Frankfurt, Stuttgart, Düsseldorf and Munich – while the remaining four bourses were allotted shares to ensure their survival. The governing body for the eight exchanges, the *Arbeitskreis der deutschen Wertpapierbörsen*, took decisions unanimously. While this structure impeded change, it enabled a comfortable lack of competition.

To make German stock markets more attractive to outsiders, the large banks resolved to end the dispersed trading. Unsurprisingly, the push to concentrate business in Frankfurt was resisted by the other seven markets. In the struggle that ensued, public officials sided with the private actors closest to them: the federal finance ministry and the regional authorities responsible for Frankfurt supported the large banks; local authorities elsewhere backed 'their' exchanges. In the end, the Frankfurt coalition prevailed. The episode was typical of German regulatory politics in that it did not pit the state against the market. Rather, facing each other were advocacy coalitions (Sabatier 1988) comprised of public and private actors.

Indeed, top-level working groups on financial reform included private sector representatives (*Handelsblatt* 1990). Such public-private cooperation was institutionalised in corporatist bodies such as the *Zentraler Kreditausschuss* (central credit committee, see Lütz 2003b: 122). Even if leading German banks were beginning to challenge the prevailing conception of control in domestic financial markets (Fligstein 2001), the most important competitive struggles still unfolded between national financial centres and the financial players wedded to them. After all, unlike in France and the UK, large domestic banks already dominated local securities markets. Rather than prying open markets from which they had been excluded , banks pushed for an incremental reform programme whose cumulative effects nevertheless changed the financial landscape.

In summary, the German financial system at the time was jointly managed by public and private actors. The 'positive coordination' of finance with national economic policy, in particular monetary and industrial policy, placed severe restrictions on admissible competition, especially for foreign firms supplying services to German clients. National public and private actors enjoyed a structural correspondence of interests. This correspondence was to disintegrate over the coming decade, largely as a consequence of banks' international reorientation. But as long as it lasted, it supported institutional structures that allowed public and private actors to coordinate their activities for mutual benefit.

REGULATORY REFORM IN FRENCH STATE-LED CAPITALISM

The 1980s also witnessed the reform of capital markets in France. While the direction of reform was similar to that in Germany, the political process differed; the differences largely stemmed from the distinct varieties of capitalism that had evolved in the two countries. This meant that national economic institutions faced distinct pressures and incentives to adapt to changes in the global economy. As a complement to general state interventionism and control over the economy, 'state autonomy' (Skocpol 1985) in financial market policy was greater in France than in Germany (Coleman 1996). The idiosyncrasies of French reforms were not only due to the specific character of French *economic* institutions, a line of reasoning which is common in functionalist comparative political economy (e.g. Hall and Soskice 2001b, Rajan and Zingales 2003). The historical development of French capitalism had produced specific *political* institutions that structured the policy process, and which influenced the French reforms.

This section also shows how misleading the distinction between private and public interests in financial market reform can be. The German case showed how private and public actors often rallied around common goals and confronted other public-private advocacy coalitions. In the French case, the public-private distinction is even less useful (cf. Coleman 1994: 48). After Mitterrand's nationalisations in the early and mid-1980s, most of the banking industry was in the hands of the state; brokers, known as *agents de change*, had the status of public officials (Cerny 1989). It is not therefore surprising that capital market reforms in the 1980s were state-driven. Most political and economic power was in one way or another incorporated into the state's structure. In addition, the government directly or indirectly controlled two-thirds of listed companies (Graham 1989a). The Trésor, the directorate of the finance ministry responsible for financial markets, was the focal point of the domestic financial elite. Often graduates of the same school (Schmidt 1996: 299), many members of this elite spent time at the Trésor before working in top public positions or heading state-run or affiliated banks.[4] Personal networks provided the social glue for the French policy community, even after formal links

---

4. An example would be Jacques Delors as European Commission president, Jean-Claude Trichet as head of the European Central Bank or Jean-Yves Habérer heading Crédit Lyonnais and Daniel Lebègue leading the Caisse des Depots et Consignations. (Cf. Coleman 1996: 101).

between the state and banks began to weaken.

Reforms were masterminded by the Trésor which meant that the motivation was specifically French. Domestic financial markets were unable to provide sufficient credit for the economy. Neither in Germany nor in the UK did the need to attract capital play a central role in regulatory reform. After the final breakdown of the Bretton Woods system around 1970, the French moved from the post-war overdraft economy (the *économie d'endettement*) to the system of *encadrement du credit* (Loriaux 1991: 38). This regime for allocating credit generated its own problems. Through attempts to keep inflation in check, some parts of the economy were chronically short of funds. No less than seventy special government-administered interest rate regimes still in place in 1981 only compounded the problem (Coleman 1997: 279). After the socialist experiment in 1982 and Mitterand's *grand tournant* the following year, the government resolved to overhaul financial markets.

Two aims of the reform programme stand out: the government wanted to end the micromanagement of credit allocation, which was the hallmark of the credit system, and to tap foreign sources of funding (Icard and Drumetz 1994). German financial reforms served as the template. Universal banking in Germany had generated measured competition between different kinds of financial players (savings, commercial and cooperative banks) in different market segments. It had further contributed to a more flexible allocation of savings. The anti-inflationary inclinations of the Bundesbank had saved Germany from the troubles France experienced in the years after the breakdown of Bretton Woods; even with growing capital mobility, it allowed the government to borrow at attractive rates. Being listed also enabled large companies to raise capital without indebting themselves. At the same time, the system of cross-shareholdings permitted a coordinated industrial policy and a high degree of national control. Finally, universal banking had brought the big German banks the type of balance sheets that allowed them to compete globally. The German model thus seemed to combine readiness for the new international situation with a degree of government discretion in economic guidance that the French cherished.

The Banking Act of 1984 tore down the barriers between the different segments of the credit market. Institutions ranging from the local Caisses d'Epargne to commercial giants like Banque National de Paris were to 'compete' and build their business where they saw fit. This did not mean that the allocation of credit was privatised: the same socialist government that introduced 'competition' between banks nationalised all but a handful of them. The conservative government that came to power in 1986 then reversed some of the nationalisations: Paribas was privatised the same year, Société Générale followed in 1987. The abolition of credit restrictions through the Banking Act now meant that banks needed fresh capital (Graham 1987d). Formal privatisation was the means towards this end.

The bank privatisations were part of a larger privatisation programme that fuelled the Paris stock market boom. Traditionally, French securities markets had played a subordinate role to banking proper, even more so than in Germany. Bank loans had often been subsidised by the state, making equity financing unattractive for corporations. In 1978, stock market capitalisation stood at a meagre 9 per cent of GDP (Graham 1987b). By 1985, this had risen to 13 per cent, still low compared to Germany's 24 per cent and 40 per cent in the USA. Government privatisations had a decisive impact: in 1987, 3.8m people signed up for Paribas shares alone, while the number of direct shareholders quadrupled due mainly to fourteen privatisations that raised FFR72.5bn (*The Banker* 1988b). While enthusiasm waned in the wake of the global crash later that year, the seeds of a stronger equity culture had been sown.

French securities market reforms throughout the 1980s can be grouped under two headings: a general updating of the market, similar to what happened in Germany, and what was soon called the *petit* Big Bang on the Paris Bourse. In the first instance, reforms consisted of admitting new financial instruments. In the mid-1980s the government approved the introduction of certificates of deposit and commercial paper and loosened exchange controls, aware that Paris might otherwise become a 'financial backwater' (Coleman 1997: 275). It thereby succeeded to repatriate much securities business to France, where many operations had hitherto not been possible (Walter 1988: 189). After all, BNP and Paribas had earlier moved their capital market operations to London in the light of their greater possibilities there (Graham 1987d).

The biggest innovation, however, was the *Marché à Terme d'Instruments Financiers* (MATIF), the new futures market opened in 1986. The MATIF was the brainchild of the Trésor and became an internationally recognised success, even as it started as an almost exclusively French affair (Graham 1987a, Story and Walter 1997: 214). Of the eighty-eight members in 1987, only one could count as truly foreign – American Express. The resolve to open the door to more foreign members was fed by the exchange's ambition to become a premier centre for the trade of ECU futures (Graham 1987a). As in so many other instances, liberalisation was strategic and controlled in the interest of French market incumbents. The idea was to selectively allow foreign financial institutions into the French market, certainly not to integrate them in a homogeneous European financial space.

MATIF's soaring trading volumes generated great profits for the *agents de change* and sparked jealousy among the excluded banks. The latter wanted their own markets in futures contracts, rather than being obliged to go through the *agents de change*. With the conflict escalating, the banks referred the problem to the Trésor. Heavy state patronage notwithstanding, this struggle fits the pattern of competition politics found in other countries where credit institutions were pushing into hitherto closed securities markets (see Fidler 1987 for Canada, Sobel 1994 for the UK, the USA and Japan). When the banks finally prevailed, the head of the stock exchange, Xavier Dupont, spoke of authorities having had to put an end to the 'civil war' (Graham 1987c).

The struggle continued as the reform initiative passed to the private sector. A mere two years after the settlement, and much to the chagrin of the MATIF and its official sponsors, a consortium of French banks and a Swedish specialist set up a rival exchange, dubbed OMF (Graham 1989b). The sponsoring banks included BNP and Paribas – the two that had already broken rank by setting up their capital market operations in London – and Crédit Commercial de France, privatised in 1987 (Graham 1988a). These cracks in the public-private front continued to widen as the direct links between the government and financial institutions weakened. But as in Germany, there remained a structural correlation between large banks' interests and those of public actors. For both, it still made sense to think in terms of 'national markets', to associate on that basis, and to form policy preferences accordingly.

The other aspect of French financial market reforms – those regarding the Paris bourse itself – was reminiscent of developments at the LSE. The Stock Exchange Reform Act of 1988 turned the *agents de change* into private enterprises and limited their brokerage oligopoly until the beginning of 1992 (Lehmann 1997). At the same time, legislation allowed the newly christened *sociétés de bourse* to raise capital from external sources, which was necessary if they were to trade on their own account. In effect, this meant that what had happened elsewhere was to be repeated in Paris: large financial players would buy themselves into the stock market by folding specialist firms into their own operations (Graham 1987b). By the end of 1990, close to 80 per cent of the small specialist firms had effectively been bought up.

The removal of bond trading from the stock exchange monopoly in 1987 was no less consequential: the market share of the large banks, which could henceforth act as market makers, surged to 73 per cent in the first half of 1988 (Graham 1988b). Again, French players got most of the action and were the prime beneficiaries of the 'liberalisation'. The development was of course hardly accidental. Up to this point, it closely followed the script written by the Trésor.

The reform of regulatory and supervisory structures informalised the closed-shop characteristics of the French policy community, but unsurprisingly failed to abolish them (cf. Coleman 1996: 97). In principle, the proposed structure again resembled the British model, featuring self-regulation plus a statutory body with punitive powers. Towards this end, the authority of the *Commission des Operations de Bourse* (COB) was expanded, giving it a role not unlike that of the Securities and Investment Board in the UK (see Moran 1991). Only France approached the model from the other side. Here self-regulation was the new element, taking the form of the Conseil de Bourses de Valeur (CBV) for stock markets with stock exchange firms as members.

'Regulatory competition' between financial centres was most palpable in the Paris bourse's rivalry with London's SEAQ International. The latter functioned as a hybrid between a conventional exchange and an information distributor. Operational since 1985 and fully automatic, it allowed market-makers – firms willing to buy and sell a specific range of shares – to quote their prices on a continuous basis, and to make these prices known to other parties through the system. Deals would then be made over the telephone; the physical trading floor had become obsolete.

By the end of the 1980s, this London-based system had attracted around 30 per cent of trading in French equities. Big players in particular liked the SEAQ because it facilitated trading large swathes of shares at stable prices, so-called block trades. French regulators had traditionally limited block trading in the name of investor protection.[5] In 1991, firms stepped up the pressure (Dawkins 1991b). The commission studying the matter was chaired by René de la Serre, head of Crédit Commercial de France (CCF) (Dawkins 1991a). A newly privatised second-tier firm, CCF was well positioned to criticise the government for dragging its feet. Leading French firms had themselves started to use the SEAQ and were ambivalent. When the report came in, the CBV quickly decided to facilitate block trading, even if it did not go as far as some reformers would have liked (Rawsthorn 1992).

The authorities knew that the half-hearted measures would be insufficient to stymie the trading of French shares in London. At the same time, it remained unwilling to copy the SEAQ model. Instead, they made the question of transparency in securities trading a central issue in European negotiations on the Investment Services Directive, a point to which we will be return in the following chapter. The episode makes clear, however, how the initiative for reform had begun to shift from the Trésor towards the financial institutions. The harmony of interests between financial institutions and public actors was showing its first serious fissures.

The French politico-economic elite continued to keep a close watch over the ability of foreign institutions to make inroads into the domestic market for financial services, and over the possibility of foreign control over important domestic financial service providers. In France's case, Vogel's qualification of the reforms as strategic re-regulation is apt (Vogel 1996). As many scholars have noted, the centralised state enabled public actors to react swiftly to perceived policy challenges (Coleman 1996, Schmidt 2002). Widespread state ownership, and later patronage, of financial institutions helped. All the same, French authorities sensed they would be unable to compete with London unless they gave up their interventionist agenda and protectionism. European policy would thus become an increasingly crucial avenue to address hitherto beyond-the-border problems.

REGULATORY REFORM IN BRITISH MARKET CAPITALISM

Capital markets in Britain were likewise overhauled in the 1980s. The politics behind the reforms again differed from those in France and Germany. Such variation should not come as a surprise: the role of capital markets in the British economy differed from that in the continental economies. There was no interventionist economic policy within which capital markets played an important role, particularly after the Thatcher government took over in 1979. The lack of such positive coordination created room for actors other than the government to play key roles in market regulation, not least the industry itself. The flip-side of self-regulation was the institutionalised incapacity of financial firms to dominate government policy

---

5. If a financial institution plans a large transaction, it is eager to hide its intentions from the market lest prices move against it. It favours lower disclosure standards and a time lag for reporting trades to the authorities, who may publish the data. If financial institutions are allowed this degree of secrecy, however, they may use it to the disadvantage of particularly smaller investors. These investors hear of transactions that may hurt their positions only long after the fact. In addition, lower disclosure rules might encourage all sorts of market rigging and other collusive behaviour among participants.

once capital market regulation appeared on the political agenda.

The reforms themselves have been well researched and documented (e.g. Moran 1991, Augar 2000). For our purposes, two aspects deserve emphasis. First, domestic factors were central (cf. Sobel 1994) – regulatory changes can only be understood by referring to the specificities of the British state and the peculiar structure of the British financial industry at the time. As with Germany and France, this belies purely exogenous, 'global' pressures as the main force behind the reforms. Second, competition politics mattered. Once change was in the air, three clusters of firms emerged: established securities markets houses, British clearing banks, and foreign (investment) banks hitherto active in the offshore Euromarkets.[6] Their conflicting interests emerged during the domestic reforms – and reappeared at the EU level in the years to come.

The capital market structures that have developed in the UK since the 1960s are probably unique in the world. By the mid 1980s, the City of London was playing host to the globally integrated Euromarkets and the top bracket of international financial institutions active there. Alongside the Euromarkets, the City also accommodated the national securities markets, including the London Stock Exchange (LSE), dominated and controlled by traditional British merchant banks, stock brokers and jobbing firms (cf. Augar 2000). There was thus not one, but two 'Cities' (Thompson 1997). While the names of those active in the Euromarkets twenty years ago still represent the top league of global finance, the names of the top British firms are now mostly forgotten.[7]

State guidance of the British economy through the financial sector was negligible (Zysman 1983: 171). There was virtually no public ownership of financial institutions, while the relationship between the national industry and the clearing and merchant banks was at arm's length. State involvement in capital markets mainly functioned through the Bank of England, which had formal oversight powers. The Bank's role, however, was ambiguous. Only nationalised in 1946, it functioned as much as an advocate of City interests *vis-à-vis* Whitehall as the other way around (Ibid.: 200). Direct government guidance was virtually absent.

The City functioned as an 'esoteric' club (Moran 1984a: 4). Market rules either took the form of industry self-regulation or informal 'gentleman's agreements' among firms or with the Bank of England. The LSE functioned as a members-only club; the execution of client orders and actual share trading were controlled by two oligopolies free to set their own rules. Other capital market functions, such as the issuance of securities, were handled by yet another group of firms, the merchant banks. Their oligopoly was slightly less formalised, but with the Accepting Houses Committee (AHC), the merchant banks had a body through which they

---

6. Clearing banks are banks in the traditional sense: financial institutions involved in deposit-taking and lending. As in the USA, they had been excluded from the securities markets business in the UK.

7. Think of the merchant banks Schroders, Hill Samuel, Samuel Montagu, Charterhouse and Robert Fleming (all among the top ten in 1982/83), the brokers Hoare Govett, James Capel, Scrimgeour Kemp Gee and Phillips & Drew (top four in 1983) and the jobbing firms Akroyd & Smithers, Wedd Durlacher, Pinchin Denny, Smith Brothers and Bisgood Bishop (top five in the same year).

could coordinate their activities and agree on common norms and rules. Because the government was barely involved in capital market policy, firms' direct political connections with Whitehall were poor. The AHC, for example, did little in the way of lobbying (Moran 1984b: 177). Other financial sector associations that later rose to prominence such as the British Bankers Association (Filipovic 1997: 125) were not yet involved in capital market matters due to the separation of merchant and commercial banking.

The government's main concern was that the City and the institutions within it should thrive. The financial industry's economic role, in terms of employment, taxes and contribution to the balance of payments, was more important than its position in economic policy (on wealth-generation in the City, see Leyshon and Thrift 1992). This explains the government's relative indifference to the problems the 1980s capital market reforms created for British firms, and why the firms lacked the institutional power to do anything about them.

The history behind the 'Big Bang', as the LSE rule changes of 27 October 1986 came to be known, differs markedly from what happened in Germany and France. The nickname reflects the magnitude of the changes the reforms triggered in the City's capital markets, but from a longer-term perspective, little about these reforms demonstrate a coherent government strategy. Two years after a change in its rules in 1976, the Office of Fair Trading (OFT), which was responsible for competition policy, more or less stumbled upon the cartel-like structures of the LSE (Moran 1991). Baffled by what it found, it referred the LSE's rule book to the Restrictive Practices Court for review. It complained about the single capacity system, fixed commissions and the restricted membership of the exchange (Sobel 1994: 37, Vogel 1996: 101). Unsurprisingly, the LSE and its members were reluctant to surrender their cartel privileges. In contrast to both France and Germany, there was no such thing as automatic government support for the financial industry. The legal proceedings started to run their course.

Almost certain of defeat, the LSE finally succumbed to the government's demands in 1983, one day before the court was to pronounce its ruling. Nicholas Goodison, LSE chairman, and Cecil Parkinson, head of the Department for Trade and Industry (DTI), struck a deal. Goodison promised to amend the LSE rule books in line with the DTI's requirements. Membership was to become more open and fixed commissions would be abolished. In return, the ministry removed the LSE from the jurisdiction of the Restrictive Practices Court.

The initial referral of the LSE to the Restrictive Practices Court was exogenous to any financial market dynamics. But once the dispute broke out, other stakeholders quickly seized the opportunity to push their own agendas. Most importantly, the clearing banks saw their chance to break into a profitable market segment from which they had been excluded. Their efforts were successful. As a main component of the Parkinson-Goodison agreement, the LSE loosened restrictions for non-members to buy themselves into stock market firms, even though the Office of Fair Trading, the initial force behind the reforms, had never voiced any complaints on this point.

It was the abolition of these restrictions that made the 'sell-out' of the old 'domestic' City possible. Even before the Big Bang, most of the City's stock market firms had lost their independence (Augar 2000). Twenty years later, a British securities industry worth its name no longer exists. In an ironic twist of fate, the British clearing banks that successfully opened British securities markets to outsiders paved the way for a third group of institutions to dominate the City: foreign investment banks. Of the British high street banks that dared to foray into securities markets, only Barclays still plays a significant role.

A spate of scandals in the years before and after 1980 had fuelled the impression that informal self-regulation combined with winks and nods from the Bank of England would no longer suffice. The government commissioned a study, which was to become the Gower Report, on how market regulation could be updated. In his report, Professor Gower asked for greater government oversight of self-regulatory organisations (SROs). Keen to preserve their independence, leading City firms opposed the plan, and with the help of the Bank of England, got their way (Moran 1991: 72). Instead of direct government oversight, the SROs came under the purview of a private organisation, the Securities and Investment Board (SIB). In view of their fate over the past two decades, the confidence of British financial institutions in the mid-1980s and their dismissal of public oversight appear misplaced; greater participation by public actors might have worked in their favour through patronage in times of crisis. Instead, the resulting cobweb of self-regulatory bodies generated few shared interests between the government and British securities firms, though it did generate ample confusion and frustration (Lascelles 1988b). A decade after the introduction of the system, it was abolished due to its deficiencies.

The UK reforms integrated the two 'Cities' – the domestic markets and the Euromarkets (Thompson 1997). London's openness since the early 1960s had made the provision of non-British financial services an important industry (cf. Helleiner 1994). Only one British firm, S.G. Warburg, played a significant role in these markets; most firms were American, Japanese, German or Swiss.[8] Their activities were deemed 'offshore', meaning that the financial flows of these markets remained outside the UK financial system (Burn 1999). The government did not intervene in them (Vogel 1996: 95). After all, continental banks alone employed almost 14,000 people in the City in 1988 (*The Banker* 1988a) and the industry was on the rise: since the beginning of the decade, the volume of international bonds had more than quadrupled, with the bulk of the activity going through London (Walter 1988: 3).

The Euromarkets functioned as an entrance to European markets for foreign firms. These firms, above all the American ones, also introduced a new business culture that was to spread throughout the continent: transaction banking. Hitherto all European financial systems had functioned on the basis of personal or institutional relationships. This was as true for the German Hausbank system as for the 'gentlemanly' capitalism that prevailed in the City. The American firms turned

---

8. Cf. the league table for Euroequities for 1986 and 1987. While the positions vary between the two years, American firms dominate in both. (Gardener and Molyneux 1990: 177). For an overview of Eurobonds, (see Ibid.: 206).

capital markets into sellers' markets: they created demand for products where none had existed, poached clients from competitors and broke conventions to boost profits (cf. Partnoy 2002). As Chapter Five will show, this increased dynamism in financial services reached European firms in the 1990s and helped inspire their reorientation towards a liberal, transnationally integrated EU capital market, setting the stage for rapid contagion when the US subprime crisis broke out.

When the domestic British debate over regulatory reform spilt over into the Euromarkets, participants there successfully kept public intervention at bay. In 1985, the top Eurobond underwriters created a new business association, the International Primary Market Association (IPMA), to fend off regulatory oversight (Urry 1985). Their bargaining position was strong: at the time, about three-quarters of global Eurobond activity was thought to go through London's markets – a business twice as large as the one in UK government bonds (Riley 1985). The Securities and Investment Board eventually appointed a weathered practitioner as director of international securities, Richard Britton of Drexel Burnham Lambert. Britton proved sympathetic to industry demands – for example, to allow 'stabilisation' in bond markets, a practice dismissed by many as simple market-rigging, and the 'soft commissions' of the leading UK investment bank at the time, S.G. Warburg (cf. Wolman 1986, Waller 1990, Waters 1991b). The IPMA was allowed to continue to write its own rules (Mügge 2006).

Domestic capital market reforms made the barriers between international and domestic industries more permeable. American firms in particular made use of looser LSE rules to either set up their own operations or buy themselves into member firms (Augar 2000). The American firms were well adapted to competition since market restrictions on Wall Street had been eliminated in 1975. Their growing role in British markets quickly fed into the political arena as well.

As the market shares of the firms it represented fell through the mid-1980s, the Accepting Houses Committee – the de facto trade association of the British merchant banks – began to look like an anachronism. In 1987 it changed both its name and structure. Together with the former Issuing Houses Association, it was rechristened the British Merchant Banking and Securities Houses Association (BMBA) (Thomson 1987, Filipovic 1997: 128). Foreign members were introduced, though the voting power of non-EU firms was capped (Lascelles 1988a). Six years later, 'British' was removed from its name (Observer 1994). The BMBA became the London Investment Banking Association (LIBA), which is one of the most influential lobby groups in the arena today.

A closer look at the changes of the mid-1980s shows that despite 'globalisation', firms with a pan-European vision were few in number. Nevertheless, the face of the British securities industry changed fundamentally in the three years between the Parkinson-Goodison agreement and the Big Bang. The majority of the jobbing and broking firms were bought by merchant, investment and clearing banks jostling for position in the post-Big Bang era. But whereas British, American and Swiss firms fought to secure a piece of the broking and market-making pie, firms from other EU countries hardly budged. German and French firms, despite their well-established positions in the Euromarkets, were conspicuously absent from the first round of the sell-out, illustrating how the Euromarkets complemented the essentially domestic focus of these institutions. Insofar as domestic clients valued access to these markets, either as buyers or sellers of securities, large banks were expected to be present, functioning as bridgeheads between national clients and global markets. But, for example, French firms had no ambition to arrange deals between two British clients and thus penetrate the *domestic* UK market. Whereas the market for financial *instruments* showed clear signs of 'globalisation', the market for financial *services* retained distinct national biases (Corrigan 1990, cf. *The Banker* 1988a).

EUROPEAN STATE-MARKET CONDOMINIUMS IN COMPARISON

Reforms in Germany, France and the UK bear the clear imprint of their respective varieties of capitalism, which informed their business models, patterns of bank ownership, overall market structures as well as political institutions. At one end of the spectrum, state control of the financial sector in France meant reforms followed a coherent plan and were (initially) dominated by state objectives. In contrast, the crucial Big Bang reforms in the UK began almost by accident; strategic objectives played a much smaller role. But as in France, market participants seized opportunities to improve their competitive positions wherever possible. At first sight, the German case seems to rest between the other two: strategic state objectives played a role, but were not the driving force behind the reforms. Yet what distinguished Germany from both France and the UK was the heavy influence of bank interests on regulatory change. Banks' organisational autonomy from the state, coupled with privileged access to policy-making, gave them more institutional power than their French and British counterparts. Table 3.1 summarises these differences.

As the analysis has shown, the competitive concerns of domestic market incumbents shaped regulatory reforms. These concerns depended on national market structures while their influence varied with domestic political institutions. State dominance in France meant that the competitive conflicts between the *agents de change* and the commercial banks only surfaced once privatisations began. In Germany the dominance of the universal banks within securities markets ameliorated competitive struggles between groups of market participants; they instead focused their energies on generating new business, both domestically and abroad. In the UK, the presence of the Euromarkets in the City allowed foreign firms to dominate domestic securities markets within a decade of the Big Bang – even though the original challengers to the domestic cartel had been British clearing banks.

Taken together, these reforms demonstrate how market incumbents' preferences were slowly shifting in favour of business internationalisation, even if reforms remained strategic and dominated by national (business) actors and the market for capital market services remained fragmented along national borders. Banks providing purely domestic services in foreign countries remained rare outside of the UK. The politics surrounding securities markets in Europe in the 1980s could still be described in traditional terms of national policy communities, national markets, national regulatory regimes and international competition (though limited in the realm of services). These politics formed the domestic side of the international constellation, the European dimension of which the next chapter addresses.

Table 3.1: Financial systems and their embeddedness compared

	Germany	France	United Kingdom
Market structures	Foreign banks play negligible role.	Foreign firms play small role; higher than in Germany because the French current account deficit necessitates capital inflows and the presence of foreign firms to sell French securities.	Divided between a relatively closed and detached domestic financial system, including the LSE, and highly internationalised Euromarkets.
Embeddedness	High. Banks and system of cross shareholdings essential for industry policy. Banks also play important role in monetary policy.	Very high. Financial system used to channel credit and for industrial policy. Extensive state ownership of financial firms.	Low
Relationship between public and private actors	Cooperative. Public actors inclined to yield to private pressure.	Almost symbiotic. Top personnel move from government to banks and back with ease. Fissures start to appear in the wake of privatisation in the late 1980s.	Mixed. No single discernible 'government' stance. Industry's relationship with BoE often cooperative, but relations with OFT and DTI more adversarial.
Policy-making community	Extensive industry self-regulation; contacts with public actors through common policy community for credit market.	Trésor at the helm; includes top-level bureaucrats and industry representatives.	Industry self-regulation; under indirect government oversight after the FSA.

chapter four | negotiating the single market

Bargaining over the single market for investment services was a protracted and acrimonious affair (Brown 1997). The Commission tabled its first proposal for the Investment Services Directive (ISD) late in 1988; it could not be adopted until May 1993. Negotiations for the second important directive for investment services – the Capital Adequacy Directive (CAD) – at times effectively broke down (Waters 1991a). It, too, was only finalised at the turn of 1992/93. Compared to other financial market sectors such as insurance and banking, the ISD did not contribute as much as had been hoped to create a single, unified market (Steil 1993, 1998). The result reflected the underlying constellation of competitive interests in Europe at the time. The protectionist impulses of national governments, and of the financial industries that their positions mirrored, were too strong and irreconcilable.

The story of the negotiations and this 'first round' of European financial market integration has been covered in detail by other authors (see Steil 1993, Brown 1997, Leyshon and Thrift 1997, Story and Walter 1997, Underhill 1997). The aim of this chapter is therefore not to rehearse yet again, but to place the initial stages of EU capital market integration on a firm theoretical footing. Its core question is simple: why did efforts to establish a single European market in investment services fail to live up to official ambitions? The answer to this question forms the backdrop against which the renewed – and this time more successful – integration efforts since the late 1990s are evaluated. Even when examined on its own, however, the failure presents a puzzle. It cannot simply have been governments' hesitancy to cede 'sovereignty' to a supranational body. In the same year that the ISD was adopted, European governments signed the Treaty of Maastricht that would lead most of them to relinquish their national currencies before the end of the decade. Also, the Second Banking Coordinating Directive, the ISD's sibling for credit markets, took less than a year to elicit agreement from European governments and was formally adopted at the end of 1989. What made investment services different?

The competition politics thesis advanced in this book points to the divergent regulatory preferences of national financial market incumbents in the central EU member states as the core obstacle to agreement. Negotiations largely depended on agreement between Germany, France and the UK. Their positions represented the spectrum of opinion at the negotiating table; the nine smaller EU members rallied around them in varying constellations. Agreement among the big three was needed to adopt legislative proposals, while the smaller countries could always be brought on board by giving them extra time to 'adjust' to the agreed measures.

Recognising the difficulty of agreeing on a single set of harmonised standards, the Commission chose mutual recognition as the way forward for the single market project, including financial services (Moravcsik 1998: 354, Egan 2001). Combined with a single passport and home country control, mutual recognition, it was thought, would unleash regulatory competition and thus further convergence. The theoretical attraction of the approach did not prevent disillusion once it was put into practice. The regulatory competition unleashed by this regime was double-edged: governments did compete, and used regulation to do so. But they used regulation not only to attract mobile business, but to give their own financial players a competitive edge. Regulation, it turned out, could be a tool for protectionism as much as for liberalisation.

This chapter details this argument in two steps. The first step places the negotiations in a historical perspective and locates financial markets in the single market project. The second step analyses the negotiations around the ISD and the CAD and the competition politics that dominated them, locating these politics in global efforts to craft common rules. In spite of their limits, the market-opening European directives sowed the seeds for the further transnationalisation of the financial industry and thus a shift in large banks' preferences towards EU rules that would go far beyond the original agreements. The regulatory structures that European public and private actors negotiated in the early 1990s thus inspired new agency half a decade later: the ISD triggered market changes that would make its own overhaul look almost inevitable around the turn of the millennium.

FINANCIAL SERVICES IN THE SINGLE MARKET PROJECT

Financial services occupied an awkward position in the single market project. Measured against the salience of financial matters in the 1990s, they were conspicuously peripheral to the project when it was initiated around 1985. Whereas large European industrial firms played an important role in re-launching the internal market – just how important a role remains a matter of debate (Sandholtz and Zysman 1989, Cowles 1995, Moravcsik 1998: 355, van Apeldoorn 2002) – financial firms were hardly visible. There is little evidence that they were a driving force behind integration.

Once the single market programme was under way, financial firms' interest in it remained subdued (de Jonquieres 1988). Only a small group of international banks took it seriously; among the most prominent were Barclays, ING and Deutsche Bank (Interview 160306.b). The City of London was digesting the effects of the Big Bang and the Financial Services Act. The Euromarkets were so far removed from any regulatory oversight that significant intervention by any public authority, European or otherwise, seemed unlikely. For securities markets, the wake-up call came once the Second Banking Coordination Directive (commonly abbreviated as 2BCD) enshrined pan-European access for universal banks in 1989 (Interview 030406). 'Europe' had left its first imprint on the competitive landscape. From the perspective of firms in the City, negotiations around the CAD and the ISD had to recalibrate the balance between bank and non-bank players. The consequences of 2BCD for securities markets provided incentives to stay at the bargaining table; without them, negotiations may well have broken down.

This was surprising as the failure to create a functioning single market in investment services came at a time when governments were anything but timid in their integration efforts. As pointed out above, the watered down ISD was adopted by the Council in the same year European governments agreed on the Treaty of Maastricht. In areas where agreement could be reached on substance, the intergovernmental nature of EU decision-making was no obstacle to the adoption of new legal regimes. The outcome in investment services was thus not due to adverse decision-making structures. In other areas, notably the launching of the single market programme itself, the Commission had played an important role as a policy entrepreneur. Yet when it came to securities markets, the Commission was sidelined. In short, the institutional make-up of the EU was not responsible for the limited success in securities markets integration. Its roots lay in competitive issues unique to the sector.

The Role of Finance in the Launch of the Single Market Project
Prior to the 1980s, the EU had achieved little financial market integration (Nicoll 1993). The First Banking Coordination Directive, adopted in 1977, granted EU financial institutions the right to open branches throughout the Union (Story and Walter 1997: 14).[9] But due to the differences between national financial regimes, it provided banks with few incentives to Europeanise. The directive's effects on the industry were minimal.

In banking as well as insurance, most EU members were reluctant to comply with the requirements of market opening legislation. Representing frustrated insurance firms, the British Commissioner, Tugendhat, initiated legal proceedings at the European Court of Justice against a number of continental EU member states in 1983 (Young and Wallace 2000). In that same year, the Commission developed plans for a single market in financial services as part of a larger package. The plans had little immediate effect.

The real push for financial market integration came with the White Paper on the completion of the internal market, tabled by the Commission two weeks before the Milan Council in June 1985 (European Commission 1985a). Compared to many industrial sectors, financial services played a minor role in the White Paper. This was even more the case for securities markets than for banking and insurance. For the 1987–1992 period, the White Paper suggested only one legislative project in the field: a directive concerning investment advisors (European Commission 1985b) – a field that turned out to be marginal to the push for integrating capital markets over the next two decades (Fisher 1988). The selling point of the single market vision was the building of an integrated economic space for the production and consumption of goods. Financial services mattered primarily insofar as they were conducive to this project.

Most scholars of the single market project agree that giving large corporations the space to organise their operations on a pan-European basis was central to the 1992 endeavour. Disagreement centres on the relative importance of different

---
9. Council Directive 77/780/EEC.

groups of actors: Sandholtz and Zysman have emphasised the 'entrepreneurial' role of the Commission, and how it could suddenly sell a long-time favourite – the single market – as the solution to Europe's economic woes, particularly rising unemployment (Sandholtz and Zysman 1989, cf. Young and Wallace 2000: 91). The Commission proposed pan-European industrial restructuring in key sectors as an answer to Japanese competition. It was aided by a 'transnational industry coalition [that] perceived the need for European-level action and supported the Commission's efforts' (Sandholtz and Zysman 1989: 96, cf. Dinan 1999: 111f).

Cowles has focused even more narrowly on support from industry, particularly through the European Round Table of Industrialists (ERT, see Cowles 1995). In her reading,

> business leaders from the ERT largely were responsible for relaunching and *setting the agenda* of the single market programme in the early 1980s. (Cowles 1995: 503, emphasis in original)

Evidence presented by Cowles and van Apeldoorn shows how the single market idea was 'alive' within corporate circles before 1985. Again, both identify 'competitive threats' from American and particularly Japanese producers as key factors (van Apeldoorn 2002: 123). In a nutshell, top European corporations wanted to exploit the economies of scale a single market would offer. In doing so, they pushed for the same kind of market re-organising that this book argues happened in securities markets a decade later (see also Fligstein and Mara-Drita 1996).

Building on a perspective with a strong emphasis on national preferences in European integration, Moravcsik's argument on the 1992 project and the Single European Act also stresses the (perceived) imperatives emanating from the restructuring of the global economy:

> [N]ational preferences primarily reflected economic interests, and in particular increasing global and regional trade and investment, which exacerbated concerns about international competitiveness. (Moravcsik 1998: 318)

In his subsequent analysis of these national preferences, the core factor is domestic industry support in the face of common competitive threats and perceived transnational opportunities. Thus, regardless of their differences, scholars agree that industry support for the project was crucial – whether it made itself felt domestically, within transnational policy coalitions, or as the avant-garde of a transnational capitalist class.

To a certain extent, financial market integration was subordinated to market integration in the interests of big industry. As Moravcsik found, 'deregulation in financial services [was] not initially the central part of Cockfield's White Paper' (Moravcsik 1998: 336). In transnational as well as domestic political contexts, banks and especially securities houses were not overly enthusiastic. Indeed, one of the earliest integration efforts in wholesale investment services came from the ERT when it set up the European Venture Capital Association to fund pan-European industrial projects in 1984 (Cowles 1995: 508).

In setting the *general* agenda – including the integration of European financial services, particularly investment banking – well-established national policy communities for financial services were minor players at best. It was only when work on individual directives began that they reasserted themselves. In this sense, the ignition of the integration process in finance came from outside the political space whose inner dynamics were later to determine its direction. Because this external impulse did not fall on particularly fruitful ground within the inner circles of financial market politics, integration remained incomplete.

More Efficiency in European Finance?

> The broad aims of the 1992 project [in financial markets] were fairly straightforward: they were to boost the effectiveness and efficiency of European economic activity through the easing of barriers to market processes. (Leyshon and Thrift 1997: 95)

With the benefit of hindsight, the picture was more complicated. In particular, Leyshon and Thrift do not adequately differentiate between the integration of the market for financial *instruments* (including currencies) and the market for financial *services*. In practice, most financial instruments are difficult to obtain without an ancillary financial service (for example brokerage); the difference may thus seem irrelevant. But the distinction becomes important in assessing alleged policy goals. Whereas policy-makers profess concern over optimising markets so financial *instruments* are priced 'correctly', financial institutions are much more interested in the prices of the *services* they sell. The two objectives can be at odds. Take, for example, stock markets: the 'efficient' pricing of shares might warrant concentration of their trading in one exchange, whereas the efficient pricing of trading services would require competition between different exchanges. So what does more efficiency in financial markets refer to – the instruments or the services? This under-appreciated distinction continues to haunt financial services integration by allowing actors to call for outright contradictory policies in the name of increased efficiency. What is clear is that as the baton was passed to members of established policy communities, concern over the price of *services* came to overshadow concerns over the efficient allocation of capital and the pricing of financial *instruments*.

Most of the studies that tried to quantify the single market's economic benefits in the second half of the 1980s were ambiguous on this point (Tsoukalis 1997: 68), combining static effects – largely one-off welfare increases through price cuts resulting from trade openness – with dynamic ones (Egan 2001: 46). In the long run, the second category was supposed to be much more important: the increased efficiency of production that was to result from the restructuring of European industry, the exploitation of economies of scale, and lower X-inefficiencies thanks to higher competitive pressures.

It was in these dynamic effects of integration that financial services gained prominence within official accounts of the single market. For example, the so-called Cecchini Report (Cecchini 1988) estimated that the economic benefits from the financial services sector could be up to a third of the total benefits from the single market project as cheaper capital would benefit all sectors (Leyshon and Thrift 1997: 83).[10] Other studies tried to estimate price decreases from heightened competition. The widely quoted Price Waterhouse study for example, calculated that integration would save consumers between 0.3 per cent and 1 per cent of EU GDP on spending on financial services (see also *The Economist* 1988). Some observers shared this optimistic vision while others remained sceptical (Grilli 1989, Walter 1989), wondering how the spoils would be distributed – something about which most studies had little to say (Tsoukalis 1997: 71).[11]

In any case, while integration enthusiasts trumpeted the economic gains to be derived from financial market integration, they failed to impress all of the parties negotiating the single market for investment services. Once discussion turned to details and core policy communities became involved, overall 'integration logics' receded to the background – never mind the abstract 'Costs of Non-Europe'. As the following sections will show, considerations over the competitiveness of national financial industries trumped all other issues. But before we turn to the negotiations, we need to understand the broader 'legislative environment' in which they took place.

Edging Towards a Single Securities Market: Capital Movements and Other Prerequisites

Once the Council endorsed the single market project in June 1985, and member states, in a radical departure, ratified the Single European Act in early 1986, the European political apparatus started to digest the roughly 300 legislative measures suggested by the 1985 White Paper. Out of the legislative flurry that ensued, two measures are particularly relevant for understanding securities markets politics: the directive that liberalised capital movements and the Second Banking Coordinating Directive (2BCD).[12]

The Capital Movements Directive showed that governments were, in principle, willing to move towards a European financial arena. This excludes general obstinacy as an explanation for the modest achievements in investment services. The directive was to abolish limits to capital flows and was agreed by the Council in June 1988.[13] Member states were given a mere two years to comply, while

---

10. Strictly speaking, the Cecchini report was a privately written study. Having been commissioned by the European Commission and arguing its case, it became closely associated with the latter. Other important publications also focused on these dynamic effects, e.g. *The Costs of Non-Europe*.

11. As it turned out, the sceptics were right; hardly any of the projected gains materialised. (See Gardner *et al.* 2001).

12. Two other directives were concluded in the field of securities – the Insider Trading Directive and the Prospectus Directive. The latter is inconsequential for our case; the former is more interesting. German recalcitrance (which had lasted for years) was broken when the banks started to fear the reputational damage to its reputation that Frankfurt might suffer from continued discussions. As it does not bear directly on the ISD and CAD negotiations, we will return to the Insider Trading Directive in our discussion of national policy change in Chapter Six. (See McCahery 1997, Lütz 2003b: 139).

13. Council Directive 88/361/EEC.

some poorer countries, plus France and Italy, were treated more leniently (Story and Walter 1997: 20). Considering how capital mobility could interfere with national economic policy, the most remarkable aspect of this directive was that it was adopted at all.[14] Surely, if governments could agree on something so fundamentally conflicting with 'economic sovereignty', more mundane questions of cross-border services provision should not pose insurmountable obstacles? The directive on the free movement of capital showed just how far governments in principle were willing to go.

The 2BCD, concluded in 1989 after less than two years of negotiations, had serious implications for competition in investment services.[15] The 2BCD applied to credit institutions the mutual recognition approach that had become central to constructing the single market (cf. Egan 2001: 109). From the envisaged implementation date, 1993, a banking licence issued by an EU member state would function as an EU-wide 'single passport', allowing financial institutions to carry out functions they performed at home throughout the EU. In negotiations, Germany had pressed particularly hard to ensure that the capital market business would be included in its purview (Interview 030406). In effect, the resulting directive gave German and French universal banks the right to engage in just about everything except insurance on a pan-European scale (Underhill 1997). For investment business, the 2BCD shifted the terms of competition among specialist securities houses and universal banks decidedly in favour of the latter.

From the perspective of our framework, trouble-free agreement on pan-European market access for banking business proper would be surprising. Were there no competitive concerns for the firms involved? There were, but they had already been addressed. To begin with, effective European competition in retail financial services had never been particularly likely for numerous reasons: customer loyalty, the role of publicly-owned financial institutions such as savings banks and cooperatives, the need to build up new branch networks, cultural differences, etc. (it has not materialised up to this day, see European Commission 2007b). In terms of the potential for pan-European competition, this left wholesale banking.

Here the central cost factor – and hence competitive issue – revolved around the reserves that banks had to set aside against loans. Just as negotiations on the 2BCD began, central bankers reached international agreement on this question in the Basle Committee on Banking Supervision (BCBS) (Wood 2005). The Capital Accord, as it became known, defined both minimum standards for how much capital banks needed to set aside and how this capital would be calculated. EU negotiators only had to transcribe these provisions into European law in the Own Funds Directive and the Solvency Ratio Directive.[16] Compared to securities, banking proved an easy nut to crack: the core competitive issues had already been solved

---

14. Some countries, notably Germany, the UK and the Benelux countries, already had a fairly permissive regime for cross-border capital flows. But even for them, abandoning national discretion on the matter was a novel departure. (Cf. Williamson and Mahar 1998).
15. Council Directive 89/646/EEC.
16. Council Directive 89/299/EEC (own funds) and Council Directive 89/647/EEC (solvency ratio).

through other means (wholesale banking) or were unlikely to arise in the first place (retail banking).

The 2BCD gave continental universal banks free access to European securities markets (Underhill 1997: 111, cf. Wood 2005: 95). Because it only applied to credit institutions, this right did not extend to the securities houses and investments banks that dominated the City's markets, both British and American. British negotiators had consciously detached the regulation of securities houses from banking negotiations in order to keep a tight grip on the former (Interview 230306.b). In hindsight, they miscalculated (Nicoll 1993). Separating banking (where continental member states were strong) from securities markets (where London was the undisputed leader in Europe) backfired. Once continental universal banks had secured pan-European access to securities markets, they had little to lose in later negotiations on investment services (Interview 020506). To be sure, calibrating the competitive balance between banks and non-banks within securities markets was only one of the two issues that came to dominate negotiations. But this competitive 'overhang' from banking sector legislation helps account for both the negotiations' difficulties and the British determination to reach a deal, even if it took another four years to materialise.

NEGOTIATING A EUROPEAN MARKET IN INVESTMENT SERVICES

When negotiations began in 1989, the UK securities industry was busy digesting the impact of the Big Bang and the Financial Services Act. That said, it would be too easy to let the changes overshadow the continuities. While ownership structures, business models and regulatory structures had indeed changed (Moran 1991, Augar 2000), the international importance and ambitions of the City remained (Bindemann 1999). In the late 1980s, the City looked as if it was simply getting better at what it had been doing for almost four decades – attracting securities business from abroad (Burn 1999). The SEAQ International trading system was but its latest success. While the institutional and policy links between public actors and the financial services industry were relatively weak in the UK, the government was committed to maintaining the attractiveness of the City as a place to do business, more so than was the case in either France or Germany.

In pushing for the interests of the City's financial services industry, two core constituencies eventually rallied behind the British government: American (i.e. non-bank and non-EU) investment banks and smaller, (still) independent securities houses that had traditionally been the core of the City's industry. Continental European banks, in contrast, tended to form alliances with their home governments – regardless of the fact that they had started to become City players in their own right. The national divisions running through the industry thus prevailed, and were clearly reflected in the intergovernmental character of the negotiations.

In France, impending EU negotiations intersected with a proactive domestic reform programme; strategic considerations were thus central to the French government's approach. In contrast, the Thatcher government had championed deregulating European services markets for years, not least to allow the 'competitive' British services industry to make headway on the Continent. At the same time, it had little use for 'positive integration', to actively use 'Europe' to achieve specific policy goals. Deregulation was part of the Thatcher government's *programme* but it, as well as its European financial market policy, was not embedded in a government *strategy*. France was different: European integration was perceived as allowing both market restructuring and continued public control. The French reforms had anticipated European integration, seen for example in steps towards loosening capital controls and restructuring the brokerage industry. French goals in the negotiations reflected reformers' ambitions: anchoring the universal banking model in Europe (achieved with the 2BCD), preserving the competitive position of French financial institutions (still state-dominated at the time) and consolidating Paris as a financial centre. This last point united the preferences of French financial institutions – their fate, it was perceived, was tied to that of Paris – and those of policy-makers who wanted to keep as much financial market activity as possible under the public eye.

In its approach to 1992, Germany found itself between France and the UK. German universal banks had embraced the single banking passport that extended to securities markets. For them, this was a major victory. But due to their relatively strong position in the British markets, German banks were reluctant to call for excessive protectionism within the European financial area. In the end, they came down in favour of laissez-faire market integration. Nevertheless, the impending negotiations presented an opportunity to push for advantage. Germany saw its banks locked in a battle with smaller British firms over 'levelling the playing field', and pushed for higher capital adequacy requirements – for all financial institutions, irrespective of where services were produced or provided. The French dispute with the British, in contrast, focused on where services could be provided. While competitive struggles were at the root of both disputes, they showed that French banks remained more wedded to their home markets than their German counterparts.

The Capital Adequacy Directive in global perspective
As an observer who was close to the negotiations around the ISD and the CAD, Philip Brown once remarked that 'any full history [of the negotiations] would require a combination of a CD-ROM and a three-dimensional chessboard' (Brown 1997: 128). Alas, Brown's assessment, which could be said to be a fair appraisal of events in the EU arena, was probably too optimistic. While EU member states were busy negotiating the provisions for the single market, no less than four other international forums were busy devising functionally similar rules in other forums – the International Organisation of Securities Commissions (IOSCO), the so-called Barnes Committee of the Basle Committee for Banking Supervision, the so-called 'Hexagonal' talks between the UK, the USA and Japan, and a European securities regulators group convening independently of the EU single market talks (Waters 1990, Lee 1992, cf. Bach and Newman 2007: 837ff). The resulting mess resembled more than a dozen actors playing chess on five boards simultaneously, with different rules governing each game.

Though EU negotiations were embedded in global developments, focusing on the competition politics of negotiating capital adequacy rules provides us with a relatively clear picture. Two arenas can be distinguished: EU and global financial markets. For the first, negotiating common rules was a *sine qua non* for issuing pan-European 'passports' to securities firms. The CAD was to provide the minimum harmonisation upon which mutual recognition (in the ISD) would be built. This provided incentives for players expecting to benefit from pan-European market access to keep negotiations alive.

This link between common minimum standards and mutual market access was absent at the global level (in IOSCO and the Barnes Committee). Internationally, negotiating capital adequacy rules is a zero-sum game: as competitive advantage is always relative, some players will gain while others will lose. With the additional transaction costs it would entail (for negotiating, implementing and monitoring), and without mechanisms for coercion, agreement appeared unlikely. In the case of capital adequacy standards for banking (Basle), there was still the 'public, common good' of allegedly greater systemic stability (Kapstein 1992). A competitively neutral regime that had something for everybody through higher system stability thus created a theoretical win-set. Even then, it took arm-twisting by the USA and the UK to force others into agreement (Oatley and Nabors 1998).

According to the wisdom of the day, such a 'systemic stability' incentive was considerably smaller in securities markets – the day that the fallout from the Lehman Brothers collapse in 2008 was to prove otherwise remained in the distant future. Policy-makers recognised that if securities firms were caught in a falling market with illiquid positions, they might falter. Compared to bank failures, however, any impact was thought to be manageable. The 1987 stock market crash had led to the failure of some securities firms, most prominently Tuffier & Associés and Drexel Burnham Lambert. Any wider effects had been limited (Bush 1990, Graham 1990). Trying to follow the Basle example in securities was bound to be an uphill struggle; it was surprising that it took IOSCO members four years to conclude that compromise was out of reach. That they kept negotiating had much to do with the awkward three-level constellation within which capital adequacy was discussed.

The core problem in the capital adequacy negotiations for securities operations was that the relevant firms had different business models and thus regulatory preferences, depending on how rules influenced their competitive positions. The main divide ran between banks and non-bank securities houses (Waters and Kellaway 1990, Underhill 1997). Firms in the securities business are normally required to maintain capital reserves to cover risks associated with market crashes, company failures, settlement problems, etc. Two questions ensued: how should the capital required for a specific market position be calculated? And what counts as 'capital' in the first place? Only equity, or subordinated debt as well?[17] These questions matter to firms because capital is a cost factor and affects their profitability. Capital

---

17. Subordinated debt leaves the creditor with fewer rights to recover the principal in times of distress, allowing the debtor company to use the money to service other liabilities first. In return, subordinated debt generates a higher yield for the creditor.

needs to be serviced, in the simplest instance through the payment of dividends to shareholders. In addition, stringent capital adequacy rules might force companies with stretched reserves to unwind securities positions in unfavourable market environments to stay within mandated limits (Filipovic 1997: 184). Such rules would thus act as a deterrent for small firms to assume larger risks, and thereby tilt the playing field against them.

The securities business was conducted under the auspices of two different regulatory regimes. On the one hand, universal banks, for example in Germany, were regulated by banking authorities. The rules for how much capital they needed to put aside to cover the risk from their securities operations was an integral part of the rules governing banks. In addition, most universal banks could use a single pool of capital to cover exposures in both their credit and securities businesses. On the other hand, non-bank securities firms – 'pure' brokers and investment banks offering a wider range of services – were covered by rules specifically devised for capital markets. In the UK, the required level for capital cushions was rather low, not least due to firms' small average size and the sector's history of self-regulation. Securities firms thus tried to influence their governments to push for standards that would skew the terms of competition *vis-à-vis* the banks in their favour. The banks, of course, were playing the same game.

The IOSCO negotiations illustrate this well (Filipovic 1997: 141). In 1989 its most powerful body, the Technical Committee, which brings together securities regulators from the core global markets, tabled a report on 'Capital Adequacy Standards for Securities Firms' at IOSCO's annual conference in Venice (Waters 1989a). At the eleventh hour, the German delegation withdrew its support for the text, claiming that the deal 'could possibly damage the vital interests of German banks'. The most contentious issue was the treatment of subordinated debt as capital and whether amounts thus recognised should be limited (Filipovic 1997: 183). The Germans – indirectly supported by other countries with universal banks (France and Switzerland in particular) – desired tight ceilings to limit capital-scarce investment firms' ability to 'leverage' their core capital in the short run.

The German representatives at the negotiating table, however, were not government regulators in the proper sense, but representatives of the Federation of German Stock Exchanges. The stock exchanges, as pointed out in the previous chapter, were controlled by the large Frankfurt banks. They regulated themselves and were thus making foreign regulatory policy, a situation which left little doubt about their own stake in it. German public actors were involved only post hoc to back the positions of 'their' private actors (Simonian 1989b). The cracks in the intergovernmental imagery now become apparent: the German government was taking a strong position on the international stage but the underlying conflict was actually a private one. In the event, the German Federation gave in to the IOSCO report's publication on the condition that further negotiations would follow quickly and that the conference made clear no agreement had been reached (Waters 1989b). The German finance ministry and the Bundesbank publicly backed their clientele less than a week later, again citing unpalatable competitive implications.[18]

Industry interests were clearly perceptible within the British delegation as well. As Filipovic found,

> [t]he [Securities and Futures Authority] maintains close links with its membership, to a degree beyond that of most regulators in other countries. This is especially the case when it comes to concrete issues of great salience. For example, commenting on the EC proposal for a Capital Adequacy Directive, the SFA International Capital Committee ... "attached considerable importance to consultation with the membership, and the Chairman of the Committee wrote to all firms on two occasions to inform them of the developments, to highlight issues of concern and to solicit their views". (Filipovic 1997: 141)[19.]

The self-regulating members of the SFA, acting as a branch of the Securities and Investment Board, were again sitting more or less directly at the negotiating table. The failure of the 1989 conference was directly attributable to irreconcilable private interests. After the collapse, IOSCO's Technical Committee made practically no movement on the issue for three years. As will be seen below, the revival of negotiations in 1992 was short-lived – a prelude to their final breakdown.

Competitive struggles between securities firms and banks equally dominated CAD negotiations in the EU arena. The conflicts were broadly similar, and led to stalled negotiations after 1989. In contrast to IOSCO negotiations, however, the promise of effective market integration gave the parties an incentive to stay at the table. The Investment Services Directive was to provide non-bank securities houses with the pan-European passports that banks had won with the 2BCD. In the words of Sir Leon Brittan, EU Commission Vice President in charge of financial institutions, the CAD was to be 'the key that [would] unlock the ISD' (Lee 1992).

The Investment Services Directive

The ISD was to enshrine 'mutual recognition' in securities markets regulation and provide securities firms with a single passport (Ashall 1993, Steil 1993: 22, Brown 1997, Story and Walter 1997, Underhill 1997, Steil 1998). In theory, the 'levelling [or rather: calibrating] of the playing field' through minimum standards was to be accomplished through the CAD. But in practice it was not simply a question of one directive building upon the other. Rather, the ISD was used to settle additional competitive issues, of which two stand out: the question of on- and off-exchange securities trading and the application of conduct-of-business-rules (CBRs) by host rather than by home authorities.

The German camp had tried to exact a price for the single passport in the form of tough capital requirements for non-bank securities firms. Their strategy

---

18. Less than two months later, Deutsche Bank board member Rolf Breuer publicly deplored the lack of public authorities representing Germany at forums such as IOSCO to better secure 'German' (that is, banks') interests. The call for 'public intervention' first came from private actors fearing the competitive implications of rule-making where private representative bodies lacked the weight to influence outcomes. (Simonian 1989c).

19. The quote within the quote is taken from a SFA report.

reflected specific German market structures: many of the financial institutions advocating regulatory protectionism were already well-established in the City (Deutsche Bank, the most prominent example, had moved its investment banking headquarters there in 1984). The perceived need to 'update' Frankfurt to repatriate or retain business was thus balanced by German banks' stakes in well-established London markets – so long as they would be allowed to operate there under advantageous conditions. The point was not that foreign firms were per se unwelcome in Germany. But the German finance ministry was clearly worried that foreign 'financial engineers', as one respondent working for the German government at the time put it, would swamp the domestic industry (Interview 020506).

The French position was less ambiguous. Furthering the interests of French banks almost fully coincided with boosting Paris at the expense of London. At French insistence, a 'concentration principle' was inserted into the ISD that basically allowed countries to oblige its residents to trade domestic securities on 'regulated exchanges'. The aim was to repatriate the trading of French securities from London's 'unregulated' SEAQ International market, where almost a third of it had migrated. Here the French were supported by the 'Club-Med' – a group of mostly southern European countries including Italy, Portugal, Belgium, Spain and Greece (*The Banker* 1991). Their motivation was similar to that of France: preventing the exodus of share trading to London.

Wedded to the 'concentration principle' was another provision aimed at London's markets: the French insistence on 'transparency' in trading. Block trading, in particular, had migrated to London because lower transparency requirements made it easier for dealers to liquidate large swathes of shares without adversely affecting market prices. Reluctant to go down the same road themselves, the French insisted on raising price transparency requirements throughout the EU to thwart SEAQ trading practices. London's financial community, unsurprisingly, was unhappy with the proposal. The British Merchant Banking and Securities Houses Association (BMBA), for example, took a very liberal position on the ISD and pressed for 'a flexible approach for information disclosure and publication of trade details on behalf of market-makers, (Filipovic 1997: 129). As with the concentration principle, the German position was closer to the British one than the French position (Waters 1991a, Ashall 1993: 99). This reflected the dominance of the big banks in the German securities business, whereas in France a separate brokerage industry still existed.[21] In addition, German banks were quite active on the SEAQ. In contrast to the French, they faced no opposition at home from a host of smaller financial institutions excluded from the lucrative SEAQ business.

The final major point of contention in the ISD concerned the principle of home country supervision. The idea was straightforward: to facilitate cross-border business operations and to relieve firms from having to report to two (home and host) authorities, home authorities would perform the supervisory function for the financial group as a whole. Together with the mutual recognition principle, this would make most dealings with the host authorities unnecessary after initial registration. Fearing the interference of foreign governments with cross-border business, the BMBA early on supported the home country control principle (Hutton 1989, Riley

1989). But in the name of protecting national investors, the French disagreed. At least retail investors, they argued, needed to be protected by host country rules lest they suffer from excessively loose regulation in financial firms' home countries. With all these conflicting interests, both 1990 and 1991 saw practically no movement in the negotiations.

The bargaining positions of the different parties reflected the interests of the most influential coalitions in their national financial industries. *Euromoney*, one of the industry's leading magazines, reached the same conclusion in 1992:

> [T]he capital adequacy directive for securities firms is not really about prudent regulation, or level playing fields. It boils down to vested interests trying to skew the regulations to obtain a competitive advantage. (Lee 1992: 33)

When the Commission submitted a revised version of the CAD in 1992, it admitted as much when it explained that 'amendments [had been] made to achieve more equality in the treatment of credit institutions and investment firms' (Filipovic 1997: 184). It was an acknowledgement that fine-tuning this balance was a major concern for the legislative process.

The regulatory protectionism dominating the negotiations was far from erratic or haphazard. Chapter Three highlighted the correlation between the embeddedness of financial markets in national economies, the institutionalisation of links between public and private actors and relative protectionism in financial market policy. The influence of private-public coalitions on the negotiations reinforced pre-existing tendencies and made the competition politics more virulent.

It was no accident that the French government intervened so vehemently on behalf of its industry. Protectionism and close public-private links were two sides of the same coin – two aspects of what Underhill has called the state-market condominium (Underhill 2001, 2003). The liberal stance of the British government *vis-à-vis* foreign firms (i.e. the weakness of protectionist impulses) was likewise the flip side of its weak links to the British financial industry. As is true for many facets of the story recounted in this book, political institutions cannot be understood independently of the concrete politics they mediate. Over time, they are mutually interdependent.

In the event, EU member states' different regulatory structures and associational institutions made a big difference. Here the contrast between the regulators' club IOSCO and the intergovernmental structure of the EU is telling. In IOSCO, the City's interests were represented through the UK SIB, a respected securities markets regulator in close contact with the industry through the remnants of the self-regulatory system (Moran 1991). The informal character of self-regulation in Germany, in contrast, saw German banks fight a rearguard action in IOSCO. Though sufficient to undermine agreement at the last moment, informal self-regulation made life difficult for the banks, ex post backing by the Bundesbank and the finance ministry notwithstanding.

Matters worked differently in the EU arena. Here German banks' informal ties with public actors proper (the central bank and the government itself) paid off because their interests were well represented from the start, not least in the negotiation of the 2BCD. In contrast, the self-regulatory structure of the British securities industry did little to help it push its regulatory cause, while its relatively weak ties to the British government, particularly the Department for Trade and Industry, reduced its access to EU negotiations.

The embeddedness of financial markets and the importance of national regulatory systems for economic policy also made themselves apparent, though less than the competition politics themselves. As pointed out above, embeddedness affected negotiations through the ties that public actors in coordinated market economies had with their financial industries. Governments sometimes invoked the 'public interest', for example to justify host authorities' retention of certain regulatory and supervisory rights *vis-à-vis* foreign firms, although for the most part they referred to 'public goods' like systemic stability or investor protection rather than to protecting nationally idiosyncratic approaches to economic policy.

A European deal shatters global ambitions

Movement returned to the negotiations on capital adequacy for securities firms in early 1992. Surprisingly, this movement was initially within IOSCO rather than the EU (Waters 1992d). IOSCO members met with representatives of the Basle Committee on Banking Supervision to hammer out a deal (Waters 1992c) and reached basic agreement on almost all issues, successfully amalgamating the different regulatory 'philosophies' that had often been invoked to justify disagreement. Only the all-important numbers remained in dispute: the precise ratio of subordinated debt to equity capital permissible for regulatory purposes and the amount of capital necessary to back up equity and other market risks.

Concerning the ratio of subordinated debt to equity, the fault line ran between banking supervisors eager to limit subordinated debt-as-capital and securities market regulators (essentially the SIB and the SEC) who favoured more generous limits. Fault lines for capital to cover market risk differed: a clear divide opened up between the SEC on one side (backed by the 'universal bank lobby', which like the SEC favoured high capital charges) and British and French regulators on the other (Lee 1992: 35). Traditionally, the SEC had required firms to hold sufficient capital to withstand firm-level 'worst case' scenarios; the British approach, in contrast, was concerned with disruption of the market at large and therefore required lower reserves. On both subordinated debt and reserve levels, negotiators once again proved to be advocates of their domestic market incumbents.

While bickering over numbers in IOSCO and the BCBS continued, the EU finally scored a breakthrough. The Commission tabled a revised version of the CAD in May 1992 that fine-tuned the question of subordinated debt-as-capital by introducing a new category: 'tier three capital', consisting of short-term subordinated debt that would be treated differently from both equity and long-term subordinated debt (Waters 1992a). The precise numbers were to be decided later by the Council but the new proposal contained a general framework: both securities houses and banks would have to separate their securities holdings and trading from the rest of their business in a 'trading book' for which the CAD charges would apply.[20]

IOSCO negotiations now stalled as the potential EU deal gained clearer contours. In particular, the SEC grew sceptical as the momentum at the European level excluded it, and the interests it represented, from the discussions (Waters 1992b). When Great Britain acceded to the EU presidency in July 1992, she was determined to end the standstill. UK negotiators managed to rally support for a common position on the CAD among all ECOFIN members by November. Agreement on a 2 per cent capital charge on gross securities holdings, which was acceptable to EU members, was far below the 4 per cent that Richard Breeden, SEC chairman, had always advocated. Now that the EU countries had locked themselves in through joint agreement, the SEC effectively withdrew support for the IOSCO-BCBS initiative (Corrigan 1992). The lock-in had decreased the EU's win-set to such an extent that compromise in global negotiations was now impossible. Indeed, less than half a year later – tellingly coinciding with the official adoption of the CAD in Brussels – IOSCO's attempts to reach a capital adequacy compromise were formally abandoned (Bacon 1993, Waters 1993).

Once the CAD was agreed, movement accelerated on the ISD as well. In fact, core aspects of the new 'Commission proposal' had been negotiated directly between the French and British delegations (Interview 030406). After the usual last minute bargains, it was finally adopted in May 1993 (for details, see Usher 2000). In the CAD, the problem had boiled down to numbers. Settlement was now reached with an approach where the capital reserves of firms with significant securities operations would consist of two 'building blocks' – 2 per cent for the gross positions and another 8 per cent for the net positions (*Euromoney* 1992). In the case of the ISD, the most sensitive questions lay in definitions. What constituted a 'regulated market' for trading? The agreed definition saw the SEAQ on the edge of inclusion. The question of who counted as a 'professional investor' was even more delicate. Market participants falling outside this designation would come under the control of host authorities, who were left free to establish rules for firms operating in their jurisdictions; the principle of home country supervision and mutual recognition of home country rules could thus easily be fudged. With a 'professional' in the field of investment services left undefined, a legal patchwork was poised to persist. While home country supervision was the official rule, '[member] states ensured that the balance tilted in favour of host country supervision' (Story and Walter 1997: 266). McCahery has argued

> that the mutual recognition approach to co-operative regulatory control is unlikely to be effective unless member states pursue similar policy interests. (McCahery 1997: 70)

Interests clearly diverged, and ineffective policy was the result.

The implementation date for the ISD was stretched far into the future. January 1996 was the deadline only for those countries that had supported relatively open

---

20. This compromise meant that securities houses were to face bank-style capital charges on those parts of their operations that were not part of the trading book itself (for example foreign exchange liabilities and expected future overheads). Again, City firms were irate. (See *Euromoney* 1992).

markets to begin with. France, Spain, Italy and Portugal only agreed to the ISD on the condition that they be granted several more years before they would have to accept 'single passports' (Steil 1993: 23). Writing in 1993, Steil aptly summed up the thrust of the negotiated results:

> Not surprisingly [..], several key sections of the ISD are political compromises reflecting the determination of member state governments to protect their domestic industry's competitive position, rather than provisions for ensuring a stable and efficient European financial market. (Steil 1993: 22)

COMPETITIVE FAULT LINES AND INTERGOVERNMENTAL POLITICS

Attempts around 1990 to create an effective cross-border capital market were defeated by the conflicting interests of financial firms, whose competitive concerns were evident in the numerous twists taken in the negotiations and in the deals that were eventually struck. What does this tell us about European integration and the relationship between market integration and levels of governance? On the surface, negotiation dynamics resembled liberal intergovernmentalist patterns. The success of negotiations depended on national governments, while intergovernmental dissent – despite the Commission's eagerness to see negotiations advance – stalled progress for several years. The prospect of overall welfare gains as identified in the 1985 White Paper (European Commission 1985a) and the Cecchini Report (Cecchini 1988) did not carry sufficient weight to elicit agreement.

Yet liberal intergovernmentalism tells us little about the underlying social forces at work. National governments acted as *de facto* agents; the interesting question concerns their principals. Moravcsik (1997) himself has acknowledged that far from being given, 'national interests' are the outcome of domestic politics. But the image he invokes of national positions formulated through domestic deliberation is misleading.

Capital market politics was not a case of top-down consultation (the state aggregating the opinions of its constituencies). Nor was it a case of bottom-up public debate. The distance separating the organised interests of the financial industry and the public actors articulating them was less than Moravcsik's imagery suggests. Through more or less explicit industry self-regulation (Germany and the UK), or the state functioning as majority owner of large financial institutions as well as regulator (France), the financial industry's interests are built into the state. Banks are insiders within the respective policy communities, not just one stakeholder among others.

In addition, financial industry interests have had a clear transnational dimension. Preferences expressed as national positions were the result of competitive struggles that transcended national and, as the role of the BCBS and IOSCO showed, even European borders. In the trade-off between effective market integration and regulatory protectionism, many actors chose the latter. Nevertheless, financial markets – notably the Euromarkets – were much more integrated than the international politics of European financial market negotiations suggest.

Governments did not act as interfaces between sheltered domestic political processes and international policy coordination. The intergovernmental character of the negotiations can be attributed to the constellation of interests within European securities markets – and not to their taking place in a world that conforms to the axiomatic division between the domestic and the international that intergovernmentalism as a theory is built on.

Put differently, the specific structure of the struggle over the terms of competition – waged on a transnational plane – was responsible for the intergovernmental character of EU capital market politics. This intergovernmental character was the *dependent* variable, and can be attributed to the overall politico-economic constellation – what we have called the 'international constellation'. This 'international constellation' combined: (1) key segments of financial markets still fragmented along national borders, (2) political institutions converging around government apparatuses, and (3) strong ties between financial markets and national 'varieties of capitalism'. As the previous chapter argued, these three dimensions had co-evolved historically – even if the increasing internationalisation of financial markets was starting to unravel the links between them.

Once the CAD and the ISD were concluded, it was up to governments to implement the measures they had agreed. This they proved reluctant to do. Nevertheless, the agreed changes set in motion a further Europeanisation of market structures. Those actors who had hoped for more far-reaching market integration did not have to wait for the ISD's lengthy implementation period to pass. As European capital market structures evolved throughout the 1990s in response to the strategic reorientation of many market incumbents, pressure was building for a second round of market integration – one that would generate not only detailed agreement on supranational rules, but a new institutional framework in which governments surrendered significant elements of national control over capital market regulation.

chapter five | the 1990s' capital market revolution in europe

The face of European finance was transformed in the 1990s. Continental European equity markets moved from the fringes of national economies into the limelight. Banks, which had previously focused on their domestic markets, began to build cross-border investment banking empires. Stock exchanges were transformed from members-only clubs into for-profit companies. This chapter explores the relationship of these changes to the supranationalisation of EU capital market governance.

Structuration in competition politics implies that the evolution of market structures, the business strategies of leading firms, regulatory policy and patterns of governance are mutually interdependent. This chapter addresses a specific part of this larger feedback loop: the co-evolution of market structures and the business strategies of core (investment) banks in Europe in the 1990s. While the behaviour of financial firms is commonly portrayed as adapting to changes in their environments (e.g. Smith and Walter 2003), changes in (macro-)market structures not only *cause* changes in firms' behaviour – they *result* from them as well. In a market dominated by a dozen (investment) banks, changes in their behaviour will translate into altered market patterns. When the financial crisis hit Europe in the years following 2007, it exposed not only how much banks' business models had changed since the 1980s, but also how broadly such changes among a handful of core firms could reverberate throughout the European economy.

This argument has important implications for both the time-span covered by this book and the subsequent crisis years: the strategic reorientation of the European financial industry has been a crucial link in the chain of events. The financial transformation of the EU was not dictated by abstract market pressures, but by firm-level preferences, which were translated into both patterns of governance and market structures. In highly concentrated sectors, firms do not confront such structures as something external to them. Rather, the *strategic* behaviour of core firms plays a central role in structuring markets and explaining changes in them (e.g. Dixit and Nalebuff 1993, Fligstein 2001). The first part of this chapter therefore takes issue with the view that market evolution 'determined' adaptation in firms' behaviour. Rather, the changes that banks perceived or anticipated in their environments inspired (further) modifications of their business strategies. In addition, changing market structures bore the imprint of both national and European-level regulatory reforms of the preceding years – reforms in which banks themselves had been key players.

This chapter focuses on the two-pronged reorientation of large European banks over the 1990s: the internationalisation of their business and the move into investment banking. Cross-border expansion was both a response to and an anticipation of further opportunities as international capital markets grew. European universal banks were inspired by past regulatory reform, US competition and the decline of profits in traditional lending. The new business interests were most apparent in the resources continental firms invested to expand their international investment banking operations.

MEASURING CHANGE IN EU INVESTMENT BANKING MARKETS

Understanding the relationships between macro market structures, business strategies and regulatory change is challenged by the paucity of reliable quantitative data. How do we retrospectively identify the business strategies of firms? While firms' documents produced at the time may seem the answer, annual reports and other public pronouncements of corporate strategy have their shortcomings. The image they provide of firms' strategies are commonly distorted by their aim to please investors (Froud *et al.* 2006). If European investment banking is the fashion of the day, managers may wish to score easy points by declaring it a priority regardless of their true intentions.

Quantitative overviews of business activities contain potentially more relevant data. For example, the relevance of international versus domestic business and capital market versus traditional banking activities might be measured by their contribution to the firm's overall profits. Such measures, however, are a weak proxy for corporate *strategy*. After all, entry into new market segments identified as strategic priorities is normally costly – such investments initially generate little revenue. It is the *expectation* of profits that motivates firms to enter new markets, not their immediate realisation.

In addition, firms differ both in the manner and the level of detail with which they report their capital market operations. They may employ different criteria depending on where their cross-border financial services are 'booked' – abroad or at home. International differences in both taxation and accounting regulation are likely to affect figures. Accounts are rarely sufficiently detailed to distinguish business segments with volatile profits (particularly proprietary trading) from others such as underwriting or brokerage. In sum, strategy announcements and operational data are not fully reliable as sources for determining corporate strategy.

Finally, the issue of time inconsistency – organisations may be motivated by their expectations of the future as much as by events of the past – complicates the task of identifying *causes* for changes in corporate behaviour more generally. For example, firms may anticipate regulatory reforms and buy into a new market before new laws come into effect. In spite of the timing, one could still argue that legal changes triggered the change in behaviour.

For aggregate macro data, the picture is also bleaker than one might suspect. Quantitative measures for all aspects of banking markets are plentiful. For example, OECD data on credit businesses have their own NACE category, allowing systematic exploration of the sector's profile over time. But no such thing exists for the various aspects of investment banking. In data collections using the NACE industry categorisation, they are likely to be lumped under 'Other monetary intermediation'. Eurostat, the leading institution for comparative data on the EU, only has financial services data for 'credit institutions', 'insurance services' and 'pension funds'. Capital market services do not appear as a separate category.[23] The absence of useful macro measures for the development of the investment banking *industry* (as opposed to capital markets, see below) explains the dearth of studies in this field, particularly quantitative ones. Again, much has been written about banking proper, but next to nothing about investment banking.

Macro measures of developments in markets for specific financial instruments offer a mixed picture: obviously, data on the issuance, stock, valuation and trading of securities are widely available, most obviously in the form of time series for stock market indexes such as those published by the World Federation of Exchanges. Obtaining data on financial *services* provision is more difficult. There is no agreement on what constitutes cross-border financial service provision or how firms should treat it in their corporate accounts (OECD 2000).[24] National accounting systems differ to such an extent that international comparison is hampered. For example, French figures for trade in financial services in the early 1990s are widely seen as unrealistic and unreliable.[25]

Valid and reliable measures of that holy grail of single market policy – market integration – are even more difficult to find. The strategy commonly used by the European Commission is to compare prices for similar products throughout the Union. However, international price differentials are influenced by numerous factors that are difficult to separate analytically. In wholesale finance, banks typically supply several services to their clients simultaneously. Even when available, the 'price tags' for individual services may not reflect the true internal cost calculations of banks. Apart from the most commodified services, products are often too complex to compare. When prices decline for these commodified services, for example brokerage or underwriting, it is likely the result of commodification itself rather than international market integration. After all, sophisticated firms, which use cutting-edge services or proprietary trading to generate profits, offer cheap off-the-shelf products to squeeze their smaller competitors out of the market. Thus even where reliable and comparable price data are available, they are not a particularly valid proxy for market integration. The first serious attempt to generate an encompassing picture of market integration in EU financial services (European Commission 2005b) therefore combined available data from different studies to

---

23. This applies to most stylised comparative overviews as well as to generalised comparisons of the 'trade openness' of European countries in these service sectors. Gjersem's OECD working paper, to give only one example, has measures for trade openness in banking (that is, credit) and insurance services only. (See Gjersem 2003: 12).

24. On how 'trade in services' defies established notions of territoriality – and thereby also measurement systems based on them – see Ruggie (1993). Ruggie approvingly quotes Jagdish Bhagwati who suggests dropping the notion altogether. (See Bhagwati 1987).

25. In the relevant OECD publication, readers are cautioned that the figures appear anomalous. (See OECD 2000: 28). In the corresponding WTO publication, they are simply omitted. (See World Trade Organisation 1997: 13).

generate an overall impression of current developments.[26] A single measure of market integration is nowhere in sight.

Due to these limitations, this chapter focuses primarily on qualitative data and existing research, even though quantitative measures (where available) will be used for corroboration. Arguably, the best indicator of a firm's strategy lies in its material investments. More specifically, heavy investment in international investment banking justifies the claim that a firm has identified it as an important part of its strategy. Luckily, the number of firms that play a significant role in EU capital markets (measured by a market share of more than, say, 2 per cent) is small; international expansion can thus be assessed on a case-by-case basis. If it emerges that all these companies invested heavily in international capital market operations, as is indeed the case, this is probably as good an indicator of a general shift in the industry's strategy as the data are likely to allow.

MARKET CONCENTRATION AS A SOURCE OF ECONOMIC AND POLITICAL POWER

Market concentration in EU investment banking heavily influences economic and political dynamics within the sector. The fact that less than a dozen firms control more than half of the market in just about every segment means that forms of economic interaction other than those suggested by traditional economic models are possible. In a nutshell, firms can interact strategically rather than just parametrically (on the distinction, see Abell 2003).[27] In highly concentrated markets, firms can collude to narrow markets and dictate prices.

Such concentration has political consequences. It gives banks considerable political clout in their home markets. It further allows the opinions of a handful of firms to stand in for what 'the market' thinks. If the top dozen banks agree on a position in consultations with the European Commission, this constitutes *de facto* consensus in the industry. Concentration also means that firms find it easy to cooperate politically: they can use industry associations to coordinate their political strategies and smooth out internal differences. As the following chapter will show, the legitimacy of the Commission's actions largely depends on the support of stakeholders. This makes a consensus that represents 90 per cent of market share in a particular market segment difficult to resist.

So how have European investment banking markets been carved up? A glance at the figures dispels the myth that the world of finance approximates the ideal of the 'market' held by orthodox economists. Underwriting in both equities and bonds is instructive: the Group of Ten found that throughout the 1990s, the top

---

26. The most comprehensive collection of data on EU 'financial integration', drawing on a variety of sources (ECB, OECD, FESE, ISMA, ISDA, etc.), has been compiled by the Commission itself. The compilations are a great step forward even if fundamental definitional issues remain unaddressed. (European Commission 2005b).

27. Under parametric conditions, the environment that actors face (for example price levels that appear as given) does not respond to the actions they take. Under strategic conditions, actors can illicit reactions from others and try to anticipate them (for example in an oligopoly).

five firms captured between 44 per cent and 50 per cent of the combined *global* market (Group of Ten 2001: 55). US firms dominated the industry, not least as the global preponderance of US stock markets grew in the 1990s due to the dot.com bubble. US equities market capitalisation as a share of global market capitalisation rose from 32.7 per cent in 1990 to 49.1 per cent in 1998 (Smith and Walter 2003: 148). In US Initial Public Offerings (IPOs), the three top firms – Merrill Lynch, Morgan Stanley and Goldman Sachs – captured more than 50 per cent of the market (Group of Ten 2001: 454).

European markets were likewise heavily concentrated throughout the 1990s.[28] In 1995, the top twenty underwriters for bond issues in euro legacy currencies commanded no less than 98.9 per cent of the market – and 95.8 per cent of that was attributable to euro area firms (Cabral *et al.* 2002: 27, see also Santos and Tsatsaronis 2003). The US firms among the top-twenty, in contrast, only had 2.1 per cent of the market. By 2000, the top twenty still commanded almost 95 per cent of the market, but now only 43.2 per cent was booked by euro zone firms whereas 40.6 per cent had gone to the American banks.[29] In absolute terms, the business volume of the European firms remained roughly constant over these five years, whereas that of the US firms increased rapidly. After 2000 matters stabilised. In 2004, the seven European firms among the top ten corporate bond underwriters in euros held 45.7 per cent of the market (Casey and Lannoo 2005: 34).[30] Equity underwriting shows a roughly similar if less pronounced picture. Between 1995 and 2000, the market share of euro zone firms among the top twenty fell from 64.2 per cent to 41.4 per cent, whereas that of US players rose from 10.8 per cent to 35.7 per cent (Cabral *et al.* 2002: 28). By 2000, US investment banks had captured an estimated 70 per cent of the fee-income on European capital markets and corporate finance transactions (Smith and Walter 2003: 367). To be sure, such concentration had a history. For euro legacy currencies between 1994 and 1998, the top five firms in countries such as France, the Netherlands and Italy never had combined market shares below 70 per cent (Santos and Tsatsaronis 2003: 10).

---

28. Examples that will not be discussed in further detail but are important to complete the picture include secured money markets, where the top quintile of participants consistently held over 80 per cent of the market share between 2000 and 2004. Over the same period, the top ten players held 60 per cent of the repo market. In over-the-counter forward rate derivatives, the market activity share of the top quintile of players approached 95 per cent in 2004. (European Commission 2005b).

29. 2001 shows a similar picture, even if slightly less pronounced. The respective figures are 46.6 per cent for euro-area firms and 32 per cent for American ones.

30. The top four were Deutsche Bank, BNP Paribas, Barclays and Société Générale (in that order); the other three EU firms among the top ten were ABN AMRO, Dresdner KW and HSBC.

THE RISE OF CAPITAL MARKETS AND INVESTMENT BANKING IN EUROPE

European capital markets came into their own in the second half of the 1990s when stock market capitalisations, share trading volumes and bond issuance skyrocketed. The opportunities created by this boom convinced many banks hitherto focused on domestic credit markets to reorient themselves. The boom was largely the result of previous political decisions: domestic coalitions had pushed through regulatory changes to enable the development of national capital markets (see Chapter 3), governments had chosen to privatise everything from utilities to telecoms, and firms had revamped business structures in anticipation of future opportunities.

The stock market boom was the most noticeable development within continental financial markets, where major stock market indexes quadrupled over the 1990s. The market capitalisation of the London Stock Exchange tripled over the same period (see Figure 5.1). Nor was the boom limited to Europe. Market capitalisation of the New York Stock Exchange (reproduced in the graph for comparison) also quadrupled over the course of the decade, reflecting the transatlantic correlation of stock market developments dating back to the 1960s (Duménil and Lévy 2005: 36). The Hong Kong market rose seven-fold; many other emerging markets showed similar increases, even if some never recovered from the crises that spread from Asia after mid-1997.

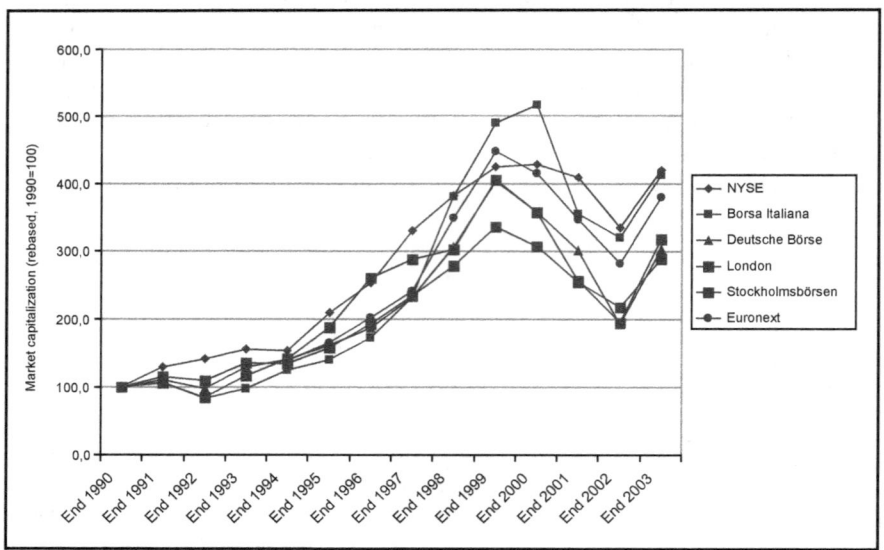

Source: World Federation of Exchanges statistics

Figure 5.1: The stock market boom

Did rising stock markets in continental Europe signal a change in financial structures from bank-based financial systems towards capital market-based systems (Rajan and Zingales 2003)? Morin has suggested that France in this period witnessed a shift from a 'financial network economy' towards a 'financial market economy' (Morin 2000, see also Clift 2004). At its peak, French stock markets reached levels that had only been known in Anglo-Saxon economies: in 1999, market capitalisation stood at 110 per cent of GDP (Commission des Operations de Bourse 1999: 18). But when broader financial structures are considered, we see that the weight of bank loans and debt securities (mainly bonds) relative to GDP remained rather stable (see Figures 5.2 – 5.4). Around 2000, roughly 60 per cent of financial flows in Europe were still passing through the balance sheets of banks; in the USA, this figure was 25 per cent, down from 75 per cent in the 1950s (Smith and Walter 2003: 361). Continental Europe in this respect was still lagging far behind the USA and the UK.

The rise in stock market valuations – one of the core business opportunities for investment banks new and old – did not imply 'deep' financial transformation. For the German case, Vitols found that

> these [changes] can be characterized as changes at the margin rather than a fundamental transformation of a bank-based financial system. Elements of a US-style market-based regulatory system have in fact been introduced in Germany, and the large banks have made considerable efforts to build up their market-based activities. However, with the exception of a flurry of new company listings on the stock market (initial public offerings, or IPOs) during the bubble years of 1998-2000 and the introduction of a moderate form of "shareholder value" by large listed companies, remarkably little has changed in the pattern of corporate finance in Germany in the past decade. (Vitols 2004: 1, cf. Deeg 2001)

Nevertheless, the stock market boom generated a kind of excitement from which governments were not immune – what Alan Greenspan famously characterised as 'irrational exuberance'. As the next chapter will show, the stock market boom also created a political window of opportunity for banks and other actors in favour of market integration. One German government official at the time recalls how

> we also had the hope that we would be able to challenge London to some degree. That was the boom of the DTB [the German derivatives exchange], also of the Deutsche Börse. And the banks were also actively playing along. That lasted for two, three years. Then we realised that we could not keep up and that in fact, we had to be careful that we didn't lose too much ground. (Interview 020506, author's translation from German)

Governments fuelled the equity boom with large-scale privatisations, which, in turn, led them and many others to believe that a revolution was sweeping European finance. The French government, for example, had already privatised some major banks and sold France Telecom (1998) and Air France (1999) on the stock markets just as the latter were reaching their heights. In Germany, the public listing of Deutsche Telekom in late 1996 was one of the catalysts for the stock market

76 | widen the market, narrow the competition

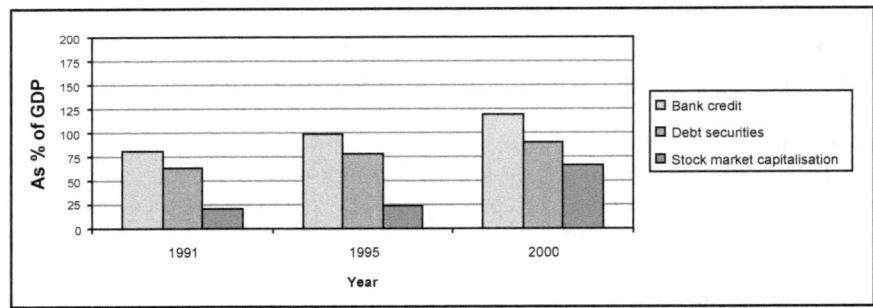

Source: European Commission 2003, also for France and the UK

Figure 5.2: Germany: financial structure

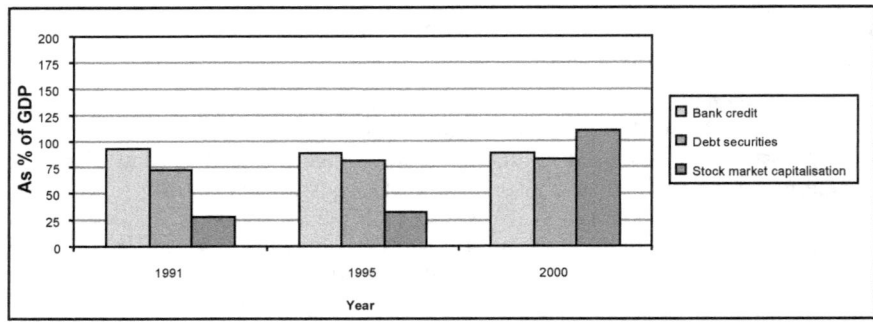

Figure 5.3: France: financial structure

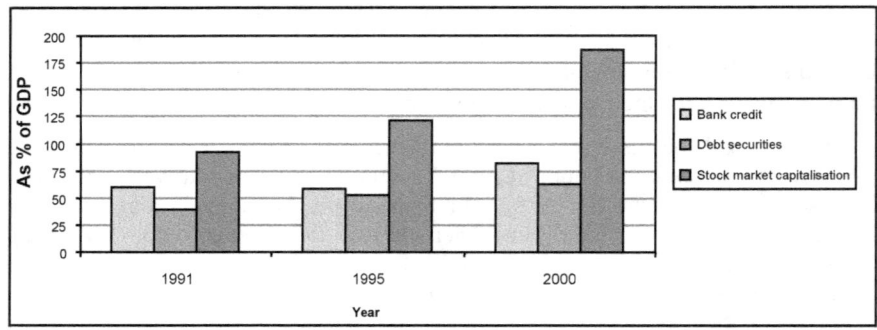

Figure 5.4: UK: financial structure

craze. The value of the company's shares rose seven-fold in less than four years and fuelled an optimism that seemed unbreakable.

The boom was still gathering steam at the end of the 1990s when key decisions were taken over the future of EU capital market governance. The issuance of European corporate bonds really took off after 1997; it rose by 70 per cent in 1999 alone (Belaisch *et al.* 2001: 37). The international portion of this business was growing as well: between 1998 and 1999, the issuance of international bonds more than doubled to over $536bn (Danthine *et al.* 2000: 57), though domestic bonds still outweighed international bonds four-to-one.

These changes were paralleled by transformations within the investment banking industry. Where the picture at the beginning of the 1990s was one of highly concentrated, nationally focused capital market industries (where they existed at all), most of the important firms developed European, and sometimes even global, ambitions over the next decade. Many of these firms had long been represented in international financial centres, particularly in London. Their foreign outlets, however, were important primarily for servicing the needs of domestic customers. At least in the ambitions of the leading continental banks, the distinction between national and international markets now vanished in favour of a transnationally integrated market place. This brought them closer to the American investment banks that had been pursuing international strategies through the City of London since the 1980s.

As pointed out above, this shift in business strategy is harder to trace than one might expect. This section therefore focuses on actual corporate expansion through overseas investment, typically in the form of corporate acquisitions. Where available, other indicators of strategy shifts will be used to corroborate the findings. In particular, Slager (2004) has studied the internationalisation strategies of the most important banks in the United States and Europe. The firms under scrutiny typically engage in both the traditional credit business and investment banking, though Slager's Trans Nationality Index (TNI) unfortunately does not distinguish between the two.[31] Nevertheless, it serves as a useful indicator of overall corporate strategy, where the trend is sufficiently clear .

European investment banking markets are concentrated, not only in a small number of firms, but geographically as well: all the relevant banks (indirectly in the case of US investment banks) are based in the UK, France, Germany, the Netherlands and Switzerland. As we will see, all domestic incumbents in the investment banking business developed international strategies in the 1990s. For the sake of simplicity, the banks are grouped by home country; the results are summarised in the book's appendix, with European market shares in 2001. Taken together with the most important US firms, these banks were responsible for around 80 per cent of the market in both bonds and equities. For comparison, the table also lists the Eurobond market shares for these firms in 1986 (or their precursors, in cases of later mergers or acquisitions). The firms that remain dominant in the

---

31. The TNI is the mean of three ratios: foreign assets/total assets, foreign income/total income and foreign staff/total staff. (For details, see Slager 2004: 555).

new millennium then had a cumulative market share of over 56 per cent. A high degree of continuity thus prevailed among US and European firms, while Japanese firms, which had more than 20 per cent of the market in 1986, hardly play a role in European markets today (cf. Augar 2005).

The Dutch banks
In both Dutch and international capital markets, ABN AMRO has been by far the most important Dutch bank. It was born of a merger between two domestic banks in 1991, which gave the new firm sufficient capital to embark on a strategy of internationalisation. Formulated in the early 1990s, ABN AMRO's strategy included becoming a 'global player' in the field of investment banking (de Vries *et al.* 1999: 463, cf. Slager 2004: 236). It was motivated by saturation of the Dutch banking market (Ibanez and Molyneux 2002: 52) and declining profit margins in the credit business that affected banks throughout Europe.

To achieve its aim, ABN AMRO invested heavily in building an international investment banking operation, even if profitability was initially low (de Vries *et al.* 1999: 471). In 1992 it bought the London brokerage Hoare Govett; three years later, it expanded into Scandinavia with the acquisition of Alfred Berg A/B. ABN AMRO then entered into investment banking joint ventures in Italy and Spain and finally started a joint venture with the Rothschild investment banks in 1996. By 2000, ABN AMRO had 60 per cent of its activities abroad (Slager 2004: 224) and its TNI rose from a little more than 30 in the early 1990s to over 70 in 2000 (Ibid.: 233).

The German banks
Deutsche Bank was probably the first continental bank that systematically expanded throughout Europe and made international investment banking one of the pillars of its corporate strategy (Slager 2004: 313, cf. also Chapter 3). By the early 1990s, it clearly had strong European and even global ambitions, though only 10 per cent of its profits came from non-German European subsidiaries (Brady 1992). One executive declared at the time that 'our aim is to become the leading banking and securities house in Europe' (Ibid.).

Two decisions exemplify Deutsche Bank's strategy: in 1989, it bought one of the leading City merchant banks, Morgan Grenfell, for £900m – a price considered exorbitant at the time (Augar 2000). Five years later, in 1994, it decided to move all of its investment banking operations to London and merge them into a single unit, thus obliterating the distinction between German and non-German business (Fisher and Cohen 1994). In the same year it also created corporate banking units in Italy (*Financial Regulation Report* 1994b).

The years that followed brought further expansion, this time into North America – a decision that was crucial for the consolidation of Deutsche Bank's position as one of the few firms still on a par with the leading American investment banks. In 1999 it bought the Wall Street investment bank Bankers Trust and the investment boutique Alex. Brown. The new head of Deutsche Bank's North America division, Carter McClelland, explained:

The US investment banks have begun to enter the European market. Only seven years ago [i.e., in 1990] firms such as Goldman Sachs, Morgan Stanley and Merrill Lynch only had small bridgeheads in Europe. Nowadays, these firms can boast relatively large and successful market positions there thanks to focused expansion strategy, extensive securities sales networks and aggressive, American-style investment banking. In such an environment, Deutsche Bank simply cannot wait. (McClelland 1997, author's translation from German

As was the case with ABN AMRO, Deutsche Bank's TNI increased significantly over the 1990s, from a little more than 20 to around 60 in 2000.

The two smaller members of the 'big three' German commercial banks also pursued Europeanisation strategies, though less ambitious than Deutsche Bank's. Dresdner Bank was late entering the acquisitions game when in 1995 it bought one of the few old City firms that had remained independent, Kleinwort Benson. The latter's prestige immediately established Dresdner Bank in the City, and towards the end of the decade it even appeared among the top ten in some league tables. Commerzbank never made any major acquisitions in the City but chose to build its own operations instead. While it had moved all of its non-DM trading and sales to London in 1994 (*European Banker* 1994b), the decision to expand only came in 1998 when it started investing heavily and doubled its investment banking staff to more than 500. Even the state-owned Landesbanken fell for the lure of investment banking: both the Hessische Landesbank (Helaba) and the Westdeutsche Landesbank (WestLB) began investing in their London operations in the mid-1990s (*European Banker* 1995a). The latter bought the City brokerage Panmure Gordon in 1996 (Slager 2004: 327). After the dot.com bubble burst, most of the smaller banks' forays into investment banking were exposed as costly and unrealistic adventures (Jenkins 2004). At the time, however, faith in investment banking as the business of the future was pervasive.

The French banks
The growing French presence abroad over the course of the 1990s featured five main players: Banque National de Paris (BNP), Paribas, Société Générale (SG), Crédit Lyonnais (CL) and Indosuez (*European Banker* 1994a). The most sophisticated and commercially oriented, Paribas, was the first to develop an international capital market focus. It set up operations in London in 1984 and in the mid-1990s extended its strategic focus to include the US market (Kraus 1994). It bought JP Morgan's European custody business in 1995 and further boosted its US securities team in 1997. The three-way takeover battle between Paribas, SG and BNP, which dominated the French banking scene in 1998 and 1999, temporarily diverted attention away from international expansion (Bream 1998). BNP's takeover of Paribas in 1999, it was hoped, would soon give it a leading position in European equities (Slager 2004: 343).

Société Générale also followed an expansion strategy that brought it within the European top twenty by the end of the 1990s. It bought the securities house Strauss Turnbull in 1993; three years later it acquired a majority stake in Crosby securities in Hong Kong. It added the banking business of Hambros merchant bank in the UK as well as two small Wall Street investment banks to its operations in 1997 and 1998.

Crédit Lyonnais internationalised even more aggressively, driven both by the state strategy to create a national champion equalling Deutsche Bank and the personal ambitions of its chief executive, Jean-Yves Haberer (Story and Walter 1997: 197). The bank, however, failed spectacularly in the mid-1990s and was dismembered by the French government, which still owned it (Coleman 2001). Indosuez, finally, was taken over by Crédit Agricole (CA) in 1996. In keeping with its status as a mutual bank, CA put less emphasis on internationalisation and used the newly-acquired investment banking capacity mainly to service its domestic clients. Nevertheless, it started to become more active internationally after it took over what remained of Crédit Lyonnais' investment banking, fused under the Calyon brand in 2004.

Banks from other European Countries
The UK and Switzerland are the only other European countries from which banks with serious pan-European or global ambitions emerged. Firms from Italy or Spain never made significant attempts to enter London's international capital markets (*European Banker* 1995b). At the time of writing, Barclays was the only British commercial bank that still played a significant role in investment banking. All merchant banks, brokers and jobbing firms were bought up by larger, mostly foreign firms in the decade following the Big Bang in 1986. With the sale of S.G. Warburg to the Swiss Banking Corporation (SBC) in 1995, the last of the big merchant banks lost its independence. Only three years later, SBC was taken over by Union Bank of Switzerland, making UBS a major player in investment banking as well. Barclays scaled down its formerly global ambitions with its subsidiary Barclays de Zoete Wedd in 1997 after poor management had led to mounting and seemingly unstoppable losses (Augar 2000). Until then, Barclays had been the most ambitious British firm, certainly the most active one in Brussels lobbying (Ipsen 1995).

The final firm with a significant role in European (and indeed global) capital markets was Credit Suisse First Boston (CSFB), formed as a joint venture between Credit Suisse and First Boston in 1978. In the mid-1990s, Credit Suisse took over First Boston and made CSFB – by then an established brand name in investment banking – its capital markets subsidiary. Even though CSFB is formally a Swiss firm, in practice it operates and is perceived as a Wall Street investment bank.

EXPLAINING INTERNATIONALISATION
The emergence of a cross-border European investment banking industry can be traced to numerous causes: the decline of traditional credit business as a source of profits, domestic and legal changes that provided new (if circumscribed) opportunities for banks, the rise of competition from US firms, the (pending) introduction of the euro, and not least the growth of business in investment banking itself. What is noteworthy about these sources of business internationalisation (discussed in detail below) is that most of them are endogenous to competitive dynamics within

the industry. Market internationalisation was bolstered by political decisions such as market liberalisation – in which banks themselves played a major role. The rise of US competition was crucial for it suggested corporate expansion and internationalisation as routes to business success for European firms. The growth of business in capital markets was itself partially endogenous to banks' changing business models as much of the international business was in fact inter-bank. In this way, regulatory developments, market changes and firms' strategic reorientations are interrelated facets of one integrated – if open-ended – structuration dynamic.

Strategic Reorientation as a Source of Market Transformation
Interest margins (in broad terms, profits made through deposit-taking and lending) in Europe had been falling since the 1970s. Throughout the Eurozone, they declined from almost 2.5 per cent in the mid-1980s to a little more than 1.5 per cent in the mid-1990s (de Haan and Prast 1999: 16). Between 1994 and 1998, they halved again in both France and Germany (Danthine *et al.* 2000: 63). Net interest margins as a source of revenue for French banks declined from 70 per cent to 53 per cent between 1992 and 1998; for Germany, the corresponding figures were 75 per cent and 63 per cent (Belaisch *et al.* 2001: 24).

The traditional basis of income for banks was thus eroding, necessitating a search for new sources of revenue. Profit margins in the highly commoditised credit business looked pale in comparison to the more 'value-added' products that American firms had pioneered in the early 1980s (see Partnoy 2002). For many firms, the strategic consequence was to refocus on these more lucrative activities, particularly in international investment banking. As Berger *et al.* wrote in 2000, this also applied to Europe:

> A wave of nonfinancial M&A activity in Europe has already precipitated fierce competition for advisory business. Intra-European merger and acquisition activity between 1985 and 1988 averaged $43 billion a year versus $280 billion a year between 1995 and 1998. In order for European universal banks to compete for this business – particularly against U.S. investment banks that have acquired substantial expertise in the M&A advisory business – they either have to develop this expertise internally or have to acquire it externally. It appears, for example, that in part Deutsche Bank has acquired this expertise by purchasing British and U.S. investment banks (Morgan Grenfell and Alex. Brown). (A. Berger *et al.* 2000: 80)

The reversal of the relative importance of credit versus fee-based business over the previous two decades (see Figure 5.5) was thus not only driven by deteriorating interest margins but by the active development of fee-generating business. Between 1997 and 1999, for example, the net commission income of banking institutions in the EU rose annually by 19 per cent (Eurostat 2001: 9). As seen previously, many of the larger European banks had identified the expansion of such business as strategic priorities much earlier.

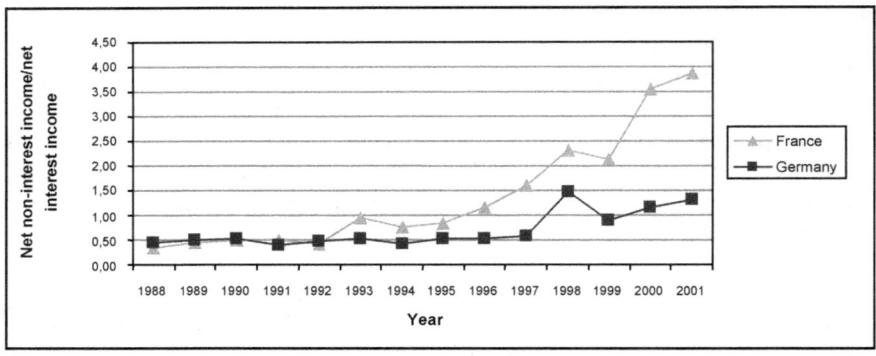

Figure 5.5: Securitisation of large commercial bank business

Unsurprisingly, this trend was most pronounced for the very largest banks (see Figure 5.6). The share of non-interest income within gross income for the six largest German and the five largest French banks reached more than 50 per cent in the period 1996–2000, compared to a little over 35 per cent a decade earlier (Slager 2004).

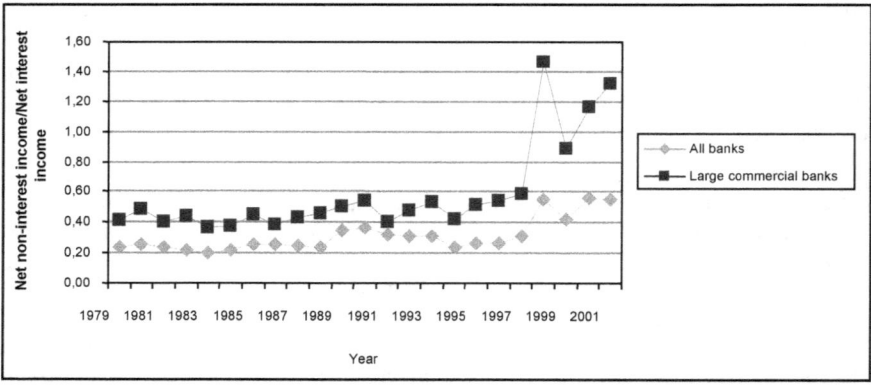

Source: OECD statistics

Figure 5.6: Comparing large commercial banks with banks in general, Germany

The rising importance of investment banking for continental universal banks had two consequences. First, they grew more interested in developing such services for their home markets. Second, they became more aware of pan-European competitive issues: the threat of foreigners taking over the smaller banks and the limitation of the cross-border market access achieved thus far for the larger ones. In this way, banks' strategic reorientations affected their regulatory preferences, a relationship analysed in more detail in Chapter 6.

Still, the question remains what motivated banks to expand as intensively as they did (Cabral *et al.* 2002, Boot 2003). The basic puzzle of consolidation is that there is little evidence that it enhances shareholder value (for such an argument, see Smith and Walter 2003); if anything, it seems to destroy it (Group of Ten 2001: 254). A large number of studies have researched economies of scale and economies of scope in financial services and in banking in particular (for an overview, see Berger *et al.* 1999). They almost invariably conclude that economies of scale only exist at the lower end of the size scale while banks with more than $10bn in assets are likely to suffer from diseconomies of scale (Berger *et al.* 1999: 158).[32] While the literature that explicitly focuses on securities markets is much smaller, findings from the early 1990s resonate with those from financial services in general, namely that the unit-cost curve is U-shaped (Goldberg *et al.* 1991). One might argue that advances in IT could have mitigated the eventual rising of unit-costs at the right end of the curve but even then it would not justify consolidation. Data processing economies of scale can often be captured through outsourcing – as indeed happened in many instances, for example in the Irish Stock Exchange using the German Xetra system for trading. Equally, economies of scope are difficult to detect; if anything, the prevailing opinion is that diseconomies of scope are more likely.

The issue looks rather different, however, if we view financial firms not only as adapters to market structures but as their makers. If there is any 'value' in consolidation, it lies in its *strategic* potential (Milbourn *et al.* 1999). Boot came to a similar conclusion:

> *[T]he* important issue is that *strategic* considerations are *the* driving force behind the current wave of consolidation. As I argue, these considerations may have rather little to do with true scale or scope economies. Rather, learning, first-mover advantages, and strategic advantages of market power and associated "deep pockets" may explain the current wave of consolidation and the broad scope of many players in the industry. [..] Strategic positioning might, for the moment, be the rule of the game and an optimal response to the uncertainties and rapid (and unpredictable) changes facing financial institutions today. (Boot 2003: 39, emphasis in original)

Banks' behaviour is thus consistent with a market structuration view in which they not only react to exogenous market changes but are themselves drivers of market transformation through their strategic behaviour. Market concentration in investment banking only amplifies the market-making effects of corporate strategy.

In light of the uncertainties Boot pointed to in the quote above, (perceived) developments within a firm's peer group are central to understanding corporate strategy. Perceived opportunity costs – the fear of 'missing out' on important trends – may be sufficient to lead CEOs down strategic paths that they would otherwise not have considered. The scramble for City brokers, jobbers and merchant banks that followed the loosening of UK rules after 1983 is instructive (Augar 2000).

---

32. For comparison, Commerzbank, a medium-sized bank by global standards, had more than $280bn in assets in 1995. (Ibid.: 189).

> Many [banks] feel that a presence in investment banking might be important for their existence as powerful banks in the future. They are willing to accept – for the moment at least – relatively low returns on those activities. The potential, but uncertain, vital role of these activities in the future defines them as a strategic option. (Boot 2003: 71)

This uncertainty stems from banks anticipating market developments or nurturing them themselves, for example in the derivatives business – rather than responding to existing demand (Partnoy 2002). After all, the investment banking strategies of the largest European players had their origins in the late 1980s and early 1990s, *before* these markets took off. The anticipatory dimension of these strategies is underscored by their frequent failure; continental universal banks, in particular, had their fingers (and money) burnt in a business of which they had little experience (see Jenkins 2004).

Even when 'markets' did develop, it would be highly misleading to think of the demand for international investment banking services – both on the sell-side (issuers) and buy-side (investors) – as exogenous to the financial services industry itself. As Berger *et al.* argue,

> the development of new financial products has primarily created markets for intermediaries rather than end users of these products. (Berger *et al.* 2000: 81)

Banks' massive exposure to complex derivatives such as collateralised debt obligations and credit default swaps, which became apparent to all in the credit crisis, only underscores this point.

In their in-depth study of European bond markets, Casey and Lannoo found the prime issuers of international bonds to be financial institutions themselves:

> International debt issues are largely, and in some EU member states overwhelmingly, dominated by financial institution issues. This result should come as no surprise, since financial institutions continue to be the main source of finance for European firms, and thereby engage in large-scale lending activities for which they must find sources of funding. Due to their expertise in, knowledge of, and experience with financial markets, banks and other financial intermediaries have a long experience of tapping international capital markets for funding purposes. (Casey and Lannoo 2005: 13)[33]

This is a well-documented but nonetheless remarkable finding. It is largely financial institutions themselves that use international markets to raise funds that they then lend on domestically. In effect this widens the pool of savers to whom financial institutions can sell their own liabilities, placing Spanish savers in competition with German and Finnish ones. In contrast, almost 90 per cent of loans in 2002 still went to banks' domestic, rather than foreign, customers (Cabral *et al.* 2002: 37). This home-bias is not surprising given the costs involved in assessing

---

33. Corporate bonds issued by non-financials account for more than 10 per cent of total international bonds in only four EU countries – the three Scandinavian members and France. Financial institutions borrow more in these markets than their respective governments in all but two countries, Greece and Finland.

the quality of (potential) loans, particularly where such information is not available 'off the shelf' through analysts or rating agencies.

In international bonds issued by financial institutions, the EU share of the global total further increased between 1999 and 2004, from 50 per cent to 60 per cent (Casey and Lannoo 2005: 14). Almost two-thirds of these bonds are European in origin. This shows that financial institutions still play a central role in channelling capital through the continent. But they mediate between savers and borrowers not by taking deposits – the lack of pan-European retail networks account for this – but by borrowing at competitive rates and using these funds to provide credit to economies and for more risky investments. While corporate bond issues increased markedly during this period, they were dwarfed in comparison to debt sold by financial institutions; in the late 1990s, corporate bonds accounted for roughly 10 per cent of total international bonds (European Commission 2005b: I-11). The demand for capital by sovereign debtors and financial firms – not corporations – propelled the growth of international markets.

Market Structuration Through Regulatory Reforms
Though the strategic reorientation of financial firms was the most visible source of market transformation, regulatory reforms pushed by public-private coalitions that had begun in the mid-1980s and continued in the wake of the ISD also transformed the market. The diverse political interests of financial market stakeholders, however, meant that these reforms often had contradictory effects. On the one hand, new rules were designed and used to defend particular financial centres and the interests of the incumbents within them. On the other hand, the largest firms pushed for and eventually exploited the opportunities the ISD gave them to expand throughout Europe. Legal changes thus both encouraged and hindered expansion. It was precisely this combination that proved unsustainable in the long run.

The ISD was meant to introduce two basic innovations: remote access to securities exchanges (discussed in the next section) and investment banks supplying financial services throughout the EU under home country rules. Relieved of having to comply with multiple rule-sets, foreign firms would be encouraged to set up branches in foreign markets. But if the service could be provided from abroad, for example electronically, firms could also close their foreign subsidiaries and service their markets from a single location.[34] In the end, agglomeration effects ensured that the latter prevailed (cf. Bindemann 1999). In the mid-1990s, both strategies were still explored.

For example, American firms, such as Merrill Lynch, were immediately encouraged by new EU legislation to spread across the continent (*Private Banker International* 1996). This, however, was easier said than done. Article 11 of the ISD stipulated that member states could draw up their own conduct of business rules. Firms trying to expand from London soon discovered that member states were ready to use such provisions to halt unwanted change. Investment banks had

---

34. One example is the Union Bank of Finland pulling out of France, for under the single market rules it could provide services from London. (*European Banker* 1995c).

to establish separate businesses in different member states, individually capitalised and with separate reports (Interview 070406). While such moves protected national incumbents, they also hampered the development of local capital markets and, in the end, helped London prevail over contenders such as Frankfurt and Paris. Some countries went so far as to dust off old laws to keep competition at bay – the SIMS law in Italy being the most extreme case. Under these rules, a firm had to be based in Italy to sell securities to Italian residents (Colvill 1995). Goldman Sachs, for example, only had one or two investment bankers permanently based in Milan; others were flown in from London when needed. The SIMS law forced Goldman Sachs and many others to build fully-fledged, operationally independent firms in Italy, which were only reintegrated into the rest of their European operations at the beginning of the millennium. Provisions such as the Italian SIMS law plainly contradicted the ISD but there was little the firms could do. In this particular case, Goldman Sachs was simultaneously applying for primary dealership in Italian government bonds. A lawsuit against the ministry of finance would not have helped its cause.

Firms soon realised that even if they were willing to pursue legal action, success was hardly assured. In a case that stuck in bankers' memories, Barclays tried to sue the French government in the early 1990s for forbidding it to pay interest on chequing accounts in its new French banking operation (Interview 160306.b, Interview 070406). The bank felt this was in clear contradiction to EU rules and sought assurances from the Commission that it would support Barclays in court. When the issue came to a head, however, the Commission backed down.

France actually met the ISD's 1996 implementation deadline (*Financial Regulation Report* 1996c) and combined this with a streamlining of supervisory structures (*Financial Regulation Report* 1995a). Yet in key respects, the French law on the 'modernisation of financial activities' violated the official spirit, if not the letter, of the ISD. Locally operating firms still had to follow the rules of the *Conseil des Marchés Financières*, an arrangement meant to undermine the competitive threat of US firms (Bream 1998). Services rendered to the state and the Banque de France, which were, after all, the two largest market participants, fell outside the scope of the new law. It also implemented the concentration rule by stipulating that most securities transactions had to be carried out through regulated markets where these existed. Nevertheless, the new law abolished the monopoly on the negotiation of transferable securities that the sociétés de bourse had hitherto held (Demarigny 1998: 277).

Events moved even more slowly in Germany (Shirreff 1997). Implementation of the ISD had been promised for 1996, which was the original target date (*European Banker* 1996b). But rule changes became law only two years later (*Financial Regulation Report* 1998a) due to the government's strategy of pushing back the 'new realities' (Interview 020506). After all, one of the ISD's core provisions allowed firms to provide services from a distance: rather than going through local subsidiaries, they could open branches or even provide services without local representation. Developments triggered by the 2BCD were worrying: Merrill Lynch, for example, had closed its subsidiary in Frankfurt in the mid-1990s to service Germany through the branch of its subsidiary in Ireland (Shirreff 1997). Indeed, of the 695 ISD passport applications the German securities supervisor received in 1996, more than 600 came from London and virtually all of them (690) were asking for permission to provide financial services across borders (Bundesaufsichtsamt für den Wertpapierhandel 1997: 33). Not all the applications were from British or American firms, but it showed that many firms preferred to provide pan-European services from a single location – the City. No surprise, then, that American investment banks were particularly irritated about the slow pace with which Germany, traditionally one of the most 'liberal' financial markets in Europe (J. Williamson and Mahar 1998), reformed its laws and regulations (Moir 1997).

That said, it would oversimplify the picture to think of individual governments as either eager or reluctant to reform financial markets. As argued in Chapter 3, reforms were above all strategic, meaning they were attuned to the attainment of specific ends and the satisfaction of particular interests. In 1994 the Second Law for the Promotion of Financial Markets had created the first German securities markets supervisor, the *Bundesaufsichtsamt für den Wertpapierhandel* (BaWe). In doing so, it acted on the realisation within both government and industry that 'internationally acceptable' supervisory structures were necessary if international business was to come Frankfurt's way (see also Chapter 4 on the CAD negotiations). For example, the Deutsche Börse in the early 1990s had sought official UK recognition as a stock exchange but was repeatedly turned down due to its lack of proper regulatory and supervisory structures (Interview 240506.b). For actors with stakes in internationalising Frankfurt, introducing oversight structures more in line with international standards made perfect sense. Also in 1994, the German government relaxed entry rules for American banks, which were henceforth treated almost as EU firms (*Financial Regulation Report* 1994c). Paralleling other market-opening steps, the decision was not unilateral but was negotiated with the US government.

At the same time, the concerns of both foreign and large domestic players often went unaddressed, particularly discrepancies between different national rule sets (e.g. for reserve requirements). As the sense of competition between Frankfurt and London grew, the German government realised that a legal environment conducive to financial innovation was crucial.

By the late 1990s London was more clearly than ever emerging as the centre of choice for wholesale business. One City investment banker remembers the development as follows:

> What was actually happening – many other investment banks did it – was to pull back trading activities from elsewhere in Europe to one location. And nearly every institution that decided to adopt this model chose to carry out their trading from London. You would keep your sales forces within the jurisdictions. But if you were trading Italian government debt or French equities, you would, so far as the law permitted you to do so, do it from London. And that has been the model. And this was driven by two things. One was the fact that the euro was coming in at the time. And everyone could see that that would create a bond

market that was driven more by maturities than by national boundaries. And that meant that ideally, all the traders who were previously trading in different jurisdictions in individual countries would go to one location. And so you had your trading desk in London transmogrified into this multicultural flower. And the other driver which was coupled with that was that most countries started to liberalise their rules with respect to who could be a primary dealer in securities. And that was driven one by the fact that the euro was coming along, two by the fact that the big international players were beginning to be recognised by the governments as the people who actually had the distribution strength to disseminate their bonds, and three by pressure from those large entities and elsewhere to open up the primary dealerships which had traditionally been held by the big banks in the particular jurisdictions, France, Spain, Germany ... The point about all of these is that the only element that was an EU element was the euro. *All the other elements had more to do with business strategies.* Having said that, the creation of the euro was a very strong element. Technology was another driver as well. It was easier to deal remotely, too. (Interview 140306, emphasis added)

As pointed out previously, legal changes in Europe invited new business strategies. But where reforms had been the result of compromise between different stakeholders – in particular between firms with different competitive interests – inconsistencies in the new legislation soon became apparent. These motivated investment firms to push for further change, which is the topic of the next chapter.

EUROPEAN BOURSES: FROM MEMBERS-ONLY CLUBS TO PROFIT-SEEKING FIRMS

The rise of independent, for-profit securities exchanges was the second major transformation of the capital market industry in the 1990s – the flip-side of (investment) banks increasingly disembedding themselves from national economies and market places to focus on cross-border business. This so-called demutualisation of stock exchanges would crucially alter the renegotiation of the ISD (discussed in Chapter 8), when the bourses emerged as fierce competitors to the new European investment banking incumbents. True to the logic of structuration, the strategic decisions made by (investment) banks in the 1990s returned to haunt them in EU-level regulatory negotiations a decade later.

As Lee has noted, exchanges occupy a peculiar position:

If there is one factor that is universally accepted as being the most important determinant of both exchange behaviour and market structure, it is competition. The ubiquity of the term has not meant, however, that its nature is clear. [..] [A] Manichean view of exchanges either competing or alternatively cooperating, is too simplistic to represent usefully how exchanges actually relate to each other. (Lee 1998: 49)

Historically, bourses have developed as members-only clubs in which competition was tightly controlled by private interests (Braithwaite and Drahos 2000: 145). Members fixed commissions and divided business amongst themselves, for example by assigning the trading of particular stocks to individual firms or persons (Pagano and Steil 1996). Exchanges, governed by the interests of their members, have always tried to protect their monopolies. In theory, this is underpinned by the tendency of trading to gravitate to the most liquid exchange (Schwartz 1996). But as Schwartz points out, things are less clear-cut in practice. Different intermediaries, and even different stock exchange members, may have diverging interests regarding the concentration of trading on a single platform.

Over time, exchanges faced creeping competition from other trading venues, first from 'alternative trading systems' (or 'ATS', such as Instinet) and later from intermediaries (Lee 2002). ATS usually have lower transparency requirements and allow intermediaries to sell large swathes of securities without prices immediately moving against them. Large banks thus have conflicting interests regarding exchanges-as-clubs. While they may appreciate exchanges limiting competition, the costs they generate, both directly for their services and indirectly through adverse price effects, may be considered too high. Large intermediaries thus often take part of their trading to alternative venues, thereby fuelling competition for the exchanges they used to dominate. The story of SEAQ International, recounted in Chapter 3, is a case in point (Pagano and Steil 1996: 5). In the early 1990s, the member firms of established exchanges opted for the application of new electronic systems to repatriate trading, for example IBIS in Germany and CAC in France. Before long, SEAQ's market share dwindled.

Once this competitive challenge to the established exchanges had been thwarted – even if large firms continued to do deals off-exchange, over the telephone – many smaller member firms saw little need for further investment in trading technology. They were, in short, quite content with the status quo. The larger members, however, were not of the same opinion. With the prevailing one member-one vote system, they regularly saw their own interests, for example in developing vibrant domestic equity markets, thwarted by what they saw as the conservatism of smaller members. These cracks grew increasingly visible in the early 1990s. In Germany, the president of the Frankfurt stock exchange was traditionally a private banker from a small firm. But in 1992, after one such president's term had ended, Rolf Breuer, board member of Deutsche Bank, took over the post in a sign of clear impatience with developments at the bourse.

Divisions further increased when the ISD – for which firms such as Deutsche Bank had lobbied – opened the possibility of granting foreign firms 'remote access'. This innovation could entail loss of business for local firms, as they would be by-passed by foreign brokers. Reaching agreement among Deutsche Börse's members to offer remote access thus proved difficult, though smaller firms were eventually convinced by arguments that the overall share-trading pie would grow sufficiently to offset the threat of growing competition. Plans were quickly made to install access points in London and Zurich (*European Banker* 1996c). For the larger firms, the overall calculation was different: while they might lose market share in their (former) home markets, they stood to gain from openness through access abroad.

Though the ISD gave exchanges the *right* to set up screens abroad, the

Stockholm exchange, which was outside the EU at the time, had already pioneered such remote access (*Financial Regulation Report* 1996b, Pagano and Steil 1996: 41). This change, however, only happened once the exchange had been privatised: with 50 per cent ownership in issuers' hands, their interest in gaining exposure to foreign investors trumped the anti-competitive instincts of local brokers. Inside the EU, the Amsterdam exchange was one of the first to make use of the new ISD rules when in 1994 it allowed CSFB to retain membership even though the investment bank had relocated its Dutch activities to London (*Financial Regulation Report* 1994a). The exception was granted when CSFB pledged to remain a market-maker for at least twenty-five Amsterdam stocks. The other companies with such a broad offering of Dutch shares were all local or at best European in reach (ABN AMRO, Mees Pierson, Suez Nederland and Van Meer James Capel). Through CSFB, an established Wall Street investment bank, Amsterdam could access a wide US investor base. Local traders were nevertheless disgruntled, pushing for remote access to exchanges abroad in return for letting the 'foreigners' in. Remote access technology was thus applied in line with the commercial and competitive interests of those who controlled the stock exchanges.

The growing split between the interests of their members led more and more exchanges towards demutualisation: they ceased to be controlled by their members or users and became private companies. The first exchanges to demutualise and modernise their governance structures were generally those that had faced most competition from ATS. The Amsterdam exchange, for example, traded numerous shares with international appeal (multinationals such as Unilever and Royal-Dutch/Shell) for which vibrant overseas markets had developed in the early 1990s. It was therefore quick to implement changes, for example by switching all operating systems to English and by demutualising in 1997 (Interview 211105.a). Other mid-sized exchanges, such as the Borsa Italiana in Milan, took similar steps in the second half of the 1990s (Steil 2002b: 26). In contrast, the world's major exchanges (the NYSE, the NASDAQ, the LSE, the TSE, the CBOT, the CME, etc.) continued to operate as mutuals, largely due to less competition and thus fewer conflicts of interest between their members.

From the moment exchanges began operating as for-profit enterprises, their own commercial interests were at the heart of their strategic positioning. Exchanges are even more highly concentrated than intermediaries: the top three exchanges accounted for over 60 per cent of global market capitalisation throughout the 1990s (Schich and Kikuchi 2003: 109). Similar numbers apply within the EU: in 1995, the LSE, the Deutsche Börse and the Paris Bourse together commanded just under 70 per cent of the EU total; in 2001, after Euronext was created, which integrated the Amsterdam, Brussels, Paris and Lisbon exchanges, the figure was almost 75 per cent (Schich and Kikuchi 2003: 110). These figures have generally remained stable over the past decades, indicating that smaller and larger exchanges, by and large, kept pace in their growth.

Exchanges have rarely managed to capture the trading of a foreign security from its home country, particularly in developed countries. LIFFE's temporary success with Bund futures was an important exception, but after the Deutsche

Terminbörse (DTB) began trading with up-to-date technology, business eventually returned to Frankfurt (Interview 020506). The episode also brought home the high costs of head-on competition. Shifting alliances notwithstanding, most exchanges respected the division of business between them and recognised what Fligstein (2001) has called the prevailing 'conception of control'. Exchanges have mitigated competition by, for example, sharing technology and forming link-ups such as the one between the French MATIF and the German DTB derivatives exchanges in 1994 (Gapper *et al.* 1996). Potential competition, and the impetus for innovation, thus came not so much from established bourses but alternative trading systems and new start-ups (Interview 240506.b). One of the more noteworthy ones, discussed in more detail in the coming chapter, was EASDAQ – an EU Commission-sponsored copy of the US NASDAQ set up in 1996 (Posner 2009b). EASDAQ was the Commission's attempt, together with the European Venture Capital Association, to kick-start the market for the kind of new 'high-tech' issues that fuelled the NASDAQ's spectacular success in the 1990s (*Financial Regulation Report* 1996a). The established exchanges, however, immediately responded by setting up their own 'new markets' such as the Alternative Investment Market in London, the Neuer Market in Frankfurt, the Nuevo Mercado in Madrid and the Nouveau Marché in Paris. EASDAQ thus never attracted more than a handful of listings; due to its Brussels location, most of these were Belgian.

Until late in the 1990s, the history of European exchanges was notable for its scarcity of successful consolidation – that is, the creation of cross-border securities exchanges (see Cybo-Ottone *et al.* 2000: 239). Most of the cross-border deals were not full mergers but joint ventures or technology sharing arrangements, and even these had a history of failures (Pagano and Steil 1996: 39). Euronext, the most prominent cross-border initiative, combined several exchanges under one corporate roof; it did not create a single entity out of them. Uncertainties over regulatory responsibilities in a truly transnational exchange did not make such ventures more attractive. Nevertheless, most takeover attempts were defeated not because they did not make sense from a wider market perspective (economies of scale, market depth, synergies, etc.), but because those controlling the exchanges felt the numbers did not add up (Lee 2002).

The most prominent example from the 1990s is, without doubt, the attempt to merge the London and Frankfurt stock exchanges. The tie-up between the LSE and the Deutsche Börse, announced in early July 1998, was a EU financial market earthquake. The big banks were strongly in favour of such transnational market integration; as chairman of the Deutsche Börse, Deutsche Bank CEO, Rolf Breuer, was one of the main driving forces behind the deal. The *European Banker* (1998) at the time was sure that such an alliance would be 'unstoppable'. But both banks and other observers underestimated just how independent exchanges had become through demutualisation. When the British-German tie-up eventually floundered, it was widely attributed to the narrow interests of both management teams rather than wider economic rationales. At any rate, the episode demonstrated to investment bankers that exchanges would henceforth be ruled by considerations that could collide with their own interests or, for that matter, with those of other stakeholders including issuers and investors. As one London investment banker reflected with hindsight,

> [t]he banks themselves did not anticipate the speed with which the new management [of exchanges] would adopt profit-maximising instincts and apply them to their monopolistic position. (Interview 300306)

The coming years would show that the rivalry between for-profit exchanges and their former members and rulers involved more than conflicting commercial interests. More important for the supranationalisation of EU capital market governance were the political differences that emerged once both groups of firms found themselves to be direct competitors for trading business. In an ironic twist of fate, the banks had created their fiercest competitors through the wave of demutualisation over which they themselves presided.

chapter six | the re-launch of financial market integration

The internationalisation of European banks and their move into investment business began to translate into regulatory change in the closing years of the 1990s. As this chapter details, these changes culminated in the Financial Services Action Plan (FSAP), a regulatory to-do list endorsed by the European Council in 1999. A milestone in the history of EU financial market integration (e.g. Bieling 2003, McKeen-Edwards *et al.* 2004, Jabko 2006), the FSAP marked the beginning of the transition towards harmonised European rules. It was also a departure in another respect: it was promoted by a coalition of firms with international ambitions and the European Commission – the first transnational public-private alliance in EU financial markets.

The 'upgrading' of the ISD was not high on the list of projects suggested by the FSAP. This is noteworthy, for the Market in Financial Instruments Directive (MiFID), as the ISD's successor was christened, later became the centrepiece of financial market reform in Europe. No directive has been more important for the organisation of EU capital markets, for the future of European financial centres and for the prospects of the financial industry's different branches. And no other directive has attracted more attention from bank lobbyists.

However, an important step remained in the transformation of EU capital market governance: the formalisation of supranational institutions, which is covered in the next chapter. The push for supranational governance depended on renewed vigour in legislative activity, fuelled by the new preferences of core constituencies. Here the FSAP played a central role in encouraging the emergence of the supranational institutions that by and large continue to govern European capital markets today.

The Commission also played an important role in the FSAP. It was, after all, a Commission product. But its agency was relevant in a wider sense as well. In the debate over the leeway of supranational institutions to affect policy independently (Moravcsik 1993, Pierson 1996, Moravcsik 1998, Pollack 1998), the re-launch of integration in financial services was clearly an area where the Commission identified room for manoeuvre – and used it skilfully (Gottwald 2005, Posner 2009b, Jabko 2006).

The European Commission's visibility in re-launching financial market integration, however, did not mean that it was the driving force behind it. As argued in Chapter 4, its support was a necessary but not sufficient condition for integration to move forward. The Commission's initiatives around the ISD and the CAD were for the most part defeated around 1990; it was left with a regime full of loopholes that fell far short of its original ambitions. What was different this time? The crucial factor governing success was widespread industry support for cross-border integration: firms exerted pressure on the Commission and convinced national governments of the necessity for change. The argument here is not that industry set the Commission's agenda. The Commission had already reached its position in favour of further integration, preferably through regulatory harmonisation (implying more competencies for EU actors). But without industry support, the integration project could never have moved forward.

There are not many written documents detailing the involvement of private actors in EU policy-making which are publicly available. As evidence of corporate influence could cause serious political damage to the integration project, even the slightly more formal consultations that the Commission had with industry representatives around 1998 were conducted under Chatham House Rules, effectively limiting what participants could communicate about what was said (Gottwald 2005). The Commission also limited the availability of written documents from these consultations, for example by producing the summaries of industry opinion itself. Given this scarcity of available material, the first half of this chapter relies on the evidence from confidential interviews with national and European public officials, regulators, and firm and association lobbyists. The chapter's second half, which focuses more on the 'official' EU policy process, again makes use of public documents and academic studies of EU policy in addition to interview material.

SHIFTING INDUSTRY PREFERENCES IN THE 1990S

Logically, the more a firm's business strategy builds on cross-border transactions, the more it should support transnational integration (Schmitter 1970, Milner 1988, Stone Sweet and Sandholtz 1998, Mattli 1999). In some cases, firm-level factors may complicate the picture. Managers may have political loyalties that contradict a firm's business interests. Or they may fail to identify promising opportunities. In general, though, strategies of business internationalisation should correlate with policy preferences in favour of easier cross-border market access.

Support for market integration, however, does not determine a firm's policy preferences. In the case of regulation for the single European market, there are at least two ways to abolish inter-state barriers. *Mutual recognition* leaves firms to operate under home country rules; *regulatory harmonisation* mandates that all firms should follow a roughly similar rule set.

What factors determine firms' support for or opposition to these alternative strategies? Other things being equal, pro-integration firms from countries with 'light' regulatory regimes should prefer mutual recognition, as potential competitors from states with more costly regulatory regimes would be disadvantaged. In contrast, firms based in countries with costly regulatory regimes should favour regulatory harmonisation, which puts them and their competitors on an 'equal footing', particularly if downward adjustment of regulatory costs associated with the home country regime is not a desirable or politically viable option. By the same token, opponents of transnational market integration will favour protectionism if the regulatory costs imposed by their home country regime are high, or will be indifferent if the regulatory costs are low, for in this scenario they will have no competition to fear. We would only expect them to voice opposition when regulatory harmonisation looms on the horizon, for it would constitute market opening on relatively unfavourable terms. These positions are summarised in Table 6.1.

Table 6.1: Hypothetical policy preferences of firms

		Relative regulatory cost of home country standards	
		High	Low
In favour of pan-European market access	Yes	Harmonisation	Mutual recognition
	No	Protectionism (= opposition to mutual recognition)	Indifference (+ wariness *vis-à-vis* harmonisation)

Whether interest in transnational market integration translates into support for regulatory harmonisation or mutual recognition should therefore depend on the regulatory regime of the home country and its competitive implications.

The political preferences of investment firms in the 1990s confirm this general pattern. City investment banks, which include American firms operating from the City, in principle preferred mutual recognition to harmonisation. It seemed unlikely, to say the least, that a single rule set would be less onerous than the existing system. This explains why many firms were ambivalent about the new legislative fervour of the Commission in the domain of investment services, even though they did support its goal of more market integration. Only the most savvy investment banks realised early on that rule harmonisation would be the price to pay for true European market integration. As one City investment banker observed with hindsight:

> We were in favour of mutual recognition and competition but the member states would not buy it without massive harmonisation. So you get a much more detailed framework. (Interview 270206)

In contrast, virtually all continental firms favouring market integration supported harmonisation as the route towards a unified market as it would, at least partly, erode the competitive advantage of the London firms.

The first to realise that the ISD and mutual recognition were not going to deliver were its most ardent supporters, firms in the City. Even then, they approached the issue with varying degrees of urgency. Many of the smaller, traditional City institutions were busy digesting the shake-up of their competitive environment rooted in domestic changes. For them, EU matters seemed a side-show to the real transformation. Without ambitions to access clients in the remote corners of Europe, many firms were content dealing in Eurobonds and Euroequities (Interview 270206). Ironically, the vibrancy of the international business, free of EU rules, allowed smaller firms to underestimate how important these rules could become in the daily running of their businesses:

> In those days, people did not realise that making one small mistake in article 11 [of the ISD] was quite crucial to consolidate the home-host distinctions and things like that. (Interview 300306)[35]

Such misinterpretations of the importance of EU level developments by the 'old guard' of City bankers were also due to another traditional advantage of the City's business environment: bankers' relative freedom from government interference in running their affairs (Moran 1991). This had left them undersensitised to the importance of public regulation, including EU rules, in shaping financial markets and poorly equipped with resources to influence government policy (Interview 300306). Hitherto the system had run largely on 'winks and nods' from the Bank of England and the personal ties that bound City bankers in self-regulatory organisations. As one investment banker graphically put it:

> We didn't do our homework, collectively, any of us. Historically, regulatory policy has had a very low economic or technical input. Regulators are poor quality people in the government world, compared to central bankers, macroeconomic people or even tax designers who are aristocrats in the system. But regulators? Who are they? They are just lawyers, degenerate commercial people… (Interview 300306)

Such attitudes meant that City firms woke up only slowly to the relevance of EU regulatory policies.

To be sure, they were not representative of all firms. The one large bank active in capital markets that was still in British hands, Barclays, tried to stay abreast of regulatory developments in Brussels (Interview 160306.b). However, it tended to espouse the EU-sceptic opinions found among the small City firms. The real exceptions were the American investment banks that envisioned European futures for themselves. Aware of what they saw as shortcomings in EU rules, they were the first to lobby in Brussels (Interview 070406).

Despite the varying perceptions of urgency, the limitations of the ISD regime did not come to most City firms as a surprise. In 1994, one year after the adoption of the directive, the Bank of England had published research documenting City firms' fears that the ISD might fall short of its goals (Bank of England 1994). The main problem was uncertainty surrounding the applicability of home versus host country rules that resulted from Article 11 in the original ISD:

> When your trader in Finland needs more than half an hour to figure out whether a trade would be legal, then you're simply not going to do it at all. (Interview 070406)

---

35. Article 11 of the ISD stipulates that member states shall draw up conduct of business rules themselves and implement and supervise compliance. With thatis stipulation, firms stay well inside the arms of the host authorities. Also, it stipulates that the professional nature of the client is to be determined by looking at the end-client, not at another investment firm through which the client may have placed his order. Because end-clients are not readily identifiable in inter-bank trades, banks could not a priori claim that they were only dealing with professionals and should therefore be exempt from local conduct of business rules.

The fact that the ISD did not harmonise conduct of business rules (CBRs) was where, in the words of a senior lobbyist from a Wall Street investment bank, 'the rubber hit the road' – a message reiterated by lobbyists to the Commission (Interview 070406). Without harmonised CBRs, they argued, running a pan-European business would induce headaches.

> In the late 1990s, one of the things that Citibank would like to do, for certain products, was build a company that could deal on a pan-European basis. And to do that, they needed regulatory approval. And they found that that was far more difficult than they had anticipated. Yes, in principle the ISD already gave them a passport, but in reality [..] how particular products had to be marketed and how you got approval varied widely. And that created a lot of difficulties. (Interview 140306)

While some of the old City firms blamed the lack of transnational market access on the faulty *implementation* of the ISD, others saw the problem in the ambiguities of the directive itself:

> [European governments] never properly accepted the concept of mutual recognition. And the Commission was too cowardly. Mogg [Commission Director General responsible for financial services] always argued: Give me evidence [of governments breaking the rules]. And we [the financial industry] produced numerous reports on evidence. And then he turned around and said... Some City lawyers said: There isn't a clear-cut case where we can build an infringement case. There was the Italian case, of course. But Mogg would argue that the directives are framed in such an ambiguous way that you cannot really guarantee that you could successfully go to court. The feeling was that in order to get such a directive as we have adopted, these ambiguities were built in. (Interview 160306.b)

It did not take long for firms to complain. As one UK government official at the time put it:

> On the wholesale issues the UK authorities, particularly the Treasury, were getting a very clear message from the industry in London that the ISD passport was very inefficient. (Interview 270206)

If opinion in the City was divided between relative indifference towards the ISD and disappointment over the lack of effective mutual recognition, continental firms were divided between favouring regulatory harmonisation – an approach that had yet to be tested in investment banking – and outright opposition to market integration. Prominent members of the 'maximum harmonisation' camp included ABN AMRO (Shirreff 1999), Deutsche Bank and ING (Interview 140306).

The German and French firms, in particular, suffered from varying degrees of what one respondent described as 'schizophrenia' (Interview 160306.b). They were torn between the growing pull of the City and a cosmopolitan business perspective on the one hand and embeddedness in and loyalty to the traditional 'home market' on the other (Brady 1992). The contradiction was much less relevant for firms from smaller countries, particularly the Netherlands, which had limited home markets (Interview 270206, cf. Jabko 2006). These differences between the banks soon became apparent in their lobbying.

THE EMERGENCE OF EU-LEVEL LOBBYING

Lobbying around capital market issues in 1990s Brussels was the preserve of large banks. The alleged beneficiaries of financial market integration – largely non-financial firms in search of capital and investment managers seeking high returns – stayed outside of the political process unfolding in Brussels. As one long-time City lobbyist summarised:

> The issuers... I mean, where were the issuers [of securities]? Every paper that we [an international trade association in finance] ever wrote talked about the supply side, trying to improve the efficiency of European capital markets. Why? Reduces the cost of access to the capital market. Increases choice, for the consumers it lowers price. Actually nothing about profits for the intermediaries. And where is the voice of the consumer? Nothing, nowhere. Absolutely nowhere in that debate. Where is the voice of even the institutional investor? Nowhere. And Europe has huge asset managers. And where were the issuers? Nowhere. (Interview 270206)

The message that 'the market' sent to policy-makers revolved around the commercial concerns of financial firms, rather than the public goods that an integrated capital market might generate.

One of the most seasoned Brussels lobbyists in financial services, John Houston, estimated in 1999 that in the financial services sector, twenty-five federations and roughly 120 individual lobbyists were present in Brussels (Shirreff 1999). Considering that this included insurance, asset management, stock exchange and many other sub-sectors in addition to banking and investment banking, this number is small. Houston also surmised that only one or two federations and not many more than seven lobbyists were actively lobbying. But given the concentration in the industry, these few could still represent a significant share of the market and hence wield considerable influence. Most of the lobbyists outside of this active group functioned largely as one-way communication channels, relaying information from Brussels trade associations to their members.

Even when second-tier banks did allocate resources to regulatory developments in Brussels, this often happened in the context of their legal departments, charged with 'keeping track of EU developments'. This was a far cry from actively trying to shape the policy agenda. After all, when continental banks had most of their capital market operations in London but were still controlled from their domestic headquarters, the identification of a clear corporate interest was no easy task (cf. Woll 2008). As was the case with securities issuers and institutional investors, 'objectively identifiable' interests and stakes in EU capital market policy were not enough to ensure that the voices of second-tier banks were heard in Brussels – if, indeed, there was a message at all.

Houston's list of pro-active firms in mid-1990s Brussels included ABN AMRO, Deutsche Bank, Barclays, Citibank, Morgan Stanley and Goldman Sachs, and among the federations, the European Banking Federation (EBF). This pattern was largely confirmed by interview respondents. When prompted for the most active lobbyists, the above list normally surfaced with minor variations: Citibank was not always included while ING sometimes was (Interview 160306.b). In 2006, one US investment bank lobbyist described the circle of 'peers' in lobbying as ABN AMRO, Barclays, Deutsche Bank, Goldman Sachs, Merrill Lynch, Morgan Stanley and UBS (Interview 070406).

Among them, the American firms were the most active and also the first to lobby in Brussels professionally (Interview 270206, Interview 021205.a). Goldman Sachs – described not without admiration by one insider as a 'very aggressive, very active, very professional organization' (Interview 300306) – is generally credited with being the first in Brussels, setting up its 'European government affairs office' in 1992/93 (Interview 070406). Morgan Stanley – the 'aristocrat' among the bulge bracket firms – followed in 1995. These banks tended to stay ahead of the regulatory curve. As one representative of a national lobbying association remembers,

> [y]ears ago our federation went to see John Mogg [the Director General at the European Commission responsible for financial services in the second half of the 1990s]. And he said: 'Oh yeah, I thought I'd see you guys.' 'Oh yeah, why is that?' 'The American investment banks came here with this problem six months ago. I can always tell the difference. They always come in before anyone knows the problem. You guys always come in afterwards.' (Interview 021205.a)

Deutsche Bank, ABN AMRO and Barclays stood out among the European firms. Deutsche Bank set up its Brussels office in the early 1990s; ABN AMRO followed with its 'Liaison Office' late in 1996 (Mijs and Caparrós Puebla 2002). Barclays lobbyists mainly operated from the City, facilitated by the completion of the Eurostar train link between Brussels and London in 1994. As pointed out above, the German and French firms were often seen as having 'two souls' in lobbying (Interview 070406). In the early days, this complicated coordination with other firms, particularly the American ones. Even if Deutsche Bank's London investment bankers shared a common position with them, 'Frankfurt' often did not. As a result, cooperation across the Channel was rare in the beginning.

Part of this split within the investment banking community simply had to do with limits to the overlap of interests. Pro-integration banks still differed on the question of harmonisation versus mutual recognition. The more savvy of the City-based firms realised that integration without harmonisation was unlikely, given the need to get member states on board. Nevertheless, they kept pushing for less intrusive EU rules, whereas the French and Germans clearly saw the advantages of far-reaching harmonisation. These views were shared by their governments. In an article co-authored by two representatives of Deutsche Börse and the director responsible for capital markets in the German ministry of finance, the goal was 'welfare-optimization through harmonization', 'the most far-reaching harmonization of rules and markets to safeguard fair and intensive competition' (Asmussen et al. 2004: 28, translated from German). The French had even stronger views, advocating not only a shared rule-set but a single European regulator.

Among the investment banks, French banks adopted a relatively low profile on policy issues. Several factors account for this. Even though French firms were not against market integration, they tended to favour it on different terms than the American investment banks. Taking a strong stand within the London investment banking community would have exposed differences without political gain. While French banks were members of the most important City trade associations, their influence was insufficient to sway these bodies. Keeping a low profile was thus a sensible strategy. More importantly, French state-market relations, themselves a product of the idiosyncratic evolution of French capitalism (e.g. Schmidt 1996), favoured opinion formation at the national level and reliance on state actors rather than trade associations or lobbyists to promote their case in Brussels.

> In the UK, if the government takes a position that the industry doesn't like, then the industry will say so very strongly. In France, there is much more discipline. If the Trésor decides a line, then that is it. That also gives them a strong position in negotiations. Whereas in the UK or in Germany they [the associations] might very well say 'Well, this is rubbish. We want something else.' (Interview 021205.a)

As French banks were privatised over the course of the 1990s, they became increasingly involved in financial sector policy. As traditional sectoral associations became less relevant for the largest banks (Interview 160506.a, cf. Lalone 2005), they founded more initiative-based organisations, most notably EuroFi, a big bank-sponsored think tank meant to emulate the Finanzplatz Deutschland initiative set up in the early 1990s to boost Frankfurt's international standing. One respondent characterised the initiative as follows:

> You had in France an American-phile faction, who were happy to learn English, who went to business schools, were in investment banking or the academic community. You then had the very big banks, like BNP and SocGen, who were aware of the need to develop an international vocation rather than just stay inward looking, and they were always keen to create a kind of internationally competitive Paris rather like Finanzplatz Deutschland. And they were quickly able to attract the support of the French institutions. (Interview 300306)

EuroFi's main aim was not to lobby Brussels directly, but to enlist domestic political support for the goals of openness and internationalisation.

Smaller financial market participants, who were likely to lose out from market integration and the concentration and consolidation it would entail, were notably absent from the Brussels lobbying game in the 1990s. The very small players, including savings banks and cooperative banks, had their own national associations which were united in the European Savings Bank Group and the European Association of Co-operative Banks. Both were relatively late to take positions on EU issues and remained largely reactive (Interview 061205).

The main reason for small firms' absence from the Brussels lobbying scene was their opposition to the European Commission's agenda. Private-public interaction in Brussels became increasingly formalised after 1999 through fixed consultations with 'representative' committees of market participants. With its agenda firmly set on integration, informal direct lobbying by firms with protectionist impulses seemed a lost cause. Their preferred route was through national associations with access to member state governments, even if collective action problems put them at a disadvantage to larger firms (there were thousands of small banks in Germany alone). Furthermore, the Commission preferred contact with European business associations to national ones (Bouwen 2002), and direct contact with individual firms to associations in general (Eising 2007). This was clearly the case when the cooperation of large banks was necessary to achieve politically important goals, for example the creation of a Single European Payments Area (Interview 231105).

The growing split between large and small firms left second-tier firms caught in the middle. National understandings about market orders – conceptions of control in Fligstein's (2001) terms – began to fray as large firms pursued their own interests. National associations such as the *Bundesverband der Deutschen Banken* (Association of German [commercial] Banks, BdB) lost their relevance *vis-à-vis* other industry-government communication channels (cf. Cowles 2001) and left second-tier firms without a body to represent their interests (Interview 220506). Mijs and Caparrós Puebla summarise the process as follows:

> In this world, only 15 or 20 years ago, the national federations represented the sector and the accumulated view was presented to the European institutions by the European federations [..]. Domestic mergers in the late 1980s and early 1990s created a number of large banks in Europe [..]. In the 1990s these banks became more and more ambitious to set up operations outside and throughout Europe. At this time these large banks started to realize the direct impact European legislation had on their business. Today most of the large banks in Europe are represented, either by an office in Brussels or by a specialized department (Mijs and Caparrós Puebla 2002: 262).

National sectoral associations such as the BBA, the BdB and the FBF were not the only ones trying to influence European politics. Other prominent organisations included the London Investment Banking Association (LIBA), the European Banking Federation (EBF) and a number of professional associations focused largely on wholesale markets such as the International Swaps and Derivatives Association (ISDA) and the body which eventually became the International Capital Market Association (ICMA). As mentioned above, LIBA emerged out of the Accepting Houses Committee, a club of leading City merchant bankers who throughout the twentieth century functioned as a quasi-trade association as well as a link to government and the Bank of England (Thompson 1997). In the course of the 1980s, this bastion of 'gentlemanly capitalism' (cf. Augar 2000) changed its composition to reflect the growing importance of foreign, particularly American, investment banks; in 1989 it changed its name to the British Merchant Banking and Securities Houses Association (normally abbreviated as BMBA) (Filipovic 1997). Five years later, the name was changed again as 'British' no longer reflected the composition of its membership (*Observer* 1994). It was now christened the London Investment Banking Association, a trade association with roughly forty members representing the top brass of global investment banking.

The high profile of its membership did not mean, however, that BMBA/LIBA was ahead of regulatory developments in Europe. To the frustration of its members who favoured integration (Interview 070406), the organisation in the mid-1990s remained absorbed in domestic issues in the UK (Interview 300306). In later years, certainly after the re-launch of EU legislative activity in 1999, LIBA shifted its focus towards European matters – with one insider claiming that they consumed 80 per cent of LIBA's resources by 2006. That said, its status in Brussels as the de facto mouthpiece of the investment banking industry remained tarred by the 'L' in its acronym. One US investment banker confided that he had repeatedly tried to have 'London' struck from its name (Interview 070406). The British firms among its members, however, were against this. Another respondent voiced regret on the same point:

> [I]f LIBA would change its name to European Investment Banking Association, that would improve its abilities in Brussels at the stroke of a pen. (Interview 021205.a)

Though the European Banking Federation (EBF) did boast an 'E' in its name, it had difficulty reaching common positions, certainly until the late 1990s. As a federation of national associations of commercial banks, the EBF needed unanimous support for its statements, which, unsurprisingly, were hard to reach. Over time, however, trade association officials became more proactive (Interview 160306.b).

> Later in the 1990s they changed their strategy. They would come out with their statement and there would be a very obscure footnote saying "Not all members agree with this..." And that was always the French, almost. (Interview 160306.b)

Recognising the authority of the EBF in Brussels, an ABN AMRO representative pioneered a separate capital markets committee to focus on investment banking issues, to reach decisions relatively quickly and to exploit the apparent representativeness of the EBF.

EU ACTION AND INDUSTRY-COMMISSION CONTACTS AHEAD OF THE FSAP

Contacts between individual banks, industry associations and EU bodies, particularly the Commission, had existed since the inception of the single market programme (Interview 030406). Yet it was only in the mid-1990s that firms began systematically devoting resources to lobbying the Commission and later the Parliament, setting up 'government affairs' offices in Brussels and charging lobbyists with influencing EU developments. Even though contacts were still irregular and informal, American firms, in particular, started to communicate their dissatisfaction with the state of affairs in EU capital market integration.

A sense of dynamism returned to financial services policy in 1995 when the Santer Commission succeeded that of Jacques Delors. David Wright, who worked as an advisor to Santer and became Director of Financial Services Policy and

Financial Markets in the Internal Market Directorate General in 1999, emerged as one of the key figures in the renewed drive towards further integration. John Mogg, Director General of that same directorate since 1993, had also played a leading role on the side of the Commission. An exchange representative remembered that they had already held informal consultations with industry representatives in the mid-1990s (Interview 240506.b). There was then interest in some sort of comitology procedure, which would allow the Commission to update bits and pieces of legislation without having to put them to the Council (Wessels 1998, Bergström 2005). Indeed, such an arrangement had been envisioned for the original ISD. But when the ISD deal was finally struck in 1993, member states' enthusiasm for collective financial services policy was exhausted (Jabko 2006) and the proposals were never followed up.

The most important communication channel between the Commission and industry representatives was an informal group that various respondents as well as four written documents referred to as the Financial Services Strategy Review Group, the Financial Services Strategy Group or the High Level Strategy Review Group (the written sources which could be identified are Shirreff 1999, Bishop 2001, Mijs and Caparrós Puebla 2002, and Gottwald 2005). For coherence, this account will use the first label, abbreviated as FSSRG, though it is uncertain whether this was the one used by its members at the time. The FSSRG was informal and meetings were held under Chatham House rules. No written records of these meetings – or of its members, the dates when it met, etc. – are available. The Commission made clear efforts to avoid publicity around this group; as soon as word spread, it established other consultative groups, at least pretending to take into account the opinions of governments and other stakeholders. Even during interviews for this book, Commission officials remained deliberately vague:

> In pre-98, there was also a discussion paper, but the process was not as developed as it is now. [..] In the past we had a document. We showed it to a number of people. We asked their reaction, and that was it. [..] There was no formal group pre-FSAP. But we had some people, meetings. It was not formally a group that was established. (Interview 141205)

The FFSRG was convened by the European Commission, and John Mogg specifically, to study 'what was wrong with the single market' (Interview 021205.a). As one member described it, the Commission established the FSSRG in 1998

> to draw together the current "wish list" of market participants in the light of the imminent arrival of the euro and the breath-taking pace of technological change since the original work on the Single Market a decade earlier. (Bishop 2001)

FSSRG members consisted of roughly twenty representatives of financial firms with stakes in a deeply integrated European financial market (Gottwald 2005).[36] ABN AMRO, for example, supplied a member to the group, which according to two people working for it at the time, was considered a major lobbying success (Mijs and Caparrós Puebla 2002: 259).

---

36. Another respondent reported eighteeen members. Interview 160306.b

The FSSRG held a little more than half a dozen meetings in which the themes were identified that were later to structure the Financial Services Action Plan. Once it became apparent that there was strong support for action within the group, Mogg informed Mario Monti, Commissioner for the Internal Market and Financial Services, that there were clear suggestions about what should be done and that current political and economic conditions provided a window of opportunity to push for change. The members of the group presented their ideas to Monti, something that reportedly helped secure his support (on this point and the following paragraph, see Gottwald 2005: 127).[37]

The fact that Commission officials felt it necessary to consult industry members and involve them in the re-launching of financial market integration already demonstrates their importance. Once the industry and the Commission had effectively joined forces, getting the Council to agree on the new legislative programme proved much less of a problem. This did not mean that the Commission simply transcribed industry demands. For both political and practical reasons, the report that was eventually put to the Council was drafted by the Commission. This also gave the Commission space to insert some of its own ideas into the document.

As pointed out previously, there was disagreement over the route to further market opening among the pro-integration investment banks: City firms (including the US banks) preferred mutual recognition as envisioned in the original ISD, while most continental firms were in the 'maximum harmonization' camp (Shirreff 1999). The question of whether new legislation was necessary or desirable thus split the pro-integration banks, with the City clearly against further legislation (Interview 160306.b). The Commission felt differently on this point as drafting new legislation is its most important power, part of its *raison d'être*. It also realised that some degree of regulatory harmonisation would be the political price to pay for effective market opening.

The question of new legislation, however, only really surfaced in 2000, and by then the re-launch was well under way. Even the FSAP only vaguely referred to an 'updating' of the ISD, tucked away among forty-two other proposed measures. One representative of the mutual recognition camp clearly realised that 'his' perspective had lost out:

[W]e [the members of the FSSRG] worked for almost a year, we identified almost all the flaws in the single market, [..] presented the results to Monti and Mogg. And we concluded there is need for very little new legislation. [..] Our main message was 'enforce', 'implement', tidy up the ambiguities. Then – and this takes us to the FSAP, around Vienna, Cardiff, the Commission wanting to relaunch the single market – then they came out with the FSAP. And we were just amazed. And they sold this to the UK Treasury on the basis of what practitioners wanted. This is not what we had asked for. We said: Hardly any new legislation. We wanted the market to work as intended. But then to say that this is what practitioners wanted is stretching the truth. We wanted a single market. We didn't want the FSAP. It came as a shock. (Interview 160306.b)

---

37. One respondent, who was a member of the FSSRG, also remembered having personally presented the findings of the group to both Mogg and Monti.

Politically, the FSAP, and the regulatory harmonisation entailed by it, became the only viable route to agreement among member states and thus to the single market.

The United Kingdom held the EU Presidency in the first half of 1998. The City had made clear to the Treasury that the single market in financial services was not working as intended. As one British respondent, seconded by the UK government to the Commission at the time, remembered,

> [t]he UK was very supportive of the whole approach [to relaunch financial market integration]. And many of the financial institutions operating in London were very much in favour. US ones, German ones, French ones. If you talk to the big banks, ABN AMRO, Deutsche Bank, BNP Paribas, quite often, on these issues, they will have the same opinion. Their respective governments may not. (Interview 021205.a)

In the UK presidency's final European Council meeting in Cardiff in June 1998, the Council asked the Commission to produce an action plan to reinvigorate financial market integration (European Council 1998a). The basis of the Council decision was a report produced by the Commission, which drew on discussions in the FSSRG. Ahead of the European Council meeting, members of the FSSRG had coordinated their lobbying: top-ranking officials wrote to 'their' ministers to point to the importance of the coming Commission communication. As planned, the European Council asked the Commission to make an official report to be presented at the Vienna Council later that year. In the run up to this meeting, industry representatives were again consulted (Shirreff 1999); one respondent working for a large exchange remembered industry members sitting down with the Commission 'around that time' and going through the articles of the ISD one by one (Interview 240506.b). The communication that the Commission presented at the European Council meeting, *Financial Services: Building a Framework for Action* (European Commission 1998), was

> the Commission-edited summary of the individual demands of the members of John Mogg's informal groups. (Gottwald 2005: 130, author's translation from German)

The Vienna European Council endorsed the *Framework for Action* and asked the Commission to draft a concrete proposal for legislative action, to be presented first to ECOFIN, the Council of finance ministers, and then to the Cologne European Council in June 1999 (European Council 1998b). These proposals were to become the *Financial Services Action Plan* (European Commission 1999c).

There was, however, criticism that the Commission's consultations had been one-sided, with too much focus on market participants from the City (Shirreff 1999, Interview 160306.b). Governments also asked for a greater voice in the preparation of the FSAP. The Commission thus established the Financial Services Policy Group (FSPG) with high-ranking government officials as members and Monti himself as chair (European Commission 1999d). It met for the first time in January 1999 but was widely seen as a form of politically correct window dressing to assuage government concerns (Interview 021205.a). The ISD, the overhaul of which eventually emerged as the most ambitious element of the FSAP, was not even mentioned in the summary of the FSPG's first meeting; it was certainly not listed as one of the priorities (European Commission 1999d). It is not implausible that the Commission, which chaired the FSPG meetings, deliberately deflected attention from the changes to the existing legislation that it had in mind. One Commission official remembers that at the time, the ISD was consciously not included:

> On [the] basis of what was in the FSAP, indeed, we [embarked on the wider reform of the ISD]. In the end, nobody really contested that it was part of the FSAP. But initially, it [as new legislation] was not part of it, because it was too recent as legislation. [The original ISD] was regarded as a failure particularly by the Commission. But it was too recent to be part of the FSAP. But we followed, and nobody said anything. [..] The FSAP has also been a success because everybody felt that it was necessary to do something. There was a consensus on the need to do something, to integrate financial services. Nobody saw a problem with incorporating the ISD. (Interview 141205)

At the third meeting of the FSPG, less than two months after its establishment, the Commission identified

> strong support for the proposal to review the Investment Services Directive to ensure that this core element of the single market framework measures up to the needs of an integrated financial market place. The idea of a single authority to monitor and enforce market rules was floated. There was support for further consideration of the appropriate infrastructure which will be needed to manage a more integrated EU wholesale market. (European Commission 1999b)

The Commission had been able to use its prior consultations with industry to argue that 'the market' was supportive of its plans, a statement which was basically correct if for 'market' one understood 'the leading firms in the industry'. As the FSAP was published a little more than three months after the first meeting of the FSPG, in May 1999, it comes as no surprise that the FSPG's influence on the document was slight. Most decisions on the list of areas that needed legislative action had already been taken. In one way or another, an overhaul of the ISD would be one of them. As it turned out, this overhaul would emerge as the single most important EU legislative project in financial services in over a decade.

THE FSAP, THE ISD AND THE FORUM GROUPS

The FSAP authorised the Commission to start work on a whole host of new directives; the action plan identified no less than forty-three areas in need of attention (European Commission 1999c, for an overview, see HM Treasury *et al.* 2003). Once the Cologne European Council had endorsed the FSAP's findings (European Council 1999), work could begin to review existing legislation or draft completely new texts. The Commission quickly highlighted the ISD as one of the core areas of concern (e.g. Monti in *Handelsblatt* 1999). The Markets in Financial Instruments Directive (MiFID), as the ISD's replacement was eventually named, emerged as the keystone of the new regulatory edifice.

State actors were hardly enthusiastic about the FSAP. The arguments with which the Commission and private actors tried to sway them revolved around two themes: 'getting the most out of the euro', which was about to be introduced in 1999, and exploiting the growth potential of vibrant capital markets, something that the US stock market boom seemed to irrefutably demonstrate.

State regulatory agencies were noticeably absent in the re-launch of EU financial market integration. In 1997, regulators had initiated their own bottom-up form of cooperation in the Federation of European Securities Commissions (FESCO), loosely modelled on IOSCO (Interview 160506.b, Interview 210306). It began work, for instance, on commonly agreed definitions for loosely-defined terms in the ISD (Federation of European Securities Commissions 2000). But due to the anticipated rivalry between the Commission and the regulators over EU rule-setting, the regulators were largely excluded from the FSAP process, which was surprising, given the stated aim of creating better and more efficient regulation.

The connection between the euro and the re-launch of capital market integration was ubiquitous: in the popular press (Davison 2001), in Commission documents such as the FSAP (European Commission 1999c) and in lobbying strategies (Mijs and Caparrós Puebla 2002). At the same time, several lobbyists confided that the euro was less a driving force for market integration than a convenient hook on which to hang it (Interview 050406, Interview 270206, Interview 070406). Discontinuities between currency areas had not been an obstacle to cross-border market integration before, although the euro did allow the convergence of interest rates across Europe and narrowed the spreads between eurozone government bond yields (European Commission 2005b). But on their own, these arguments did little to strengthen the justifications for deepening market integration that were already on the table.

Nevertheless, governments in Paris and Berlin saw the UK's decision to stay outside the eurozone as an opportunity for their national capital markets to compete with the City. In the late 1990s, the prospect of London losing business in the wake of the single currency was still taken very seriously (*Handelsblatt* 1998), a point that was also raised in several interviews. Combined with the location of the European Central Bank in Frankfurt, the potential boost to the German 'Finanzplatz' was a major incentive for the German finance ministry to support the FSAP (Interview 020506). It is ironic, then, that many of the leading corporate proponents of the euro-argument in support of capital market integration had their bases outside the eurozone – in the City. They correctly foresaw that in an age of electronically-integrated financial markets, the location of a bank *vis-à-vis* a currency zone mattered little. With the benefit of hindsight, the euro was a blessing for the City: national foreign exchange markets were turned upside down, as were futures markets for currencies (much of the currency derivatives business did actually end up in Frankfurt). Many firms integrated their national bond trading desks into one eurozone trading desk and relocated their traders from national financial centres to their own European headquarters, normally in London (Interview 140306). By increasing the scope for conglomeration through the choice of business location (cf. Bindemann 1999), the euro probably did more to hurt than aid Frankfurt and Paris.

Just as the euro was a discursive window of opportunity, the argument linking rapid capital market development to higher economic growth must be taken with a grain of salt, certainly with the benefit of post-crisis hindsight. At the time, however, the impressive growth in the United States was seen as a result of the boom in capital markets, particularly the provision of venture capital to young, 'innovative and high-growth' companies (e.g. Rajan and Zingales 2003). As pointed out in the preceding chapter, continental European governments were susceptible to reform agendas that promised to create a similar dynamic in Europe, something that became clear in the Lisbon Agenda of 2000 (cf. Sapir 2004). Commission president Santer himself made the case for the importance of risk capital to finance SMEs in front of ECOFIN less than two months before the Cardiff Council (ECOFIN 1998), while similar arguments were used to push for a European version of NASDAQ (Posner 2009b). National stock exchanges, too, were quick to set up their own 'growth markets'. Risk capital provision was seen as a crucial issue and financial market integration sailed easily under that banner.

Getting and keeping governments on board, however, was only half the work: in addition to the FSPG, the Commission set up five so-called Forum Groups in the summer of 1999. This was in part due to continental criticism that there had been an Anglo-Saxon bias in the Commission's consultations with industry. John Mogg thus invited industry associations covering the whole breadth of financial services to nominate members to the Forum Groups, including one on 'updating the ISD' (Shirreff 1999), in which the Commission would consult market participants to identify concrete future steps. The group concerned with the ISD first met in October 1999, at which point the Commission unveiled a Green Paper that set out the issues for discussion (European Commission 1999a). Several respondents who had been involved in the pre-FSAP consultations, however, felt that the Commission had already reached its own conclusions, even as the ABN AMRO representatives considered it a great success that they were present in four of the five Forum Groups (Interview 160306.b). One US lobbyist showed clear disdain for these Forum Groups, pointing out that his bank had 'gotten involved' much earlier (Interview 070406). Another complained that

> [t]he agendas [of the forum groups] were drafted by the Commission and the papers were drafted by the Commission, supposedly on the basis of what the experts said but sometimes that was not the case. [..] The classic one was market abuse where the industry had a very strong opinion, finding that there was absolutely no benefit to European legislation on market abuse. What was needed was better enforcement on the national level. And the Commission comes out with a directive. No one on that group thought that that was a good idea. In other groups, it was less clear-cut. You always get some industry people who are in favour and some who aren't. So the Commission is free to pick and choose. (Interview 021205.a)

The question of mutual recognition versus rule harmonisation was a good example: for its own reasons, the Commission sided with those in the industry who preferred the latter. By 2000, it was busy drafting a new directive to rectify the ISD's shortcomings. Before the end result was to see the light of day in 2004, however, it was the EU policy process itself that was subjected to serious overhaul.

chapter seven | the emergence of supranational governance

This chapter traces the creation of the supranational institutions that have come to govern European capital markets in the new millennium. Central to the story is the adoption of the so-called Lamfalussy process by the Council in 2001 and the European Parliament in 2002 (see Committee of Wise Men 2001). This new legislative procedure was crucial in institutionalising the role of two new European committees, the European Securities Committee (ESC) and the Committee of European Securities Regulators (CESR). Whereas national financial industries earlier relied on national governments to represent their interests, larger firms now preferred a supranational and much more technocratic approach to rule-setting. This, it was thought, would enhance the 'quality' of regulation while reducing the scope for protectionism.

Theories of supranationalism suggest that supranational governance will be supported by actors who prefer supranational solutions to policy problems (Stone Sweet and Sandholtz 1998). Supranational governance, it is argued, will more likely overcome collective action problems and distributive struggles and thus generate efficient solutions (Scharpf 1997b, 2001). In the economic realm, in consequence, we would expect that the larger the transnational component of a firm's business or ambitions, the more it will support some form of supranational governance (Schmitter 1970, cf. Weber and Hallerberg 2001). In Mattli's words,

> [as] new technologies increase the scope of markets beyond the boundaries of a single state, actors who stand to gain from wider markets will seek to change an existing governance structure in order to realize these gains to the fullest extent. (Mattli 1999: 46)

This idea is both plausible and borne out by the evidence presented in this chapter.

At the same time, it needs refinement. States and political institutions are not just empty shells occupied by societal actors who arrive at collectively-binding decisions, as some of the game-theoretic models of multi-level governance suggest (cf. Scharpf 1997a). States, and by extension EU bodies, are large organisations run and controlled by people who themselves have bureaucratic and political objectives (Nordlinger 1981, Krasner 1984, Skocpol 1985). For large firms, patterns of governance should match the scope of their preferred policy solutions, but the public actors within them should not become too powerful in their own right. In most cases, societal actors with a stake in transnational integration will favour supranational governance *without* a single supranational entity free to ignore societal pressures. This is particularly true of actors who hope to exert influence. Consumers of financial services may feel that they are best served by a Leviathan to protect them from the vagaries of financial innovation and charlatanry. Large firms, in contrast, prefer an institutional architecture made up of competing public actors whose bureaucratic power depends on industry support. With the complex EU governance structures that still rule EU finance today, this is exactly what they got.

SUPRANATIONAL COOPERATION BEFORE LAMFALUSSY

The idea of supranational cooperation in the field of securities markets dates back to the first round of capital market negotiations which produced the ISD and the CAD. The draft directives had envisioned a 'Securities Committee' staffed by member state representatives able to update specific pieces of legislation together with the Commission. The Commission would draft these updates; the Securities Committee would adopt, reject, or if necessary, amend them. Though this foreshadowed the comitology procedures implemented a little less than a decade later, it differed from it in important respects: the Securities Committee would have allowed member states to renegotiate small, previously decided bits of legislation without having to reopen the overall bargain. In contrast, the Lamfalussy process went a step further and saw member states transferring this power to supranational actors, not least the Commission itself.

While the implementing powers built into the ISD and CAD were limited, distrust between member states nevertheless led to the scrapping of any reference to a Securities Committee in the directives' final versions. They only stated that the Council would retain implementing powers until another arrangement was agreed through a separate directive (*Financial Regulation Report* 1995c). The idea of a Securities Committee had already elicited industry support in the mid-1990s (e.g. Interview 240506.b). As implementing powers were clearly circumscribed, technical aspects could be updated without upsetting the fundamental bargain.

Member states' appetite for further financial market integration ebbed following agreement on the ISD (Jabko 2006). Nevertheless, the Commission proposed a separate directive to establish a Securities Committee in 1995, reminding member states that it was only implementing that which had been agreed two years earlier (*Financial Regulation Report* 1995b). Given the extensive powers of the new committee – it promised to keep national governments in control of changes to existing legislation – member states were largely in favour of it. The European Parliament also indicated its support for some form of a Securities Committee (*Financial Regulation Report* 1996e). But sensitive to the balance between its own competencies and that of the member states represented in the Council, it envisaged a committee with fewer powers than that proposed by the Commission (*Financial Regulation Report* 1996d). This conflict remained unresolved in the following years (*Financial Regulation Report* 1997, 1998c), with no actor on the European stage compelled to cut the Gordian Knot. By the time the Commission tabled the first draft of its Action Plan in 1998 (European Commission 1998), the 'committee' directive had effectively disappeared from the EU agenda.

Partially in response to this lack of progress within the EU architecture, national regulators began to coordinate their activities. The Federation of European Securities Commissions (FESCO), as mentioned already in the previous chapter, was a joint initiative of the *Commission des Operations de Bourse* (COB), the French capital market regulator, and Tommaso Padoa-Schioppa, who at the time worked for the Italian regulator CONSOB and is often credited with being one of the visionaries of EU financial market integration and an architect of the euro (Interview 210306). Early in 1997, the COB organised a dinner to which it invited the heads of all European capital markets regulators as well as Commissioner Monti. At this occasion, it floated the idea of some sort of institutionalised cooperation. Eight months later, FESCO was officially established with a secretariat at the COB in Paris (Interview 190506).

FESCO's practical achievements were, however, limited, largely owing to the regulators' lack of legal and institutional leeway. It had no formal powers to make rules; at best it could try to agree on common interpretations of European rules where national legislation left it sufficient room. FESCO's main accomplishment was a multilateral Memorandum of Understanding (MoU), an agreement for cooperation in the fulfilment of regulators' supervisory tasks that replaced previous bilateral ones. More importantly from the perspective of the financial industry, it tackled the vague definitions that had circumscribed the market-opening effects of the ISD. Article 11 of the directive allowed member states to impose 'host country rules' on firms dealing with residents if the latter were 'retail' rather than 'professional' investors. These terms were not defined anywhere, effectively allowing governments to enlarge the former category as they wished. FESCO tried to find common definitions and indeed published a compromise in 2000 (Federation of European Securities Commissions 2000). In spite of heavy lobbying by financial firms, the agreement still fell short of the changes for which leading banks had been hoping (Interview 270206, Mijs and Caparrós Puebla 2002).

With hindsight, one of the most remarkable things about FESCO is that before 1997, there was no forum in which European regulators could coordinate their activities. This shows how far matters have since evolved: national regulators today are embedded in a network with their European partners, while supranational cooperation has become an integral part of regulation, both as a set of rules and through the actual day-to-day operations of national authorities. The Committee of European Securities Regulators (CESR) is now a central actor in EU capital market politics; at the time of the FSAP's adoption, its predecessor FESCO played no significant role in the Commission's efforts to reinvigorate EU financial market integration.

However, it would be wrong to judge FESCO's impact solely by the material changes it produced. FESCO was the first embodiment of a nascent transnational epistemic community for securities markets regulation in Europe (P. Haas 1992, Kapstein 1992). It provided a forum for regulators to meet, exchange ideas and formulate common positions with fewer hesitations than in actual negotiations. As regulators discovered how far their ideas had already converged, FESCO spurred on their *esprit de corps* (Interview 210306).

LAUNCHING INSTITUTIONAL CHANGE

Following the adoption of the FSAP, there was widespread feeling that some sort of institutional change, in order to finish its work programme within the envisaged six years, was desirable. The Commission had indicated as much in the report itself (European Commission 1999c). One lobbyist for a large bank confided that, for him, institutional change had always been an integral part of the FSAP enterprise and thus for effective market integration and the reordering of the competitive landscape (Interview 231105). Support for some form of supranational governance was widespread in the industry, even among firms that were otherwise competitive rivals, such as large investment banks and stock exchanges. On the question of supranational governance, their transnational business ambitions brought them together.

Many continental firms supported institutional change due to their interest in pan-European rule harmonisation. The Conseil du Marchés Financiers' president, Lepetit, supported rule harmonisation in the light of announced stock market consolidations in 1998 (*Les Echos* 1999). Deutsche Bank's Rolf Breuer decried the 'regulatory nightmare' in European securities markets and called for a single regulatory institution (*The Economist* 1999), while French banks presented a list of grievances reminiscent of the complaints coming from the City of London (Association Française des Banques 2000c). Even the otherwise cautious European Savings Bank Group called on the Commission to 'examine the burdensome legislative process and in particular the length of the entire procedure' and suggested the use of comitology (European Savings Banks Group 1998).

The necessity for EU rules to pass through the regular co-decision process, often taking many years, was suitable for the low degree of top-down harmonisation envisioned at the time of the ISD. Co-decision now proved unable to cope with detailed legislation. The Association Française des Banques, hitherto one of the more protectionist forces in the field, described its support for change as follows:

> Private firms have now begun to think in European terms. They are in need of a secure and unified legal framework in order to let the European financial market function efficiently. French banks in particular have developed European and international strategies in the fields of fund management, commercial and investment banking and custody. Thus current regulation lags behind market developments. The [ISD] is seven years old. It currently constitutes an inadequate response to the changes of the last few years, and therefore a range of legal and regulatory problems currently remain unresolved. (Association Française des Banques 2000b, translation from French by the author)

The Brussels lobbyist for a large European bank came to a similar conclusion:

> The main advantage of this procedure is its flexibility. [..] When we change a directive according to EU procedures, that is, in co-decision, then that is not only the framework directive. But the discussion in parliament goes down into the tiniest detail of a technical nature. (Interview 231105)

The gap between market evolution and EU provisions widened precisely where detailed European rules were needed. This comes as no surprise, as Story and Walter found the 'average adaptive efficiency' of international public bodies to be lower than for any other group (national authorities, SROs, etc.) (Story and Walter 1997: 131). Frustration in the industry grew to the extent that a group of investment banks, headed by the bulge bracket firms, Morgan Stanley, Goldman Sachs and Merrill Lynch, reportedly entertained the idea of drafting their own standards which could eventually form the basis of a pan-European rule book (*The Economist* 2000).

In its report, the European committee charged with proposing avenues for institutional change came to similar conclusions, finding that drafting detailed agreements in the Council more often than not added unnecessary complexity to the attempt to fit fifteen regulatory regimes into a single set of rules (Committee of Wise Men 2001: 14). The resulting ambiguity of the provisions made it easy for them to be stretched to fit local arrangements. The Committee report in its final assessment aptly described the situation:

> Whilst part of the problem concerns the incomplete regulatory coverage at European level, the greater part of the responsibility lies in the way in which European Union legislation has been decided (or left undecided) and 'implemented' (or not 'implemented'). The problem is the system itself. (Committee of Wise Men 2001: 13)

Chapters 3 and 4 examined the links between interest constellations filtered through national policy communities, the desire to create a single market without rule harmonisation, and intergovernmental negotiations as the preferred route to manage regulatory interdependence. With the two former conditions now outmoded, it left only an institutional arrangement unable to live up to changed expectations. While the creation of FESCO was a step in the right direction, it did nothing to change the cumbersome and inefficient co-decision procedure.

NEGOTIATING LAMFALUSSY

Institutional overhaul was to prove difficult. Even when wide-ranging reforms appear sensible from the outside, they tend to be considered in policy-making circles only after solutions within established frameworks have been found grossly insufficient (Hall 1993, Crouch and Farrell 2004). While the overall conditions highlighted the sensibility of basic change, distributional conflicts and distrust resurfaced within negotiations. Even as the financial industry pushed for change, the power to implement the desired change was essentially in governments' hands (cf. Quaglia 2008).

In the FSAP the Commission had again raised the issue of *institutional* change in the governance of securities markets, tentatively proposing the creation of a single regulatory authority, while lamenting 'the absence of a committee of appropriate standing to assist the EU institutions in the developing and implementing of regulation for investment services and securities markets' (European Commission 1999c: 14). The idea of installing a regulatory committee following comitology procedures was likewise raised by Howard Davies, head of Britain's FSA (Financial Services Authority 1999). In March 2000, the European Council convened in Lisbon in an ambitious mood. But while it acknowledged the problems listed in the FSAP and called for their solution over the following five years, it failed to propose institutional mechanisms to achieve this, calling only for 'more intensive co-operation by EU financial market regulators' (European Council 2000).

Whenever institutional change in the governance of European securities markets was debated, one of the hotly-contested options was the creation of a single regulatory authority. Proud of their newly established FSA and generally wary of European institutions, British authorities in line with most market participants, while in principle supportive of more pan-European co-ordination, disliked the idea (Financial Services Authority 1999). Apart from rare exceptions such as Deutsche Bank's Rolf Breuer, industry response was muted. The Federation of European Securities Exchanges (FESE), for example, voiced its belief that a 'European SEC' was *not* the way to go (Federation of European Securities Exchanges 2000). Contrary to Quaglia's (2008) findings, this was not an isolated view within the European financial industry. An overly powerful pan-European regulator potentially threatened industry interests while its advantages over a well-thought out committee system were far from obvious.

The idea of a single regulator did, however, find favour in the French financial establishment, notably in political circles (Interview 190506). One of the main reasons for this was that according to 'European logic', the location for such an institution would be Paris, almost by default. Germany had only managed to bring the European Central Bank to Frankfurt after a face-off with France, while the UK, not being a member of the eurozone, had practically watched from the sidelines. France was thus next in line. France was also already hosting FESCO, making Paris the natural choice for a more formalised body for regulatory cooperation in Europe.

One month before France assumed the EU presidency in July 2000, Laurent Fabius, the French finance minister, proposed to his ECOFIN colleagues a 'Committee of Wise Men' to study the governance of capital markets in Europe. As one Commission official closely involved with the Committee of Wise Men recollects:

> The idea was explored – and is still there – of a single regulator for Europe. The French were working at the time to create a single regulator. By creating such a group, one of its resolutions or conclusions would be to have a single regulator. That was why it was the French. (Interview 141205)

Although the single regulator was rarely mentioned explicitly, Fabius' initiative was widely perceived as a step in this direction. Suspicion heightened when the name of Alexandre Lamfalussy surfaced as chairman of the committee. Lamfalussy was known as a federalist and a strong supporter of supranational arrangements. Britain and Germany, which opposed a single regulator, were cautious about mandating a report. The core issue was again one of competition: paralleling the tension between mutual recognition and harmonisation, City firms thought a single regulator would erode their competitive advantage (Interview 141205). Most of the smaller EU members felt that they stood to gain from the French initiative. For them, the eventual choice would be between moving closer to the regulatory structures of the large European markets, leaving them with most of the costs of convergence, or all parties making concessions to create a single regulatory authority within the EU framework.

But without British *and* German support, the initiative for a pan-European regulator stood little chance. Rather than abandoning the committee in the face of resistance, Fabius took a more cautious approach and retreated from the idea of a single EU authority (Crooks and Norman 2000). Michel Prada, head of the French *Autorité des Marches Financières*, conceded late in 2000 that the time for a pan-European regulator had not yet come (Prada 2000). The French climbdown on the issue gained the backing of almost all EU members for a committee of 'wise men' – only the UK still voiced formal opposition (Osborn 2000). As noted above, comitology procedures had been advocated by Davies the previous year; for the British authorities, the problem had been how to pre-empt a report advocating a single regulator. Changing strategy, the Treasury now pushed for the committee's mandate to be as wide and vague as possible and for Sir Nigel Wicks to be one of the 'wise men'. Wicks, who had served as the head of the powerful EU monetary committee, shared the general British line of caution in conferring regulatory powers to 'Brussels' and to more integrated forms of regulation.

EU finance ministers finally agreed to establish the committee at the ECOFIN meeting on 17 July 2000. Several aspects of the mandate are noteworthy. In its definition of the problem to be tackled, reference was mostly made to unsatisfactory implementation and transposition of EU rules; institutional arrangements for rule-*making* were not explicitly criticised (ECOFIN 2000). The committee was to have seven members, instead of the initially envisaged five, due to the British insistence on having Nigel Wicks included. The mandate to consider institutional adjustments was almost hidden at the end of the document; it asked the committee to propose 'scenarios for adapting current practices to ensure greater convergence and co-operation in day-to-day implementation'. As a disincentive to any proposals for a single authority, prudential supervision was explicitly excluded from the scope of the inquiry.

Less than two months after the mandate was given, the Committee of Wise Men made it clear that it was no longer pursuing the idea of a single regulator (Norman 2000a). The reason given in the first report, published in November 2000, was that it would require a change in the Treaties, and would thus take several years and an intergovernmental conference to accomplish (Committee of Wise Men 2001: 67-114). Lamfalussy himself reiterated the point in an interview with *Business Week* in January 2001 (Echikson 2001). Political will was simply lacking, with most stakeholders pushing for a comitology solution of some sort. As the head of one business association remembers,

> In Europe, we need a system that is not too rigid. If you have a long-term, almost eternal piece of Community legislation, a Directive, you must have the flexibility. And when Lamfalussy and David Wright [Director in charge of financial services at the EU Commission] and his team came here, they sat upstairs and we had them for five and a half hours, we took them straight through this model, and it is pretty much what they came out with. Now whether that was our brilliance I have no idea, but what I am able to say is that we were very heavily involved with Sir Nigel Wicks and some of the other key members of the Lamfalussy group. Once it began to generate activity

we were very enthusiastic. And once it began to gather speed we coordinated with our fellow associations in Europe to improve the consultative procedures. (Interview 300306)

As the respondent points out, it is difficult to establish with any certainty how much credit his organisation and its allies deserve in giving the Wise Men's committee its ideas. At the very least, the result was clearly in line with industry thinking. When the preliminary report was published on 7 November 2000, it was met with wide sympathy, as well as relief in its absence of a call for a single authority, by financial industry associations such as the Federation of European Securities Exchanges and the London Investment Banking Association (Norman 2000b).

The essence of the Wise Men Committee's suggestions came to be known as the Lamfalussy process. It split the policy cycle into four 'levels' (Committee of Wise Men 2001) and had already been outlined in the initial report; the final version, published in mid-February of the following year, altered it only slightly. With minor deviations, this is the legislative procedure that was implemented, and which remains in use at the time of writing, even as the credit crisis has jump-started debates about future reform (High-Level Group on Financial Supervision in the EU 2009).

The approach favoured by the Committee of Wise Men can be characterised as 'comitology-plus'. In common with procedures widely applied in the EU (Bergström 2005), comitology places the legislative process on two levels: on level 1, the European Parliament and Council decide on 'framework legislation' through the regular co-decision procedure, on the basis of drafts prepared by the Commission. Such framework legislation consciously brackets specific supposedly 'technical' questions. For these, it confers implementing powers to the European Commission, which can then 'fill in the details' on level 2. In the variant adopted for capital markets, the Commission's implementing measures are scrutinised by a regulatory committee, in this case the European Securities Committee (ESC).

The ESC, consisting of member state delegates, is meant to function as the Commission's 'watchman' (cf. Dehousse 2003), ensuring the latter uses its implementing powers in line with the mandate conferred upon it in the framework legislation. Following the general rules agreed by the European Parliament, the European Council and the Commission on the functioning of comitology in 1999,[38] the regulatory committee needs a qualified majority – a supermajority of more than 70 per cent of the weighted votes – to stall the Commission's plans to adopt a particular implementing measure (cf. Inter-Institutional Monitoring Group 2003: 40). The measure in question is then put before the Council, which has three months to reject the measure definitively, again with a qualified majority. Otherwise the Commission can proceed to adopt the measure in its original form. The ESC and the Council can thus reject Commission proposals, but cannot amend them or make suggestions of their own, at least not formally. The bluntness of the ESC's policy instrument is meant to deter its excessive use.

The real innovation of the Lamfalussy process, however, lies in its creation of a second committee, one which easily overshadows the ESC: the Committee of

---

38. Council Directive 1999/468/EC.

European Securities Regulators, commonly known as CESR. Like its predecessor FESCO, CESR brings together capital market regulators from all the EU member states. But in contrast to FESCO, CESR has a formal role in the European legislative process. Officially it fulfils two functions. First, it advises the Commission on the implementing measures to be adopted on level 2. In concrete terms, it makes suggestions for the gaps that have been left open in framework legislation at level 1. The idea is to have experts, i.e. the regulators, deal with the technical details instead of the Council, the EP or the Commission. Formally, CESR's role is only advisory at this stage. In practice, however, the Commission is expected to justify its deviations from CESR's advice, giving CESR a central role in capital market legislation.

CESR's second function is placed on level 3 of the new procedure. There, CESR is meant to coordinate the transposition of European legislation into national law lest discrepancies in national implementation defeat the goal of a harmonised rule set. Again, CESR cannot exert any formal pressure on member state parliaments when it comes to the adoption of national laws. The idea is to use moral suasion to ensure smooth transposition, and to detect potential deviations from commonly agreed rules as early as possible. Finally, on level 4, the Commission is charged with systematically monitoring implementation and, if necessary, using its legal powers to challenge members states in front of the European Court of Justice (ECJ).

Industry response to the publication of these ideas was overwhelmingly positive as they resonated with firms' preferences. Praise came from both Paris (Association Française des Banques 2000a) and the City. The latter made its views known through the Federal Trust, a UK think-tank. The Federal Trust report on the Lamfalussy procedure was written by a working group of seventeen people, including the chief EU lobbyists of many of the most active banks and business associations, the most prominent of which were Goldman Sachs, Morgan Stanley, Barclays, LIBA, the International Securities Markets Association and the International Primary Market Association (Federal Trust 2001a). The secretary general of the Federation of European Securities Exchanges (FESE) and the former head of the Amsterdam Stock Exchange were also part of the group, which showed that despite the competitive struggles between investment banks and stock exchanges, these organistions were in agreement regarding supranational governance. Other prominent lobbyists soon joined the group, including representatives of the two most active continental banks, Deutsche Bank and ABN AMRO (Federal Trust 2001b).

The working group's evaluation of extant legislation was damning:

> The initial directives were fudged. They were slowly implemented by most governments and weakly enforced by the Commission. National bargaining in Council led to a protectionist atmosphere. Regulators did not trust each other and so Directives became excessively detailed. (Federal Trust 2001a: 1)

It therefore welcomed the thrust of the latest report. Among the shortcomings it nevertheless identified, one was most obvious: the lack of transparency in the proposed process and institutionalised industry consultation. Indeed, ever since the publication of the first Lamfalussy report, the issue of formal private input into policy-making had been one of the focal points of industry concern. Lobbyists kept emphasising the point. One of them, who was also a member of the Federal Trust working group, found that

> [i]nsisting on that sort of discipline [that consultative procedures are adhered to] has been one of the single most important things I have ever done in my life. Because it is alien to any organisation that wants to retain its power [..]. So we would constantly be talking to Alexander Schaub [EU Commission Director General for financial services at the time] and asking: why didn't we see that thing in advance? Could we please have longer to reply to it? (Interview 300306)

After the publication of its first report, the Wise Men committee held extensive consultations with both industry groups and national governments in an effort to make its recommendations more acceptable.

The final report was published on 15 February 2001 and addressed many of the issues that had been raised in the consultations. It clarified the roles of the different parties in the procedure and formalised private sector input (for industry evaluations of the final report, see e.g. Federal Trust 2001b). The British Bankers Association (2001) praised the degree to which industry concerns had been incorporated. It was now up to governments and the European Parliament to sign on to the Wise Men committee's suggestions.

While the enthusiasm European leaders had mustered at the Lisbon summit had already cooled, momentum was maintained in the overhaul of securities regulation. It was only shortly before the Stockholm Council in March 2001 that governments' adoption of the proposals was again placed in doubt. Given the prominence of British officials in the securities markets department in DG Internal Market, the German government was wary that integration privileging the role of the Commission would benefit the City more than Frankfurt (Brown-Humes and Norman 2001). It resolved to accept the new process only if the bar for member state intervention on level 2 measures was lowered. Fearing yet another deadlock after the take-over directive had been blocked by the German government for years, the financial industry demanded adoption of the report without delay, with individual companies as well as the European Banking Federation publicly voicing their concerns (de Larosière and Lebègue 2001, Norman 2001a, Walker 2001). As was the case with legislation, firms were ahead of their governments on institutional issues (Quaglia 2008). Agreement was reached at the last minute when the Commission committed itself 'to avoid going against predominant views which might emerge within the Council' on 'particularly sensitive' issues (European Council 2001, Groom and Norman 2001). This so-called 'Aerosol clause' was widely interpreted as meaning that a simple majority would be enough to block proposals in the Council (Inter-Institutional Monitoring Group 2003), circumventing the 'official' comitology rules that required a qualified majority to reject the Commission's implementing measures. The effect of this nebulous phrase remains unknown – at the time of writing it has never been invoked.

Nevertheless, the political repercussions were enormous: supranational bodies and institutions had escaped the grasp of their former principals and had begun to live lives of their own (cf. e.g. Pollack 1997, 1998). The European Parliament had already felt under-represented in the proposed legislative procedures before the Council negotiated extra concessions from the Commission and endorsed the Lamfalussy process (Norman 2001b). After inclusion of the Aerosol clause, the EP clearly saw the inter-institutional balance upset between itself, the Commission and the Council. From the EP's perspective, it was a matter of principle; it demanded influence equal to that of the Council, including over implementing measures. The political sensitivity of power-sharing between the different Brussels bodies delayed adoption by almost a year.

In effect the EP was demanding the right of 'call back', that is to be able to review the Commission's implementing measures. Its position was spelt out in an April 2001 letter from Christa Randzio-Plath, chair of the EP's Committee on Economic and Monetary Affairs, to Frits Bolkestein, who was the Commissioner for the Internal Market (Randzio-Plath 2001). In its reply the following month, the Commission suggested a range of 'trust building' measures between the institutions but refused to give in to the EP's main demand (Bolkestein 2001). To make matters worse, the Commission had already included comitology procedures within its drafts of the Market Abuse and Prospectus Directives in May 2001, long before institutional matters had been settled (Interview 221105). A month later, it established the ESC and CESR, again before any formal agreement had been reached with the EP (European Commission 2001). Both of these steps only increased the EP's resistance.

In this spat, the industry largely sided with the parliament (e.g. Federal Trust 2001a). Lobbyists saw the EP as one of their major partners in Brussels. The EBF, for example, had repeatedly found the EP a crucial ally (Interview 221105), while another lobbyist had similar experiences over the Prospectus directive in particular (Interview 140306). Yet another respondent reported a similar conclusion regarding work on the MiFID, adding that

> there is definitively a shift of power, towards the EP. [..] The EP is one of the main ways to get legislation changed. All the amendments are published, and MEPs are quite open to discuss things. In the parliament it is much more clear on the trade-offs. National trades are not that common anymore. (Interview 021205.a)

Indeed, industry representatives in 1998 had already taken the initiative to set up a so-called 'inter-group' on financial services, a public-private forum 'composed of several MEPs and several banks and financial services associations' (Mijs and Caparrós Puebla 2002: 263). The body's name was later changed to the European Parliamentary Financial Services Forum (EPFSF), whose members included many of the most important EU lobbyists in finance. But despite the breadth suggested by its name, the EPFSF has no consumer representatives or other non-corporate stakeholders among its members.

As pointed out previously, private actors have an interest in the fragmentation of supranational power among public actors and a system of checks and balances that prevents the excessive autonomy of any single actor. Public bodies are consequently not only forced to listen to private interests; in a conflict between public actors, industry support may become crucial. This is particularly true for the EP, which generally commands less expertise than the Commission or CESR. Within the legislative process, the EP's power lies largely in the amendments it can make. More than once, amendment proposals were copied directly from lobbyists' suggestions (Interview 021205.a). This turned into particular embarrassment when several MEPs tabled identical proposals, suggesting a common source outside the EP.

As the dispute between the Commission and the EP continued to smoulder during the summer of 2001, it became clear that the call-back right demanded by the EP would, in all likelihood, require a change in the Treaties, particularly Article 202 concerning the delegation of legislative powers to the Commission (Inter-Institutional Monitoring Group 2003: 41). The search for a different arrangement led finally to a compromise in the form of a 'sunset-clause' limiting the Commission's implementing powers to a four-year period (European Parliament Committee on Constitutional Affairs 2001). Implementing measures would then have to be renewed which would act as a deterrent for the Commission to adopt them in the face of EP opposition, particularly in cases where the EP felt that the Commission was acting *ultra vires*. Two weeks after the group of MEPs charged with finding a way out of the impasse had published its report, its suggestions were officially adopted by the EP. The Commission gave its assent without delay and the new Lamfalussy procedure could finally be implemented (European Commission 2002).

SUPRANATIONAL GOVERNANCE IN PRACTICE

On the drawing board, the Lamfalussy process has clear supranational elements. But these are tempered by the fact that the two new committees, the ESC and CESR, are composed of member-state representatives. How radically does the Lamfalussy process depart from previous governance arrangements?

By agreeing to both the FSAP and the Lamfalussy process, member states have effectively Europeanised capital market governance. With the FSAP completed and the updating of its provisions in the hands of the Commission and CESR, the scope for independent national action in the field of capital market regulation has been seriously curtailed. Only in fields where competitive differences remain strong – clearing and settlement is a clear example – have no legislative powers been transferred to the Commission. At the very least, governments have 'pooled' their sovereignty (Hoffmann 1966), notwithstanding the differences of national opinion that emerged in the post-crisis reform debates.

At least until these debates gathered pace, the *practice* of contemporary capital market governance has deviated significantly from what the formal process suggested. This has been particularly true in two respects: first, the ESC – officially the 'watchdog' of the Commission's use of its implementing powers – has widely been seen as failing in its function. Providing its chairman and effectively running its meetings, the Commission has managed to co-opt the ESC in questions of policy (Interview 131206). The ESC has had no independent staff, consultation procedures or powers to propose changes to implementing measures – it has not, in short, functioned as an instrument of member-state control. Indeed, one member-state representative worried that regulatory authorities, joined in CESR, were de facto assuming legislative tasks (Interview 071205.b). The relative weakness of the ESC resonates with what other scholars have found regarding the functioning of comitology in the EU. For accountability and democratic control, both Rhinard (2002) and Dehousse (2003) remain highly sceptical of whether comitology committees are nearly as effective as they seem on paper.

Lobbyists agreed that the ESC played a small role in capital market governance. In most interviews it was never mentioned, whereas CESR always received considerable attention. In the words of one respondent,

[t]he ESC is for when we have a big problem. They don't do consultation or anything. It is really CESR... (Interview 211105.b)

Where, after all, would the ESC get its cue to intervene? National regulators – the experts in the field – are already active in CESR and the issues most dear to national finance ministries have already been addressed in framework legislation at level 1. The ESC, at best, is an additional veto point which stakeholders can use to stop unpopular rules – hardly an instrument of 'national' oversight.

Second, CESR functions much more as a single, supranational entity than its official committee structure suggests. Representatives of national, regulatory authorities expressed a strong *esprit de corps* in interviews while parties involved were unanimously impressed by the level of cooperation achieved thus far (Interview 160506.b, Interview 160306, Interview 030506, Interview 190506). In the execution of their tasks, BaFin and the FSA still function as national authorities. But in policy-making, they invariably see themselves as part of a larger European network. This resonates with the well-established, if elusive, neofunctionalist claim that the supranationalisation of institutions is capable of generating shifts in loyalty among bureaucrats (Haas 1958, Risse 2005, Niemann 2006). Collaboration has allowed regulators to assert themselves in the face of increasingly integrated financial markets. Regulatory structures were indeed 'behind the curve', and for those regulators who took their tasks seriously, being organised on a European level made sense. It also boosted their standing in the wider world of public actors.

This is particularly relevant given the competition among the different bodies involved in European policy-making. Various respondents have pointed to the cool relations between CESR and the Commission; the tension is unsurprising as both feel themselves to be at the centre of EU capital markets regulation (Interview 190506). The Commission, wanting to keep the drafting of legislation to itself, solicits 'reports' from CESR for its level 2 work rather than suggestions for draft legislation, whereas CESR clearly feels it performs more than an 'advisory' role. On several occasions the Commission has significantly amended CESR's advice for level 2 implementing measures (notably for the MiFID), prompting

CESR members to claim that 'politics' had unduly trumped 'expertise' (Interview 160506.b). More positively, competition between the Commission and CESR has fostered close cooperation among regulators.

Indeed, regulators themselves appear to have become a force for further integration. While few would espouse the establishment of a pan-European regulator which would abolish the independence of national authorities, intensive cooperation has created possibilities for new arrangements, for example the supervision of cross-border stock exchanges such as Euronext. Close cooperation within CESR has furthermore encouraged the sharing of competencies in ways that would have been considered intrusions onto each other's turf just a few years earlier. CESR's Himalaya Report (Committee of European Securities Regulators 2004) has been a clear initiative in this direction. Even before the crisis, leading European firms had long been calling for a 'lead-supervisor' (European Financial Services Round Table 2004), meaning a single authority to supervise a financial conglomerate's activities throughout Europe. In effect, this would extend the idea of the European passport for services provision to supervision as well. Though it was quickly realised that the lead supervisor idea in its pure form would run foul of the present treaty and national laws, CESR's Himalaya Report outlined possibilities within the legal framework for working towards a similar sort of supervisory structure. Even among leading firms, this was seen as a progressive move.

In a similar spirit, CESR initiated a mediation mechanism among European regulators in 2006 (Committee of European Securities Regulators 2006b). CESR members thereby commit to a procedure for solving disputes among themselves, for example over the interpretation of common positions. The industry was again delighted by the prospect of a mechanism to iron out mismatches among national rule-sets. Even though mediation was not meant as an appeal mechanism, industry firms have asked CESR to allow them access to mediation when they have grievances against the local implementation of EU rules. CESR not only granted such access, even if indirectly, but also allowed firms to use host country regulators to raise problems with their own home authorities (Committee of European Securities Regulators 2006a). Though not an appeals process in name, CESR's mediation mechanism comes close to one in practice. With it, firms have further emancipated themselves from their home regulators and reinforced the supremacy of CESR as a supranational body.

INDUSTRY INTERESTS AND INSTITUTIONAL REFORM

With the coming into force of the Lamfalussy process, EU capital market governance has largely been supranationalised, creating at least a temporary equilibrium between market structures and patterns of governance. Policy-makers stopped short of creating a single European regulator, a step that would have required changes to the treaties of the European Union. Formally, member states retain significant influence in the two new committees at the core of the Lamfalussy process. One of them, the European Securities Committee, has largely failed to fulfil its function as a 'watchdog' over the exercise of implementing powers delegated to the European Commission. The second, the Committee of European Securities

Regulators, has been very active and visible in EU capital market policy. Though made up of member-state regulators, it functions more like a single supranational entity than its design suggests. CESR's evolution fits the neofunctionalist notion of *engrenage* – the supranational socialisation of bureaucrats involved in collective governance (Niemann 2006).

Member states retain significant influence over EU capital market policy – the current decision-making process much more closely resembles Scharpf's image of 'joint decisions' than that of 'hierarchical direction' (Scharpf 2001). Given the centrality of financial markets in economic policy, this is not surprising. Within the financial industry, only a small minority of firms favoured more far-reaching steps such as a single European regulator. In an industry consultation on the functioning of the Lamfalussy process in 2003, European banks submitted a positive joint response, together with the Federation of European Securities Exchanges and a whole host of other transnational professional associations, demonstrating the breadth of industry support for this kind of arrangement (FESE *et al.* 2003). Multi-level governance suits transnationally-active firms, particularly in the light of the perceived danger of an overly powerful EU regulator at liberty to ignore industry positions. The present system is replete with access points for industry lobbyists, while political competition between public actors turns financial firms into potential allies. This, however, does not mean that the supranationalisation of capital market policy has been a smooth and automatic process as the agency of specific actors remains crucial for understanding the timing and process of change. Looking back on the emergence of the Lamfalussy process, one Brussels lobbyist observed that

> [i]t is like all great plans, and lobbying is the same. If you have great plans and you try to lobby on something, usually you will achieve something, but it often isn't really what you set out to do. And that is true of the French, who saw [triggering institutional change] as a means to get some more control of [EU financial market politics]. And to a degree that has happened. Because the Lamfalussy committees are taking back some of the power to the member states. But in practice, because it is a collective taking back, it has not given the individual members states back so much control. (Interview 021205.a)

Strong industry support for integrated governance was a crucial precondition for its emergence. In keeping with the argument advanced in the previous chapter, such 'private influence' is impossible to isolate as an explanatory factor, and hence cannot be measured. However, it is indisputable that financial firms were core proponents of the kind of governance structure that eventually emerged. Given firms' ability to insert their preferences into the EU policy process, it is implausible that member state governments would have endorsed such a process in the face of industry opposition. Indeed, the following chapter will show that even with the governance of EU capital markets being heavily supranationalised, the ability of firms to dominate rule-making did not disappear. In the renegotiation of the ISD, competition politics still ruled – only this time with transnational alliances rather than national blocks.

chapter eight | renegotiating the ISD in the supranational constellation

The introduction of the Lamfalussy process was only one side of the institutional changes that marked the transition of capital market policy in Europe from the 'international' to the 'supranational' constellation. Alongside changes in formal governance structures, state-market relations in the capital markets domain became increasingly transnational. The industry was now largely organised on a European basis and used regional trade associations to assert its policy preferences. 'Brussels' emerged as the focal point of lobbying and decision-making. The degree to which public-private interactions have been institutionalised at the European level is evidence of the (temporary) equilibrium that emerged between new supranational patterns of governance and transnational market structures. The first half of this chapter shows just how far this process has evolved.

The chapter's second half analyses the regulatory changes that have largely completed the cross-border market integration that began two decades earlier. Transposed into national law in 2007, the Markets in Financial Instruments Directive (MiFID) has replaced the ISD. This chapter traces the process from the Commission's initial proposals in 2000 to the MiFID's endorsement by the Council and the European Parliament in 2004. This case study of 'Lamfalussy in action' illustrates how the pre-crisis political climate had shifted from a preference for nationally idiosyncratic regulatory regimes towards supranational harmonisation. ISD negotiations had been hampered by the divergent interests of national financial industries, in particular their protectionist impulses. MiFID negotiations, in contrast, featured competition between regulated exchanges and large investment banks. Both camps favoured cross-border market integration. But they disagreed on the terms under which investment banks would be allowed to act as marketmakers in competition with securities exchanges. This resulted in negotiations that were even more drawn out than those for the ISD. MiFID negotiations showed that competition politics had anything but disappeared with the cross-border integration of the industry: they were now truly transnational.

This new competitive constellation, which structured negotiations and shaped regulatory outcomes, is a good example of structuration at work within EU capital market integration: the consequences of strategic decisions made by the banks a decade earlier now informed competition between investment banks and regulated exchanges. When the banks demutualised the exchanges, thereby turning them into independent for-profit entities, they created a new brand of actor in European financial markets. Regulatory politics after 2000 can only be understood against the background of the earlier strategic restructuring of the financial industry and its corresponding shifts in preferences. The chain of events, in which core actors set the stage for each following integration step, cuts across states and markets.

Clearing and settlement is one important area in which the EU still has no competencies at the time of writing. The fragmentation of the industry in this sector is widely seen as a major impediment to the kind of market integration envisioned by the European Commission. As before, appeals to wider economic goals were insufficient to sway governments in favour of EU-level action. Instead, the clashing competitive interests of a small number of firms prompted their respective governments to veto the further supranationalisation of policy-making. Given incompatible competitive interests, Internal Market Commissioner, Charlie McCreevy, was forced to admit defeat in 2005, announcing the Commission would abstain from proposing a directive for the sector. Competition politics still trump where interests remain opposed to the pull of massive institutional change.

EUROPEAN LOBBYING TRANSFORMED

The flip side of the formal and informal institutionalisation of supranational governance has been a shift in the way private actors interact with public policy-makers. This process began in the mid-1990s, as private actors' preferences swung in favour of transnational market integration and supranational governance, leading to the opening of lobbying offices in Brussels and cooperation on an European level. The Europeanisation of public-private interaction in capital market policy was driven by the mutual reinforcement of the supply and demand for EU-level policy as supranational institutions grew stronger. Again, structuration is at work: the growing relevance of EU bodies demanding input from supranational trade associations has itself been a function of the growing market-integration preferences within the industry. In this way, Schmitter and Streeck's (1981) 'logic of access' and 'logic of membership' in the structuring of private sector input into public policy are two sides of the same coin – even if other factors play a role, their co-evolution is plain to see.

In capital market governance, these two logics have been expressed in the growing transnational organisation of business interests and the formalisation of public-private relations at the supranational level (cf. Streeck and Schmitter 1991, Cowles 2001). Taken together, these two trends show how after a decade of transformation, private-public associative patterns stabilised once more in the years preceding the crisis. As if in a new equilibrium, the scope of investment banking markets, political institutions and private-public interactions have complemented each other in the 'supranational constellation'.

To begin with, the European scope of much of the legislation imposes a new focus on formerly nationally-oriented lobbyists. One representative of a City association found that:

> [w]hen I arrived here [at the association in 2000] I probably spent 10 per cent of my time on international issues, of which 9 was on Europe and one for the rest of the world. By the time I gave up last year [2005], the figure was probably 80:20, 80 per cent international, 20 per cent domestic. That partially reflects the fact that domestic matters were becoming more routine and we got the full flood of European measures. (Interview 300306)

The growing relevance of EU-level measures led to more lobbying in Brussels, though lobbyists from individual firms tried to avoid acting on their own (Interview 231105). Instead they sought the broadest possible consensus, if possible through some EU-level association, and then tried to insert their own preferences.

> People [lobbyists] know each other's positions. In Brussels they play with open cards. [A Commission official] has enough to coordinate already. What is important for him is that he does not have seven people from different banks come to him with the same message on the same day. So everybody, also the Commission, plays very open. People ask 'Listen, this is my position.' If you have one, that is. 'What is yours?' And then people will be very honest. 'On this issue, we cannot follow you because we have a different business position, different business interests.' Or maybe you even say 'Our opinions are diametrically opposed here.' That was the case for example with the Capital Adequacy Directive between the savings banks and the private banks. But of course, that weakens the voice of the banks as a whole. And where the industry does not speak with one voice, the room for manoeuvre of politics increases. I don't think... It is not impossible, but it is of course more difficult for the Commission and later for the [European] Parliament to push through a proposal that is rejected by all [banks] across the board. (Interview 231105)

Finding such broad industry consensus can be a laborious process, well-illustrated in an example given by Mijs and Caparrós Puebla (2002: 265). As recounted previously, one of FESCO's main achievements was agreement on a common definition for professional and retail investors (Federation of European Securities Commissions 2000). The original definition proposed by it, that only financial institutions could be professional investors, was less inclusive than the industry had hoped. Even large non-financial corporations fell into the 'retail' category, meaning host country conduct of business rules applied (Interview 270206). In response to FESCO's proposal, ABN AMRO prepared a classification of its own to submit to the European institutions. It presented the proposal to the International Swaps and Derivatives Association (ISDA), LIBA and the EBF, but found that getting their approval was more difficult than anticipated.

> Even if the primary goal was to obtain broad support for our alternative [classification], even in an amended version, from associations, time was running fast and further pressure on FESCO was needed. We therefore decided to engage, parallel to our discussions with associations, in negotiations with other European banks where decisions could be made in a speedier way. (Mijs and Caparrós Puebla 2002: 266)

Again, this took more time than ABN AMRO imagined. Because of the level of detail, each bank had to consult internally on whether the relevant business units 'could work under the terms proposed'.

> In July 2001, eight leading European banks agreed a joint paper proposing to FESCO and to the European Commission an alternative classification. [..] At the same time, the European Banking Federation (EBF) had successfully convinced all its national associations of the merits of proposing an alternative

definition of professional investor and was discussing in detail our joint paper. The [EBF] finally agreed to send the joint proposal, agreed by eight leading banks and its national associations, to the European Commission and to FESCO in July 2001. (Ibid.: 266)

Using consensus among core players to get whole associations on board could also work the other way around, with the urgency coming from EU bodies rather than industry. One lobbyist gave the example of the Single Euro Payments Area (SEPA), a favourite Commission project due to its (hoped for) visibility for EU citizens (see European Commission 2008):

> Let's assume that Commission really wants a single European payments area. Then it says: 'We want that.' Then the industry says: 'Hmm. That's difficult, that is going to be expensive.' Then the Commission says: 'Yes, but you do have to move a little [on this issue].' Then the industry says: 'Okay. We all get together and we build a sort of interest association where we discuss this. That is the European Payment Council, EPC.' Then every now and then the [European] central bank or McCreevy [Commissioner for the Internal Market at the time] tells you: 'Now, you should hurry up, otherwise we come with a regulation.' And then you maybe realise: 'Oh, now there are very, very many players in the EPC.' There is no real movement. That means, maybe they are doing good work where they agree technical standards but in essence, they cannot cut the Gordian knot. At that moment it is of course attractive for the Commission to talk, not with us, but possibly our board members and to say 'Now, you guys have contacts to the other large banks. [..] You are the large players. How do you see all this? What should we believe of these things that we are being told? Where do you see the problems?' And then it could possibly happen that several large banks say: 'Well, in principle we understand where all this is going but here and there, there are simply insurmountable obstacles. But if it is really the case that either we get a regulation or we move some, then this is how far we can go.' And if then you can tell the Commission: 'We have the largest twenty players,' or even only the ten largest players in Europe behind such a proposal, then the chance that such an EPC will agree to such an informally agreed thing is of course much larger. Now that is the game. (Interview 231105, author's translation from German)

In addition to collective action problems, the overlap of commercial interests among members of an association such as the EBF are crucial in determining its ability to act: on the issue of internalisation (central in MiFID negotiations and discussed in more detail in the following section), the interests of European banks diverged (Interview 211105.b). In contrast, the EBF was effective in generating consensus on the Market Abuse and Prospectus Directives:

> Prospectus is an example. I know that going into the Council meeting people have told me that they could see that the EBF position paper was on the desks – not on every desk – but a whole range of governments were using that as an element of their briefing. And you are aware that in the prospectus directive, the whole approach completely switched around, and that was the result of an awful lot of lobbying that was given the parliament. Particularly on the fixed income side. The EBF, with IPMA – lobbying from a more London perspective – put in very substantial amendments and lobbying points. (Interview 140306

The demand for EU-level private sector input has led to the creation of many new bodies and associations that complete the supranational organisation of industry interests. In contrast to old national corporatist associations, these are either forums for consensus-finding or single-issue associations. The European Payments Council is a good example of the former, as is the European Banking Industry Committee (EBIC), the most encompassing trade association in EU banking. The latter was launched in January 2004 (European Banking Industry Committee 2004) in response to the Commission's desire to hear from the industry in a single voice. Unsurprisingly, the range of issues on which there is sector-wide agreement is relatively limited; most of its output therefore tends to be framed in rather general terms. At the same time, that the EBIC exists at all says much about the consolidation of interest representation structures at the European level.

The European Securities Forum (ESF), also set up in 2004, is one of the more prominent single-issue associations in EU capital markets. It pushes for consolidation in the clearing and settlement industry (Interview 220206). The interests of the investment banks are divided on this issue; the French banks, BNP Paribas in particular, have commercial stakes in the continued fragmentation of the clearing and settlement market. The ESF thus brings together the major investment banks active in Europe, with the exception of the French ones.[39] It exemplifies the new geometry of interest representation where loyalties and shared background play less of a role than commercial interests. Rather than being channels for top-down communication, ad-hoc interest associations, such as the ESF, are used instrumentally by shifting alliances of market participants. They complete the spectrum of private EU-level sector associations that meet the public sector demand for policy input.

In addition to the field's Europeanisation, the second major trend in EU capital market lobbying has been the formalisation of industry ties with the Commission, CESR and the EP. This mainly comes in the form of regular public consultations and fixed-membership advisory groups. The formalisation of public-private relations largely reflects the desire of firms to be heard and informed at all stages of the policy process.

> [T]here was a problem before because [..] it took ages to have a directive adopted and then when it had to be implemented it was already outdated. That was something that everybody recognised. And when Lamfalussy was created, we were still really supportive of that. It is a good thing to have a EU culture in supervising. By working together, they are forced to develop common interpretations, common guidelines, common advice to the Commission. I think [our bank] is one of the few lobbying offices where we really were strong in [replying to] nearly all CESR and CEBS [Committee of European Banking Supervisors] consultations. On MiFID, we have one person working on MiFID, level 2 [of the Lamfalussy process]. So CESR consultations. For CEBS consultation, we did not respond directly, we gave our input to [the EBF]. Yes, it is a lot of work but it is what we have been asking for. So we have to be consistent. It is much more transparent than before. (Interview 211105.b)

---

39. ESF, 'Members', Availble http:<//www.eurosf.com> (accessed 19 May 2004).

The opportunity for input that CESR offers is indeed considerable. In 2007 it launched no less than twenty-one consultations, normally in the form of highly technical documents published on its website. 'Interested parties' were then invited to comment. As these documents are usually long, formulating appropriate responses that reflect corporate interests is a full-time job. It is thus hardly surprising that responses only come from the financial industry, non-financial issuers of securities and supervisory bodies. Nevertheless, for large investment banks with transnational operations, having CESR produce countless consultations is preferable to monitoring the proceedings of more than a dozen national regulators (Interview 070406). As one lobbyist observed,

> [t]he industry demand was also more consultation, more transparency. And CESR has given it to them in bucket loads. There is so much consultation. Also, the CESR members are closer to the industry than to the Commission. In that sense, the industry is quite pleased. Of course, sometimes CESR comes up with rules that are more detailed than the industry thinks are necessary. (Interview 021205.a)

The degree of detail in common rules, another industry representative found, was partially the fault of industry itself:

> So we are talking not only about the framework, but MEPs who are beleaguered by firms and lobbyists, who arrange things down to the smallest technical detail for very different motives. There are, for example, people who come here and complain that the Commission makes such complicated laws. On the other hand, they come here to try to get things into the directive, because they don't want their supervisor at home to have too much leeway. They try to arrange things here in Brussels so they don't have to arrange them in England or in Germany. (Interview 231105, author's translation from German)

For another industry representative, EU-level rule harmonisation was part of the overall shift in capital market governance:

> [T]hat is the price you pay for increasing recognition. The price is everybody levels up. Now as it happens, for the big firms, it probably doesn't matter too much. Because they were already pretty levelled up anyway. If you give them cross-border access, that is a price they are willing to pay. This is a huge political problem for the 99 per cent of banks who are domestically active and will have to pay the price, too. You will see in the next two years a huge outcry from retail banks [..]. The stockbrokers – why should they have to do all this? They don't trade across borders. It's all for the prize of the big firms. The other part of the deal is the Lamfalussy process. He said that there should be mutual recognition based on trust. It hasn't so far delivered. We were in favour of mutual recognition and competition but the member states would not buy it without massive harmonisation. So you get a much more detailed framework. That on the whole is working. The deal there is [..] we got the transparency. Because our only chance really was to stop the regulators stitching us up in private and imposing... So we desperately wanted public accountability and EP accountability. Some of the bizarre things you have seen in the FSAP is the industry supporting the EP which is not always very reliable. Supporting

transparency in the Commission. The Commission did not like it at first. It is still slightly uncomfortable with the length of time it takes to go through this transparency process. And to be fair to CESR, Fabrice [Demarigny, secretary-general of CESR] did a great job. They really do now operate in a transparent manner – and they did not like it in the beginning. (Interview 270206)

Most of the battles over consultation and representation have already been fought. All public bodies hold regular hearings and have their expert groups; the majority of these external 'experts' are industry representatives. The membership list of the European Securities Markets Expert Group (ESME), the official advisory committee to the Commission, is instructive: at the time of writing, all of its twenty members came from financial firms (European Commission 2006b). As expertise is defined in technical terms – and the problem to be solved is nothing less than the optimisation of capital markets – the Commission finds the group representative. Other formal 'advisory groups' to the Commission and CESR are similarly composed. For example, only one of the twenty-six members of the Securities Markets Expert Group that evaluated progress in market integration and legal harmonisation was not directly or indirectly an industry representative.

The influence of these expert groups should not be underestimated. According to ESME, they should provide 'technical advice [..] on issues of contemporary relevance in EU securities markets' (European Commission 2006a). This broad mandate included the role of credit rating agencies (CRAs), in the public spotlight since the summer of 2007. In August of that year, the Commission publicly questioned their role in the credit market crisis that spread out of the US housing market (Buck 2007); in November 2009 the European Parliament and the Council adopted a regulation placing them under European regulatory oversight.[40] Back in 2005, however, heavy industry lobbying had deterred the Commission from attempting to regulate CRAs (*The Banker* 2004). The seemingly technical can rapidly assume highly political proportions.

On the whole, lobbying has come a long way since the early 1990s (Interview 070406).

> Back in the days, you could go and lobby the Commission fairly directly, and that was that. Now you have to lobby CESR, the individual member states, the EP. On the one hand, you have a lot more opportunity to lobby, on the other hand, you need to do it well, there is a lot more you have to do. That is one change to ten years ago. Back then, you basically just went to the person on the Commission who was writing the directive. And you succeeded or you failed. But you knew there was one person or a couple of people dealing with this. And the parliament only advised… (Interview 021205.a)

With the multiplication of relevant actors, the frequency of interactions has increased. A lobbyist from a large US investment bank estimated that his firm talked to the Commission 'basically every week' (Interview 070406). Sometimes 'Brussels' calls on its own – something he claimed was unthinkable a decade earlier.

---

40. Regulation (EC) 1060/2009.

> It brings the EU more towards the US level of legislation. More lobbying. More PR. Government relations work. The whole thing becomes much more professional. Back then it was much more informal, behind closed doors. That is gone. (Interview 021205.a)

Within the architecture of European public-private relations, the role of the European Parliament has grown over the past decade, even if the Commission still stands at the centre of Brussels lobbying (Interview 211105.b). This reflects its increased powers since the Amsterdam Treaty; it will have to be seen how the Lisbon treaty may affect this balance. Already now MEPs are also popular targets for lobbyists, however; the other EU bodies can draw on more in-house expertise than MEPs, making the latter particularly susceptible to external influence:

> The MEPs, their main problem is lack of resources, but they want to be seen to be active. So they are quite keen to meet people. You state the case and present your argument. It is still very much how good an argument you can come up with. You sometimes still end up with some maladroit lobbying where you have four or five MEPs putting forward exactly the same kind of amendment [to a Commission directive proposal] in the same language. (Interview 021205.a)

The more experienced parliamentarians are aware of this vulnerability (Interview 071205.a, Interview 120106.a). Lobbyists have also found that manipulating MEPs can quickly tarnish their reputations and forfeit their most valuable asset: access to policy-making (Interview 011205). One MEP confided that he received so many invitations to London on the back of EU efforts to curb insider trading that he stopped accepting them altogether (Interview 071205.a). There seem to be unwritten rules about how far lobbyists can go. Nevertheless, MEPs, in particular, remain exposed to corporate influence; their relative lack of expertise makes them dependent on industry 'experts'. Given the vagueness of the overarching goals in capital market policy, the key for lobbyists is often to connect their specific proposals to general themes that resonate with MEPs:

> For some [MEPs], efficiency is the main thing. The next level is that this will create jobs. For some, you will need to link it to why this is good for your constituency. And in financial markets, the arguments are fairly straightforward. Who could really be against efficiency? You would have a much harder time if you came with a protectionist view. Then you would have to spin some sort of cultural argument. That this would destroy national tradition... But even on consumer protection, some of the more far-sighted firms understand that that is in their interest. They want happy, confident consumers. Otherwise, they are not going to sell anything across borders. (Interview 021205.a)

In sum, EU-level public-private interactions approached the level of routine that they had hitherto only had within national policy communities. The establishment of new transnational trade associations, fixed-membership 'expert' panels and formalised consultative procedures completed the supranationalisation of EU capital market governance. This novel pattern of governance once more matched the effective scope of many core firms' business operations and of market structures in which a new group of market incumbents – a European 'Champions League' – had emerged in investment banking and securities trading.

LAMFALUSSY IN ACTION: RENEGOTIATING THE ISD

The renegotiation of the ISD, which led to the Markets in Financial Instruments Directive (MiFID), is a case study of the implications of the Lamfalussy process for the governance of European capital markets. The MiFID is widely considered the most important directive for capital markets since the ISD, and probably the most important for European financial markets as a whole. Negotiations for the MiFID not only showed the Lamfalussy process at work; the substantive rules contained in the directive also reflected stakeholders' changed preferences. The previous chapter showed how the interests of most large firms had coalesced around the further cross-border integration of markets and governance, even if some were more enthusiastic about new legislation than others. Once it was decided that the directive was to be rewritten, discussions immediately shifted to the content of new legislation.

The fault lines in the discussions showed how much the competitive landscape and preferences had changed over the preceding decade. Traditional, national protectionism on the part of banks and stock exchanges played only a minor role. Within these two groups of firms, competitive struggles remained subdued. Regulated exchanges with de facto monopolies over the on-exchange trading of their home market shares posed little threat to each other. Sporadic attempts to break into each other's markets – as the London Stock Exchange did with its offer to trade Dutch shares in 2003 – invariably failed. Among the large investment banks, business models had grown sufficiently similar to make EU-level regulation an ineffective tool for competitive struggle: firms would be affected by regulatory changes in roughly similar ways.

This did not mean that competition politics had been superseded. One source of resistance to the large banks' preference for market integration – smaller firms – were too few in number and too ineffectively organised to mount a significant defence. As Chapter 5 showed, the number of firms holding significant market share in Europe was small to begin with, and transnational market integration meant many of the small brokerage houses in Paris, Frankfurt and London were bought up (e.g. Augar 2000 in the UK, Jabko 2006 in France). Most other EU member states had no investment banking industry. In addition, the growing divergence between the interests of large and small firms weakened national alliances; the positions of national sectoral associations often remained vague or reflected larger firms' preferences. In short, smaller firms were too weak, both economically and politically, to counter the wave of regulatory harmonisation about to sweep over them. As one Commission official concluded, forging agreement on a 'true' passport was helped both by the increasingly global nature of firms in the business and the fact that fewer and fewer of them remained (Interview 141205).

The real competitive struggle in negotiating the MiFID took place between stock exchanges and investment banks over share and bond trading: where was the future of European securities business going to lie? To understand the core issue, it is useful to take a step back and consider the evolution of share trading over the previous decade. Historically, bourses functioned as clubs of brokers and market makers (Lee 1998, Braithwaite and Drahos 2000). As owners of the exchanges, member firms invariably pocketed any profits that accrued during share trading – whether through their own fees or those charged by the stock exchange. In addition, monopolies on the trading of domestic shares limited competition for trading services: as rulers of the bourse, market incumbents could control access to the business.

Chapter 5 recounted how stock exchanges demutualised over the course of the 1990s. Brokers turned members-only clubs into for-profit firms and sold them, often by listing on the same stock market (Steil 2002a). The new businesses quickly tried to secure as large a share as possible of the revenues associated with securities trading (trading revenues, but also listing fees, clearing and settlement fees, custody fees, etc.). This took the investment banks by surprise. One investment-banking lobbyist argued that two decades earlier, national exchanges had been

> [o]ld boys clubs with a license to effectively print money, probably protected by law. Then, they were refusing to move with the times. They were very reluctant to set up sensible governance structures internally. They failed to get the right chief executives. And then people said 'It can't get much worse than it is now.' But then, we [the investment banks] should have made sure that we had it right. [..] The banks themselves did not anticipate the speed with which the new management [of exchanges] would adopt profit-maximising instincts and apply them to their monopolistic position. (Interview 300306)

Demutualisation thus gave a new competitive, political salience to the question of why securities markets should be organised around national exchanges. Investment banks felt they could perform many of their functions. For listing – effectively 'vetting' issuers of securities – and for clearing and settlement services, some central entity was desirable. But trading services could just as well be performed by investment banks as market makers. Trading could thus be 'internalised' by banks and bypass bourses altogether. It was clear that the old concentration rule would fall in renegotiating the ISD; securities trading on alternative venues would be enshrined in EU law. What remained undecided, however, was how high the bar for non-bourses would be set. Given the commercial stakes for both the stock exchanges and investment banks, 'systemic internalisation' dominated the negotiations. A Commission official had no doubt on this point:

> On MiFID, the real problem was internalisation. Because it was about competition, and the competition was between stock exchanges and other forms of markets. That was really the main aspect. (Interview 141205)

The initial Commission proposal, discussed in the Forum Group on the ISD, placed the bar for systemic internalisation relatively low. There had never been much doubt that trading data would eventually need to be aggregated at some central point to aid price formation and efficiency, and to allow effective supervision. The argument for market efficiency was hard to trump (cf. Jabko 2006); it was, after all, the official rationale for creating a single European capital market in the first place. Efficiency, however, said little about how information was to be aggregated or about when such information would have to be communicated to a central authority. The details – and costs – of such 'post-trade transparency' were still up for grabs.

'Pre-trade transparency' was even thornier: the question of how systemic internalisers would ensure that their clients were receiving the best available price (Interview 021205.b). Given the enormous volume of securities traded each day, even tiny price differentials would generate significant profits for banks and, by implication, damage to their clients. At the same time, by endlessly complicating requirements to 'shop around' before matching two trades in-house, pre-trade transparency could be used to make systemic internalisation altogether unattractive. Proposals went so far as to require brokers to tape all telephone calls with clients, which could then be used as evidence against investment banks in court.

Although the eventual rules did not include this obligation, investment banks were surprised by the effectiveness of the stock exchanges in mobilising political actors for their cause. The Federation of European Securities Exchanges (FESE) is widely credited with having played a central role. As its name suggests, it began as a federation in the early 1990s. But its character changed over the following decade. As one investment banker observed, not without admiration:

> FESE is no longer a club that has national monopolists as members. Rather, FESE is now a political association of financial services companies which are above all competitive. (Interview 021205.b, author's translation from German)

This did not mean that FESE members had identical interests. Depending on their business models and home regulatory regimes (cf. Lee 1998), some bourses were more intimidated by the prospects of systemic internalisation than others. The application of the concentration rule, which forced share trading onto exchanges, was not required under the ISD: member states were free to apply it or not. Among the larger European markets, France and Italy had put it into effect. Thus shielded from competition, the Paris Bourse and Borsa Italiana in Milan had the most to lose from internalisation. For them, the MiFID had the potential to, as one exchange lobbyist put it, 'destroy the market' (Interview 021205.b).

> In MiFID terms, there is no question that the two key jurisdictions in terms of politically lobbying from a different perspective to that of the City were France and Italy. And the other key player in the politics of MiFID was FESE. Driven not just by concerns of, say, Euronext-LIFFE or, say, Borsa Italiana, but also by Deutsche Börse's concerns. (Interview 140306)

The Deutsche Börse, Germany's central stock exchange, was already functioning in a regulatory environment that permitted off-exchange trading. Trades through alternative channels were reported directly to public oversight authorities, meaning that off-exchange business completely bypassed Deutsche Börse. Investment banks and alternative trading venues such as Instinet were its direct competitors. While the MiFID was unlikely to heighten competition, it had the potential to increase the regulatory burden on off-exchange trading, and thus bring business back to the exchange (Interview 021205.b). Deutsche Börse therefore supported stringent pre-trade and post-trade requirements and, as one stock exchange lobbyist found, it 'could hide its own commercial interests rather well behind the investor protection argument' (Ibid., author's translation from German).

The London Stock Exchange was different again, largely due to the regulatory regime under which it operated. A remnant of the times of self-regulation, the LSE still functioned as the central authority through which trading data was aggregated and price information was provided back to banks and other trading venues. For this service it charged its clients. Because London had known no concentration rule, the LSE had shifted its primary sources of revenue towards those functions where there was less competition than for trading services (Interview 130306). As with other exchanges, the LSE was not hostile to the idea of rules that would let it keep or regain liquidity (Interview 140306). But getting the London bourse to join most other FESE members in opposing internalisation was no easy task (Interview 021205.b).

This was the competitive landscape as the Commission drafted its legislative proposal. In many respects, the Commission was on the side of the investment banks and the City. The introduction of pan-European competition for trading services was its goal, and this meant abolishing the exchanges' monopolies on the trading of securities and the tearing down of regulatory barriers. Investment banks were pleased with the early proposals. Yet national governments, particularly the French and Italian ones, together with FESE managed to tilt the Commission's text in favour of the exchanges. In a move that saw European capital market politics at its most dramatic, the Commission amended its legislative proposal on the MiFID the night before it was sent to the Council. It once again increased the burden of pre-trade transparency, a shift that was widely seen as a nod from the Italian Commission President Romano Prodi to the interests of his home government and Borsa Italiana (Ibid.). Investment banks were astonished; the MiFID had taken a very different direction from what it had seemed at the outset (Interview 231105). As one Commission official phrased it,

> the idea of pre-trade came in last minute, just before the Commission finalised its proposal. It was actually... Some people say it was produced at the last minute. I suppose... That was not completely untrue, I would say. At some [earlier] points it was not there. (Interview 141205)

The interviewed officials working in DG Internal Market did not seem particularly happy with the last minute changes. But as bureaucrats they had to follow the orders of politically chosen Commissioners. In this case, the national loyalties of the Commissioner in question still seemed to trump commitment to the supranational project.

In the Council negotiations that followed, the banks found themselves fighting a rearguard action. The UK government still took what one representative called a 'City view' on the MiFID (Interview 120106.b). But with its strong pro-internalisation stance, it was alone among the larger member states. Whereas Deutsche Bank had bet on its contacts with policy-makers in Brussels, the Deutsche Börse relied on its connections with the national government; as mentioned earlier, it had not even set up a representative office in Brussels (Interview 240506.b). Though the German government did not take as strong a position as either the British or the French ones, it still came out in favour of pre- and post-trade transparency rules that were much more demanding than the investment banks had hoped for (Interview 231105). The big French banks likewise had much less political capital with their national government than had been the case a decade earlier. A lobbyist for one of the large French banks felt that the French position on the pre-trade and post-trade issues was 'nonsense', based on 'fantasy, not facts' (Interview 160506.a). The French government, he argued, bore significant responsibility for many of the 'bad' things about the MiFID.

This disjuncture between the large investment banks and their governments on the continent reflected the disembedding of national financial industries from what Hall and Soskice have called coordinated market economies (Hall and Soskice 2001a, cf. Story and Walter 1997). While most scholars agree that continental varieties of capitalism have not converged on an 'Anglo-Saxon' model (Schmidt 2002, 2003, cf. Glyn 2006), the role and positioning of their national financial industries certainly have changed – both in Germany (Vitols 2003, 2004) and in France (cf. Morin 2000, Clift 2004, Culpepper 2006). In both countries, the leading international banks have increasingly concentrated on their business and left their wider economic functions behind. The relevance of cross-shareholdings and the role of banks within them, for example, has clearly decreased since the mid-1990s. In the competition with the bourses, which were still closely wedded to national financial centres, investment banks could no longer count on their governments' support to see their positions through in EU multi-level governance.

Instead, their hopes rested with the European Parliament to demand amendments that would soften the pre- and post-trade transparency requirements. But it took the banks some time to organise again, as one representative of a trade association remembers:

> I would say we really started working quite effectively some time at the beginning of 2002. Already in 2001 we were starting to have meetings [..] different representatives of industry, banks, [EBF], all kinds of things, together, from the end of 2001 until the directive finally got adopted [..] For more than a year, we organised a lot of meetings with presidencies, so each time there was a new presidency we would lobby them, we went to the Commission together, we wrote letters together, and most importantly of course we were able to convince the Parliament, and lots of different groups in the Parliament, as a whole [..] that in all those key areas the Commissions proposals had made the wrong decisions. [..] In the end, a very good number of our suggestions ended up being proposed by the Parliament. In the Parliament's second reading and then in the end, no, in between in the revised Commission proposals, because the Commission actually withdrew its proposal and actually [came out] with a new one. (Interview 221105)

One problem the banks faced was the number of firms standing to profit from internalisation, which was less than a dozen. Therefore uniting the European Banking Federation behind their interests was not going to be easy. Both the French and Italian national banking associations refused to sign up to the pro-internalisation line, even if the largest French banks were now in favour (Interview 140306). The recalcitrance of the associations restrained the EBF in the statements it could make on behalf of the European commercial banks. With hindsight, another banking lobbyist felt the inability to present a unified position was a missed opportunity:

> We were too late dealing with certain conceptual aspects. Had we started hard on the best execution [a central aspect of pre-trade transparency] right at the beginning, there would have been much more of a chance to get the intermediaries largely to agree. But the design [of EU rules] had gone far too far by the time we got in. [..] We started talking seriously, with the French [associations] particularly, in 2002, 2003, but that was too late, already. But it's a question of personalities. We wouldn't have talked to the right person if we would have tried earlier because he wasn't there. The French have gone through a large temperamental change in recent years. The boss of the AFEI [the French association of investment firms] has long despaired over his own government's inward-looking, protectionist philosophy. He says. 'We must compete, otherwise we will wither all.' But he doesn't control the system. The Trésor, the Banque de France, the big commercial interests don't always agree [with each other]. (Interview 300306)

The compromise that emerged from the co-decision procedure between the Council and the European Parliament smoothed the rough edges of the transparency requirements. The competitive struggle between the investment banks and the exchanges ended without clear victors, even as observers were clearly impressed by the political defence the exchanges managed to mount. In any case, as a banking analyst summarised, 'the margin of benefit of being a systemic internaliser has been significantly eroded, it would appear' (Interview 140306). Another lobbyist for a large European bank concluded:

> For us the MiFID is not really [a great business opportunity]. That is simply the way it is. For us it is, if you are really mean, we're speaking among ourselves, for us the only advantage is, that the small brokerage houses will suffer much more under the new rules and this transparency with best execution because in relation to turnover and profit the investment expenses are higher for them. (Interview 231105, author's translation from German)

Implementing measures for the MiFID were only published in early 2006, so at the time of research, respondents were in no position to comment on the result. Nevertheless, almost a dozen London-based trade associations, including the London Investment Banking Association, had already launched a project called 'MiFID Connect' to develop industry standards for the even implementation of the new rules and to forge a consensus among firms on how MiFID provisions should be interpreted, especially in dealings between financial firms (Interview 140306). The industry stood ready to take the baton of rule harmonisation from European regulators.

CLEARING AND SETTLEMENT: THE PERSISTENCE OF NATIONAL COMPETITION POLITICS

One crucial area in European capital markets has thus far remained largely untouched by European regulation: clearing and settlement (C&S). Both the fragmentation of European post-trade services and the lack of competition in the domain have repeatedly been identified as barriers to cross-border market integration (e.g. The Giovannini Group 2001, Goldberg *et al.* 2002). Two competitive issues still divide the financial industry and obstruct government agreement on EU-level action: governance structures and consolidation.

The firms providing post-trade services fall under two categories: central counterparties (CCPs) and central securities depositories (CSDs) (see Cox *et al.* 2005). When two parties agree on a securities trade, for example on a stock exchange, the transaction is commonly arranged via an interlocutor, the CCP, which becomes the actual counterparty to both the seller and the buyer. One to three days normally elapse between the agreement to trade and the actual transaction; in order to minimise risk in this time-lag as well as to allow the 'netting' of buy- and sell-transactions by the same broker, all trades in a particular security are cleared through CCPs. In Europe, the biggest ones are Clearstream, owned by Deutsche Börse, and LCH.Clearnet. Central securities depositories hold the actual securities; they keep book of their ownership and 'deliver' them against payment, even if the securities, as tangible pieces of paper, remain immobile in the CSD. Euroclear is the largest CSD in Europe. Finally, market participants who cannot or do not want to deal with CCPs and CSDs directly (for example pension funds) use custodian banks to take care of the payment for and delivery of securities; custodians also collect dividends on shares and perform related services. Custody services are normally provided by large banks. In Europe, at the time of writing, the largest custodians are State Street, Bank of New York, JP Morgan and Citigroup. Coming in fifth place, BNP Paribas is, by far, the largest European firm providing custody services.

From the perspective of efficiency, it is suboptimal to have several CCPs and CSDs in Europe (Goldberg *et al.* 2002). Banks have to keep balances at all of them. More money has to change hands than would be the case if a single European CCP existed; only then would it be possible to net for example the sale of Portuguese shares against the purchase of German ones. In short, many observers see the fragmentation of C&S markets as a barrier to true financial market integration. Most large banks would also like to see further consolidation in the field as it would lower their post-trading expenses. The political question is whether consolidation could be forced on the sector for the sake of financial market integration.

The issue of consolidation is wedded to the second stumbling block, governance structures. Formally, most clearing houses (which often also provide settlement services) are independent from the stock exchanges they serve. For example, Euroclear handles the settlement for trades on Euronext and the London Stock Exchange (LSE). It is largely owned by the users of its services – large banks – and neither the LSE nor Euronext can dictate the prices Euroclear charges for its services. Nor can they legally force parties trading on their systems to use Euroclear for settlement. In contrast, Deutsche Börse owns Clearstream, the company that clears and settles the shares traded on its system. Similar 'silo' models that integrate trading and post-trading services exist in Italy and Spain. This vertical integration of the value chain has attracted much criticism: banks and other exchanges claim that Deutsche Börse, in particular, uses its monopoly over the clearing and settlement of German shares to subsidise services in which it competes with other firms. Deutsche Börse's clearing and settlement system is widely seen as the central obstacle to pan-European consolidation in the industry. Unsurprisingly, Deutsche Börse denies the veracity and relevance of both claims (Viermetz 2006).

Seeing both the lack of consolidation and the vertical integration in some countries as impediments to financial market integration, the Commission was eager to see movement in these areas. While clearing and settlement appeared as a separate agenda point in the Commission's first 'issues paper' for the Forum Group on the ISD (European Commission 1999a), it was dropped from later meetings (e.g. European Commission 2000); where clearing and settlement was still mentioned, the Commission emphasised that it remained outside considerations for future legislation (Ibid.: 4). As one Commission official remembers:

> At one point we had a provision in the MiFID concerning C&S. In the discussion it was there. That you should have free access to C&S systems. But immediately during the debate... Because many member states said 'It is a difficult issue. It's not appropriate to deal with it simply with an article in the MiFID.' That is why what was in the MiFID disappeared. (Interview 141205)

The German government, in particular, remained obstinate; it was clear that it would not accept legislative action in this area (Interview 240506.a). Its position largely matched that of Deutsche Börse – the welfare-enhancing prospects that experts commonly associate with consolidation in the industry notwithstanding.

The German government was not alone in opposing legislation. The French government was also hesitant, though this had less to do with the interests of Euronext than the commercial interests of the French banks (the largest custodians in Europe), and of BNP Paribas in particular. The fragmentation of clearing and settlement systems in Europe means that many settlement-related services are handled by custodians. In effect, the latter profit from what is, for the rest, an inefficient system. As recounted above, the rapport between the largest French banks and the government had been deteriorating (cf. Lalone 2005). But on this particular issue, a lobbyist from a French bank with high stakes in the field reported that his bank and the Trésor had reached a 'good understanding' and that the latter had finally arrived 'at the right position' – meaning scepticism towards EU-level legal action (Interview 160506.a). Lobbyists from non-French banks also observed the influence of BNP Paribas on the Trésor's position (Interview 231105). Firm loyalty to the home state or to European integration thus depended on the issue at hand. As another lobbyist noted: 'on the investment business [the French banks] are [European], on C&S they are not' (Interview 021205.a).

Most investment banks of any standing in Europe were united in the European Securities Forum (ESF), a single-issue association that lobbied for more 'efficiency' in the clearing and settlement industry. Only the French banks were absent. BNP Paribas left the ESF in the fall of 2003 because its commercial interests as a major custodian were no longer compatible with the goal of the abolition of barriers in the sector. Likewise, in the post-FSAP Expert Group on Securities Markets, which gathered industry representatives to advise the Commission, there was only superficial consensus on 'tackling' clearing and settlement.

> Everyone agrees on that. But tackled – for some people that means a directive, for others it means doing nothing and letting the 'market' do its work. (Interview 141205)

In late 2007 the Council of EU finance ministers had abandoned initiatives to force change on the industry through a directive and concentrates (Council of the European Union (ECOFIN) 2007); instead, European bourses drew up a voluntary code of conduct (Buck and Cohen 2006). The example of clearing and settlement shows how a small number of firms – only two in the eyes of many observers – could stall the Europeanisation of an issue area if it went against their competitive interests and if they happened to have access to powerful member state governments. Competition politics and material interests still trumped the supranational push of the institutions created by the Lamfalussy process.

THE SUPRANATIONAL CONSTELLATION IN EU CAPITAL MARKET GOVERNANCE

After twenty years of transformation, the dust appeared to be settling in the mid-2000s. The work programme of the Financial Services Action Plan had basically been completed (European Commission 2007a) while member states were busy implementing its centrepiece, the MiFID. For the years to follow, the Commission committed itself to a 'regulatory pause' (European Commission 2005c). Instead of making new rules, both Brussels bureaucrats and industry representatives emphasised the need to improve the 'quality' of existing rules. A new balance emerged between market structures and the level and scope of capital markets regulation in the EU. The emphasis on 'improving' regulation meant that much of the work to come would take place on 'level 2' of the Lamfalussy process where implementing measures can be adapted without renegotiating entire directives. Until a wholly new directive was to replace the MiFID, both the Council and the European Parliament would largely be excluded from the evolution of EU regulation. Instead, the Commission, CESR and the core private stakeholders – a small group of transnational financial firms – were destined to decide collectively the direction of further change. This is where the most radical supranationalisation of policy-making lay.

The financial crisis starting in the summer of 2007 has upset this arrangement. Capital market governance has been repoliticised. National governments, parliaments and citizens in general have woken up to the centrality of financial regulation for the well-being of whole economies. Inevitably, the formerly cozy patterns of supranational policy-making have been disturbed. At least until a temporary regulatory fix is agreed, the dynamics of rule-making will diverge in important respects from those described in this chapter. Irrespective of whether even tighter EU cooperation or a re-nationalisation of policy will emerge as the regulatory answer, national governments are once more directly involved in capital market policy. That does not mean that competition politics have been superseded. Quite on the contrary. In dire straits, banks have rediscovered their home governments as crucial allies in their fight for survival. Governments have grudgingly acknowledged how dependent they are on a well-functioning financial sector. In the European and global regulatory negotiations ongoing at the time of writing, this mutual dependence will induce governments to side with their own industries once again, simply to insure their long-term survival. Preliminary evidence on revised capital adequacy rules, but also hedge funds and credit rating agencies, reveals close matches between national positions and industry structures and hence preferences (Mügge and Stellinga, forthcoming 2010). If competition politics remained a constant force in the two decades of radical capital market transformation covered in this book, it also stands a good chance to survive post-crisis regulatory reforms.

chapter nine | conclusion

Over the two decades covered by this book, capital markets were governed by a small group of insiders. Bankers and stock exchange operators employed their political leverage to shape market rules and regulatory institutions to their own advantage. Adam Smith's elegant summary of their motives warrants reiteration: 'To widen the market and to narrow the competition, is always the interest of the dealers.' When Smith wrote these words, the complexities of contemporary finance and the bureaucratic apparatus governing it were two centuries away. Nevertheless, it is these two considerations – market-widening and competition management – that have guided the fate of EU capital markets.

When formulating their regulatory preferences, European firms face a trade-off between greater market access abroad and limiting foreign competition in their home markets. EU decision-making requires a majority of member states to support changes to common market rules, meaning that firms cannot expect more liberal access abroad without ceding ground at home. Sufficient support for market opening did not materialise until the late 1990s as fear of the mighty investment banks operating out of the City of London was too strong. On the continent, it was felt that market integration would inflict heavy losses on most financial firms; only a small number of banks stood to gain.

This perception shifted dramatically in the run-up to the new millennium. In the brave new world of the Internet boom, everyone could be a winner. Staid German Landesbanken hired glamorous City investment bankers; even Crédit Agricole, hitherto dedicated to serving French farmers, entered investment banking. Opposition to an integrated European capital market crumbled, while a transnational coalition of leading European and American banks emerged as the leading advocate of concentrating rule-making powers in Brussels. By 2001, EU governments had endorsed the Lamfalussy process for capital market regulation. Three years later, they adopted legislation that replaced most of the former regulatory patchwork with a single European rule-set. Capital market governance had been supranationalised.

BANKER INTERESTS IN EU CAPITAL MARKET INTEGRATION

One of the main themes of this book is structuration: the agency that effects change in economic and political structures is not reducible to these structures, even if it is clearly influenced by them. In order to remain true to the dynamics of political economy as they unfold in practice, models that place all emphasis on politics (in a narrow sense) or on economics are not appropriate – whether their focus is on national or supranational actors, or on agents or structures. The evidence presented in this book suggests that the transformation of market structures cannot be understood without examining the institutions and politics that govern them and vice versa, underlining Underhill's (2001) thesis that state-market condominiums need to be studied as integrated wholes. Nevertheless, the common social science division of labour that assigns regulation, political institutions and corporate strategy to disparate disciplinary branches hinders the study of markets in the way Adam Smith still understood them – as politically structured social spaces of production and exchange.

The focus on structuration within EU capital market integration holds insights applicable to a wider range of cases. First, though we saw that private interests had a decisive impact on public policy-making, the standard Stiglerian concept of 'regulatory capture' is imprecise. Stigler argued that producers have higher stakes in public policy than consumers, and can more easily manage collective action problems. While both points are valid, they ignore how particular political interests may already be 'built into' the state (Lindblom 1977). This particularly, though not exclusively, applies to banks due to their central role in economic policy (Zysman 1983). To borrow Krasner's (1984: 227) metaphor again, states are not neutral 'cash registers' that add up the vectors of political power and preference. States are made up of political institutions that maintain relationships with diverse societal constituencies; the institutions co-evolve with these groups, who use them to advance their own political interests (Skocpol 1985, Cerny 1990). In the case of economic policy, this includes the state as the codifier and enforcer of limits to inter-firm competition (Fligstein 2001). If political institutions are indeed 'frozen politics', the institutions that govern competition are frozen competition politics.[41]

State-market relations varied considerably across the three countries at the heart of this study: Germany, France and the United Kingdom. So did their institutions regulating market structure and access. But in all three cases, financial firms were closely involved in financial sector policy-making, whether through corporatist structures, through a tight state-business nexus or through self-regulation. Political institutions allowed banks to use regulatory policy to further their economic objectives. This did not entail private actors coaxing government officials into policy positions inimical to their own convictions. More often than not, the long-established proximity between governments, banks and, later, stock exchanges made the public defence of private interests appear almost natural. Even when the lobbyists interviewed for this book were unambiguous about the self-interested nature of their policy positions, they still betrayed a sense of entitlement to support from public actors.

Second, Stiglerian thinking envisions interest politics as battles between large groups of actors, primarily producers and consumers. Stigler clearly realised that group size was inversely related to their effectiveness in political organisation. Yet capture theory did not envisage an insider politics in which a handful of firms – no more than two dozen in Europe – would drive political dynamics within the sector. Incumbent firms from the most important EU capital markets formed the core of the private half of the policy community. The political struggle over regulation

---

41. I owe the 'frozen politics' metaphor to Brian Burgoon.

did not involve large societal groups such as producers, consumers, investors, or classes.

EU capital market politics around 1990 still fit Moravcsik's (1993, 1997) liberal model of international politics. But as this book has shown, the intergovernmental character of the two-level game did not last. The political transformation over the next decade revealed that intergovernmental politics was contingent upon the division of regulatory preferences along national borders. Whereas around 1990 many continental firms perceived the City investment banks as a threat, less than a decade later they had become models to emulate. As the constituency in favour of institutional change grew, associational patterns in the industry began to change as well. Transnational business associations such as the European Banking Federation and the London Investment Banking Association supplanted national trade associations as the primary vehicles for lobbying. The European Commission emerged as the most sought after partner for the transformation of EU capital markets.

The role of the Commission deserves special attention. As the most fully developed of the EU's supranational bodies, it is the institution that neofunctionalists have most expected to drive EU integration (Haas 1958, Nugent 1995, Pollack 1998). But, it would be a mistake to equate the Commission's visibility with its capacity to propel integration forward. The Commission functioned as a catalyst by providing a focal point for societal actors who favoured further integration. While it was able to use what leeway it had to insert its own preferences into policy, it proved unable to advance integration if this went against the preferences of the core stakeholders in the field: the financial firms. Even rudimentary comitology procedures had not elicited agreement before 1998. Yet, by 2000, financial firms were the most vocal champions of a much more far-reaching form of comitology, complemented by a powerful 'expert' committee of national regulators. A year later, further integration was in place.

What does all this imply for established theories of supranational integration? In essence, the competition politics approach proposed in this book has a materialist core: the main factor first obstructing, and later furthering, integration was the (perceived) material interests of a relatively small group of firms. The ideational or institutional dynamics emphasised by neofunctionalism have played subordinate roles. Even though these latter have their place in the developments recounted in this book, neither adequately explains the political struggles and outcomes in the field.

The theoretical approach of this book also highlights the growing importance of transnational politics and alliances. Contemporary patterns of governance, including formal institutions, go far beyond the inter-state arrangements that continue to constitute the intellectual anchor of liberal intergovernmentalism (Moravcsik 1997, 1998). The societal actors that matter are organised transnationally, while policy-making power has been concentrated among supranational actors even more than suggested by formal flows of accountability. Member state control over capital market policy has been seriously curtailed. This suggests that, in the long run, institutional arrangements, including the state itself, reflect underlying constellations of social forces. As these forces change, so do the political institutions that channel them. Without denying the stickiness of institutions, there is nothing immutable about the state, as we know it today, as the primary forum of preference aggregation.

At the same time, the structuration perspective exposes the open-ended dynamics of political economy (cf. Cerny 2006). Actors miscalculate the results of their actions, as demonstrated by the stark example of the financial crisis that hit global finance in 2007. Bankers did not foresee that by demutualising stock exchanges, they would create fierce competitors. Second-tier banks vastly overestimated their chances in European and global investment banking; they nevertheless provided crucial political support for integration in the late 1990s when they still saw themselves as potential winners in a transnational market place. The broad structural trends that unfold over decades notwithstanding, the complexity of political economy imbues it with unpredictability. This, in all likelihood, will always remain the case.

The second main debate of this book focuses on financial liberalisation and market integration. While individual theories here do not fall under neatly circumscribed headings, the focus on competition politics highlights core weaknesses shared by most of these approaches. Most importantly, scholarship on financial liberalisation rarely has much to say about the political *process* through which it is effected. For large-n studies that try to capture the dynamics of liberalisation in quantitative terms (Quinn 1997, Abiad and Mody 2003), correlation between variables need not imply causation. When rival hypotheses remain plausible in the light of the available evidence, we need to examine the actual policy-making process to trace political change rather than just hypothesising it. This is not to deny the value of such studies, but it is useful to point to gaps that their methodologies are unable to bridge.

The same criticism applies to leading comparative case studies in the field which contain relatively 'thick' descriptions of their variables but insufficient attention to conceptualising, or even exploring empirically, the connection between them. Laurence (2001), for instance, has convincingly laid out the liberalising trajectories of British and Japanese capital markets. His conclusion that the global rise of capital mobility was responsible for this shift, however, remains insufficiently substantiated. Capital mobility is not a 'thing' in itself – it is the result of government policy. But nowhere is it empirically demonstrated how investors' preferences translate into political action. This book found that European investors' access to policy-making was much weaker than is often suggested, and that the interests of political insiders – banks in this case – were much more important. Vogel's (1996) analysis, which highlights the importance of political and economic institutions in government responses to globalisation 'pressures', also falls short in this respect.

The competition politics approach, which sees the regulatory preferences of firms as an integral part of market functioning (Underhill 2006), contests the notion that markets tend towards greater efficiency. Here theories that conceptualise markets as pre-set social spaces in which goods, services and labour are exchanged (normally against money) miss a crucial point. Markets are populated by political actors, often large organisations, which have goals that regularly defy the logic of markets as pure spaces of flows. These actors, including the state itself, use both collectively-binding rules and 'economic agency' to attain their goals and to tilt the terms of competition to their own advantage. How they do that, and how along the way they craft political institutions to solidify their grip on power, remain core questions for political economy (Underhill 2006).

There is no reason why the dynamic identified in this book as the underlying force that has led to the emergence of supranational governance should be limited to the European Union. In line with regional integration theory more generally, the demand for economic governance beyond the nation state is seen as a function of the transnational integration of market structures or, more precisely, industry structures (Mattli 1999). Such integration can take a variety of forms, ranging from simple market access abroad via the mutual recognition of home country rules to transnational rule harmonisation. The question is: when does an industry's demand for overseas market access translate into mutual market opening through regulatory means?

In order to answer this question, the argument in this book has pointed to the structure of competition in the relevant sector. We expect mutual market opening when the most important firms are no longer competing with each other on the basis of their provenance and support a transnational 'conception of control' (Fligstein 2001). This means that a new group of transnational market incumbents must have evolved for whom regulatory barriers are no longer a means for managing competition but rather obstacles to further expansion, particularly at the expense of smaller firms that continue to thrive in national market niches. If former national incumbents have either developed such a business perspective or have lost their economic significance, we can expect united calls for the demolition of regulatory barriers and, in more radical cases, integrated institutions for market governance.

In the field of transatlantic investment banking and capital markets, there is strong evidence that precisely this had been happening in the years preceding the crisis (Mügge 2006). The largest global investment banks operate from two hubs – Wall Street and the City – irrespective of their national backgrounds. Globally, less than a dozen banks dominate the business, and apart from Deutsche Bank, UBS and Credit Suisse, all these banks are American. Exchanges have also strengthened their transatlantic ties. The New York Stock Exchange took over Euronext in 2006, while NASDAQ made serious overtures to the London Stock Exchange the following year. For these firms, the regulatory barriers that still existed between the United States and the European Union were no longer competitive assets but a hindrance to the seamless integration of operations in their two most important markets. Competition politics suggests that the next steps towards integrated market governance would emerge along the Washington-Brussels axis.

Pre-crisis evidence supports this intuition. Whereas the SEC had long been loath to coordinate regulatory policy with authorities abroad (cf. Simmons 2001), it began to make concessions to EU demands in the name of transatlantic convergence, for example in the field of accounting standards (Bach and Newman 2007, Posner 2009). CESR entered negotiations with the Commodities and Futures Trading Commission, the US derivatives regulator, on the subject of facilitating transatlantic market access (Commodities and Futures Trading Commission 2005). With most of the legislative work from the FSAP completed, one of the key areas for future work identified by the Commission in its 2005–2010 White Paper was the 'external dimension', with particular attention to the EU-US regulatory dialogue (European Commission 2005b, Interview 091205).

In 2007, slow progress in transatlantic harmonisation prompted the foundation of the US-EU Coalition for Financial Regulation, a lobbying body that has its headquarters in London (Grant 2007). In April of that same year, the American Securities Industry & Financial Markets Association issued a statement calling on the US-EU summit to move forward on regulatory convergence. But just as US-EU negotiations on freer market access were getting underway, the US housing market showed its first signs of cooling after years of boom, creating ripples in the market for securitised mortgages – for most policy-makers a remote niche of little material relevance for global finance governance. Little did they realise that these ripples foreshadowed the most serious financial crisis of the post-war era, one which would call into question the project of transatlantic and, indeed, European cross-border integration.

EU CAPITAL MARKET GOVERNANCE AND THE CRISIS

This book has covered the transformation of EU financial governance until the mid-2000s – that is, just before the crisis hit; the reform proposals that have since been tabled (e.g. Financial Services Authority 2009, High-Level Group on Financial Supervision in the EU 2009, Ricol 2008) therefore fall outside its ambit. Nevertheless, the current crisis poses three pressing questions: first, did insider politics contribute to it? Second, if past policy-making has fallen short, will the future be any brighter? And thrid, will insider politics prevail in post-crisis reforms?

The current crisis is a complex phenomenon. No single theory or driving force can explain the toxic cocktail of personal greed, global imbalances, run-away financial 'innovation' and the continuing widespread faith in the regulatory prescriptions emerging from liberal economic thinking (Morris 2008, Gamble 2009, Schwartz 2009). The challenge is not to present yet another explanation of what happened, but to examine how the transfer of policy-making competencies interacted with the other factors that made financial meltdown possible.

The uploading of policy-making to Brussels was part of the political project to integrate EU capital markets across borders. The financial firms identified by this book as the driving force behind this shift had two aims: first, by freeing themselves from the shackles of regulatory fragmentation, they could pursue aggressive strategies of internationalisation. Banks embraced competition in the belief that they would all emerge as winners. Even though common sense would suggest that where some would win, others would lose, in the heady days of the European capital market boom such cautionary thinking was out of style. With the capital market pie growing so rapidly, it was thought that there would be enough for everyone to get their share. The banks' second aim was thus wedded to internationalisation: the expansion of capital market activity, including listing firms on stock markets, underwriting tradeable bonds, trading in securities, and engineering mergers and acquisitions. Banks across the continent felt the lure of the City, and were willing to open their borders to foreign competition to secure part of the fortunes being earned there.

For many European banks, the new competitive environment – in which they confronted Wall Street firms like Goldman Sachs and Morgan Stanley – was much harsher than they had anticipated. Particularly since the dot com crash, originating and trading over-the-counter derivatives, including the now infamous collateralised debt obligations, had become a leading source of profits. Gone were the days when initial public offerings and stock trading for retail investors or pension funds could secure banks a top slot in the league tables. In the new competitive environment that the European banks had themselves created, many felt that they had to emulate the most lucrative business strategies or perish. Few of the big firms were immune to the credit derivatives virus that swept investment banking. In cumulative terms, write-downs on securities holdings were much lower in Europe than in the USA (IMF 2009: 28). But as the banks themselves were much smaller, the losses were often at a level to trigger government intervention. Financial system collapse was only staved off through rock-bottom interest rates, lax central bank rules for collateral, and government promises that they would not let banks implode. In a nutshell, the banks ushered in the brave new world of European finance which turned out to be an environment too fraught with risks and dangers for them to withstand. They sowed the seeds of their own demise.

How has the supranationalisation of governance affected European countries' ability to formulate adequate regulatory responses to the crisis? As is true for supranational governance more generally, current patterns of capital market policy-making have both their strengths and weaknesses. On the one hand, they are an antidote to dissonant national responses. Financial governance is wrought with collective action problems, and the eagerness of firms to exploit regulatory arbitrage could militate against reforms unless supranational institutions enable cooperation in the formulation of new standards. In principle, a tightly integrated policy process is a boon when governments agree on what needs to be done.

It may be a bane when they disagree. Governments have locked themselves into a set of institutions that allows little room for opting out without endangering the whole regulatory edifice that supports European finance. Answers to numerous regulatory challenges will have to be European in scope, for the simple reason that they require changes to EU legislation. The need for consensus, or at least a supermajority, to legislate, complicates efforts. The UK government, concerned over the City's future as a global financial centre, will try to block any legislation which it suspects will endanger the City's position. By implication, countries wishing to pursue more far-reaching reform programmes will find their policy space severely limited.

Global agreement, should it be feasible, is the obvious way out. But here as well, the uneasy combination of supranational governance and diverging member state positions hampers effective reform (see Mügge forthcoming 2011). At the G20 summits of 2009, there was no European voice to be heard; member states were in control. But how can governments commit to international reforms when their implementation at home is contingent upon intra-European bargaining?

All these observations point to a fundamental problem in contemporary governance arrangements: they functioned smoothly as long as financial regulation remained depoliticised. However elaborate the organisational charts appeared on paper, the small size of the policy community and its members' shared framing of policy challenges allowed technocrats to move policy forward. In the case of capital markets, member states reserved the right to intervene in the work of the Commission and CESR through the European Securities Committee. But when all was plain sailing, such interventions were rare at best. The strength of supranational governance rested not only on its formal institutional design, but on the tightness of the Brussels-oriented policy community. The crisis and its attendant politicisation of regulation, however, have upset this structure. Fundamental differences between governments have emerged, with finance ministries attempting to claw back the initiative on reforms. What may have been a workable institutional arrangement in calmer times is now tested by strong, divergent government opinions.

Does this mean that insider politics in EU capital market governance is a thing of the past? It is too early to give a definitive answer. On the one hand, the financial industry has been vilified for its role in the crisis, for pushing regulatory regimes that served its own interest while betraying that of the wider public. The public trust in banks has taken a serious hit and that if for no other reason than populist electioneering, politicians on both sides of the Atlantic have doled out highly symbolic forms of punishment. Several countries decided in 2009 to impose onerous taxes on bonus payments; at the time of writing, the US administration plans to raise $90bn from banks in 2010 to pay for the costs of the crisis.

The intellectual cocoon in which regulatory policy was made has also been pried open. As head of the Financial Services Authority, Adair Turner has initiated a debate on which parts of the financial system are socially useful and which ones are not. The era in which financial innovation and expansion were automatically equated with economic progress is over. Even if regulatory answers that effectively address the reflexivity of financial markets (e.g. Soros 2008) are hard to find, the debate over policy has once again widened to include more repressive proposals than were previously acceptable.

On the other hand, the centrality of financial institutions in contemporary capitalism remains unchanged. For better or for worse, governments and non-financial firms still depend on banks and exchanges. The rescue of their financial industries has also given governments a greater role in this sector than most of them have had in decades. With the survival of core national banks at stake, governments have strong incentives to take their well-being – and regulatory preferences – to heart. As banks scale down their international ambitions, their interests may also swing back in favour of clandestine regulatory protectionism. Indeed, national positions within contemporary conflicts over hedge fund regulation, bank capital requirements and credit rating agencies betray significant overlap with the competitive preferences of domestic firms (Mügge and Stellinga forthcoming 2010). Only the future will tell whether post-crisis regulatory reforms will supersede competition politics or whether the latter will persist – now only in reverse as weakened national players come to rely on government intervention to fend off foreign competition.

GOVERNING FINANCE IN THE INTEREST OF ALL?

What are the normative implications of the changes recounted in this book? Put simply, has the supranationalisation of capital market governance in the EU been a good thing?

The *raison d'être* of the whole single market programme was to boost economic growth and thus employment (European Commission 1985, Cecchini 1988); financial services were no different (European Commission 1988a, 1988b). In economic theory, these are plausible effects of market integration. The classical political economists had already pointed to the welfare-enhancing potential of cross-border market integration, though they tended to ignore the potentially uneven distribution of the spoils. The empirical evidence on the welfare-enhancing effects of EU financial market integration is thin on the ground. Methodological problems militate against unambiguous conclusions, even when we disregard the complications the financial crisis has generated for establishing clear causal links. Existing studies already see it as a success when they are able to trace increases in financial market integration to legislative change (European Commission 2003, 2005a); the impact on welfare in the EU remains a matter of informed speculation. Evidence from the USA, however, suggests that the expansion of the financial services sector is more a sign of an upward redistribution of welfare than of its overall increase (Krippner 2005). It is far from clear that the supranationalisation of EU capital market governance has generated societal economic benefits that would justify the enterprise.

The impact of supranational governance on other goals of financial market policy is equally ambiguous. As argued above, increased cooperation among regulators has been integral to the political project of transnational market integration itself so that the net effect of the transition from the international to the supranational constellation for the public oversight of financial markets remains doubtful. They have also revealed the tight link between financial regulation and other policies, particularly those of public treasuries and central banks. As long as nationally organised tax payers provide the ultimate safety net for bank bankruptcies, it comes as no surprise that governments are reluctant to cede completely supervisory powers to supranational bodies. Supervisory fragmentation, in turn, sits uneasily next to much more integrated forms of rule-making. Institutional reforms that boost the effectiveness of one particular policy may well undermine that of another. There is no obvious way out.

In addition, supranational governance has formalised the disembedding of capital market policy from national economic policy as a whole, further shrinking the leeway for national governments to coordinate capital market regulation with other policy domains (cf. Jayasuriya 2001). Strengthened forms of supranational or international governance in the wake of the crisis will reinforce this trend. To the extent that positive coordination across policy domains was necessary for the successful functioning of social or industrial policy in coordinated market economies such as Germany or France, supranational capital market governance spurred on their transformation (cf. Schmidt 2002). The capacity of multi-level governance to coordinate across policy domains is limited. In much the same way that trade policy takes precedence over EU development policy where the two are linked, financial market policy produces policy-externalities for other issue areas that are, and remain, difficult to internalise given the EU's already complex institutional structure.

Highly technocratic, supranational policy-making limits governments' abilities to manage the externalities generated by capital market policy such as its effects on employment, the availability of credit throughout society, states' (in)ability to tax particular kinds of capital income (cf. Seabrooke 2006). Over the two decades covered by this book, a skewed version of the 'public good' has been enshrined within the rules and institutions governing European capital markets: policy was meant to ensure market stability, support economic growth and protect the users of financial services. Other societal preferences were mostly ignored.

The removal of capital market policy from effective democratic control has aggravated this trend. By definition, the rise of supranational governance decreases the scope for action by national governments. This process has gone further in practice than suggested by formal flows of accountability. At the national level, political influence has shifted away from parliaments towards executives. National parliaments still have to 'implement' EU-level decisions. But the whole Lamfalussy process is designed to minimise the scope left to them to adapt supranational rules to national imperatives. Certainly at the national level, the democratic deficit has increased (Mügge forthcoming 2010).

The complexity of EU capital market policy, both in substantive and procedural terms, makes it all but impenetrable to ordinary citizens. Existing consultation mechanisms provided by the Commission or CESR do little to change this complexity; they are de facto heavily tilted in favour of industry. Hopes for a broader democratic legitimisation of policy therefore rest on the European Parliament. The EP, however, has serious limitations. In addition to its circumscribed role in policy-making, its capacity to process information is limited. Capital markets are only a small part of the brief of the EP's Economic and Monetary Affairs Committee, while MEPs typically have no more than two or three assistants to supply them with expertise and background information on all the fields they cover. MEPs are thus at a serious disadvantage to other public actors such as the Commission, the securities regulators and national finance ministries.

On the whole, the supranationalisation of capital market governance exhibits serious legitimacy deficits: a skewed vision of legitimate policy goals has been institutionalised without installing mechanisms that would allow EU citizens to discover their own policy preferences, let alone inject them into the policy process. The lack of concern evident among members of the Brussels-focused policy community is as good a sign as any of this democratic deficit.

As for institutional reform, the dilemma can be stated simply: in the face of globalised financial markets, can political institutions be at high enough a level of aggregation to allow effective public control over these markets and at the same time be close enough to citizens to safeguard the democratic process? If the answer is no, it may be time to re-examine the case for the unhindered flow of financial funds around the globe. This book opened with the observation that in many ways, a bank like ABN AMRO today looks more like it did two decades ago than it did just before the crisis. It may have become more boring again. But this may be for the better. The financial system is too important for the public interest to allow bankers to tweak the system to their own advantage. To quote Adam Smith a final time,

> [t]he proposal of any new law or regulation of commerce which comes from [the dealers] ought always to be listened to with great precaution, and ought never to be adopted till after having been long and carefully examined, not only with the most scrupulous, but with the most suspicious attention.

As this book has shown, this warning is no less relevant today than it was when Smith first published it in 1776.

appendicies

OVERVIEW OF THE INTERNATIONAL EXPANSION OF EUROPEAN BANKS

Name	Home country	Cross-border expansion	Other indicators of internationalisation	Market share in 1986 eurobond book running market[1]	Book running market share for euro-denominated equities issued by euro-area resident firms, 2001[2]	Book running market share for euro-denominated bonds issued by euro-area resident firms, 2001
ABN AMRO	Netherlands	Acquisition of Hoare Govett in 1992, Alfred Berg A/B in Scandinavia in 1995. Joint venture with Rothschild merchant banks in 1996	60 per cent of activities abroad by 2000	1.9	7.9	4.8
Deutsche Bank	Germany	Acquisition of Morgan Grenfell in 1989, Bankers Trust and Alex. Brown in 1999	Decision in 1994 to concentrate all investment banking in London	9	7.9	9.8
Commerzbank	Germany		Moved non-DM trading and sales to London in 1994	1.5	0.4	na
Dresdner Bank	Germany	Acquisition of Kleinwort Benson in 1995		1.2	7.5	3.1
Barclays	UK	Had already bought De Zoete and Wedd Durlacher in the 1980s		0.5	na	2.5

Name	Home country	Cross-border expansion	Other indicators of internationalisation	Market share in 1986 eurobond book running market[1]	Book running market share for euro-denominated equities issued by euro-area resident firms, 2001[2]	Book running market share for euro-denominated bonds issued by euro-area resident firms, 2001
UBS	Switzerland	Bought Swiss Banking Corporation in 1998, which had itself bought S.G. Warburg in 1995		5.8	4.1	0.9
Credit Suisse	Switzerland	Control over First Boston in 1988; European presence primarily through this US firm		11.2	9.9	7.2

1. Rounded to one decimal and based on the market shares of the listed firms plus that ones that were later acquired. Data is from Ingo Walter, *Global Competition in Financial Services* (Cambridge, Mass.: American Enterprise Institute/Ballinger, 1988), p. 93.
2. 2001 data is from Inés Cabral, Frank Dierick and Jukka Vesala, *Banking Integration in the Euro Area*, December 2002, (Frankfurt: ECB, 2002).

Name	Home country	Cross-border expansion	Other indicators of internationalisation	Market share in 1986 eurobond book running market[3]	Book running market share for euro-denominated equities issued by euro-area resident firms, 2001[4]	Book running market share for euro-denominated bonds issued by euro-area resident firms, 2001
BNP	France	Buys Paribas in 1999, which has a strong international investment banking presence		1.2	2.6[5]	12.53
Paribas	France	Acquisition of JP Morgan's European custody business in 1995	Boosted its US investment banking team in 1997	3.7	na	na
Société Générale	France	Acquisition of Strauss Turnbull, a London securities house, in 1993, Crosby Securities in Hong Kong in 1996, the banking business of Hambros merchant bank in 1997 and two small Wall Street investment banks in 1997 and 1998		0.3	9.8	8.1

Name	Home country	Cross-border expansion	Other indicators of internationalisation	Market share in 1986 eurobond book running market[3]	Book running market share for euro-denominated equities issued by euro-area resident firms, 2001[4]	Book running market share for euro-denominated bonds issued by euro-area resident firms, 2001
US investment banks, added for comparison and completeness						
Morgan Stanley				4.8	11.5	8.2
Goldman Sachs				2	10.4	2.6
Merrill Lynch				3.2	9.9	2.7
JP Morgan				5.4	na	6.1
Salomon Smith Barney (later part of Citigroup)				4.6	4.2	10
Cumulative market shares of the firms listed above				56.3	86.1	78.5

3. Rounded to one decimal and based on the market shares of the listed firms plus ones that were later acquired. Data is from Ingo Walter, *Global Competition in Financial Services* (Cambridge, Mass.: American Enterprise Institute/Ballinger, 1988), p. 93.
4. 2001 data is from Inês Cabral, Frank Dierick and Jukka Vesala, *Banking Integration in the Euro Area*, December 2002, (Frankfurt: ECB, 2002).
5. Figure is for BNP Paribas.

references

Abbott, K. and Snidal, D. (2001) 'International "standards" and international governance', *Journal of European Public Policy*, 8(3): 345–70.
Abdelal, R. (2007) *Capital Rules. The Construction of Global Finance*, Cambridge MA: Harvard University Press.
Abell, P. (2003) 'On the prospects for a unified social science: economics and sociology', *Socio-Economic Review*, 1(1): 1–26.
Abiad, A. and Mody, A. (2003) *Financial Reform: What shakes it? What shapes it?*, IMF working paper 03/70., IMF, Washington DC.
Adler, E. (1991) 'Cognitive Evolution. A dynamic approach for the study of International Relations and their progress', in E. Adler, B. Crawford and J. Donnelly (eds) *Progress in Postwar International Relations*, New York: Columbia University Press.
Akerlof, G. (1970) 'The market for "lemons": Quality and the market mechanism', *Quarterly Journal of Economics*, 84: 488–500.
Allen, F. and Gale, D. (2000) *Comparing Financial Systems*, Cambridge MA: MIT Press.
Amable, B. (2000) 'Institutional complementarity and diversity of social systems of innovation and production', *Review of International Political Economy*, 7(4): 645–87.
Andrews, D. (1994) 'Capital mobility and state autonomy: Toward a structural theory of international monetary relations', *International Studies Quarterly*, 38(2): 193–218.
Ashall, P. (1993) 'The Investment Services Directive: What was the Conflict all about?' in M. Andenas and S. Kenyon-Slade (eds) *EC Financial Market Regulation and Company Law*, London: Sweet and Maxwell.
Asmussen, J., Mai, S. and Nawrath, A. (2004) 'Zur Weiterentwicklung der EU-Finanzmarktintegration', *Zeitschrift für das gesamte Kreditwesen*, 4: 28–34.
Association Française des Banques (2000a) 'Intégration du Marché Européen des Services Financièrs et des Capitaux: La Profession Bancaire Juge Positief le Rapport Préliminaire du Comité de Sages', *Actualité bancaire*, 445: 1.
Association Française des Banques (2000b) 'Présidence française de l'union européenne. Les priorités des banques françaises pur le secteur financier', *Actualité bancaire*, 440 (20 July).
Association Française des Banques (2000c) *Réponses de l'Association Française des Banques au questionnaire de la Commission Lamfalussy*, 27 September, Paris.
Augar, P. (2000) *The Death of Gentlemanly Capitalism*, London: Penguin Books.
Augar, P. (2005) *The Greed Merchants. How the Investment Banks Played the Free Market Game*, New York: Portfolio.
Augar, P. (2009) *Chasing Alpha. How Reckless Growth and Unchecked Ambition Ruined the City's Golden Decade*, London: Bodley Head.
Bach, D. and Newman, An. (2007) 'The European Regulatory State and Global Public Policy: micro-institutions, macro-influence', *Journal of European Public Policy*, 14(6): 827–46.
Bacon, R. (1993) 'EC finance rules face fresh obstacles', *Euromoney*, May 1993.
Bank of England (1994) 'The developing Single Market in financial services', *Bank of England Quarterly Bulletin*, 34(4): 341–46.
Barnett, M. and Duvall, R. (2005) 'Power in International Politics', *International Organization*, 59(1): 39–75.
Belaisch, A., Kordes, L., Levy, J. and Ubide, A. (2001) *Euro-Area Banking at the Crossroads*, IMF working paper 01/28, IMF, Washington DC.
Berger, A., Demsetz, R. and Strahan, P. (1999) 'The consolidation of the financial services industry: Causes, consequences, and implications for the future', *Journal of Banking & Finance*, 23: 135–94.
Berger, A., Deyoung, R., Genay, H. and Udell, G. (2000) 'Globalization of Financial Institutions: Evidence from Cross-Border Banking Performance', *Brookings-Wharton Papers on Financial Services*, 3: 23–158.
Berger, S. (2000) 'Globalization and Politics', *Annual Review of Political Science*, 3: 43–62.

Bergström, C. F. (2005) *Comitology: Delegation of powers in the European Union and the Committee system*, Oxford: Oxford University Press.
Bhagwati, J. (1987) 'Trade in Services and Multilateral Trade Negotiations', *World Bank Economic Review*, 1(4): 549–69.
Bieling, H.-J. (2003) 'Social Forces in the Making of the New European Economy: The Case of Financial Market Integration', *New Political Economy*, 8(2): 203–24.
Bindemann, K. (1999) *The Future of European Financial Centres*, London: Routledge.
Bishop, G. (2001) *Reflections on Two Years of the Euro Bond Market*, European Policy Centre, Brussels.
Bolkestein, F. (2001). *Letter to Christa Randzio-Plath*, 19 April 2001, Brussels.
Boot, A. (2003) 'Consolidation and Strategic Positioning in Banking with Implications for Europe', *Brookings-Wharton Papers on Financial Services*, 6: 37–83.
Bouwen, P. (2002) 'Corporate lobbying in the European Union: the logic of access', *Journal of European Public Policy*, 9(3): 365–90.
Brady, S. (1992) 'Deutsche makes its mark', *Euromoney*, June 1992: 24–9.
Braithwaite, J. and Drahos, P. (2000) *Global Business Regulation*, Cambridge: Cambridge University Press.
Bream, R. (1998) 'The calm before the storm', *Euromoney* (354).
British Bankers Association (2001) *Wise Men Final Report*, BBA, 27 February 2001, London.
Brown-Humes, C. and Norman, P. (2001) 'EU's single financial market in the balance', *Financial Times*, 23 March 2001.
Brown, P. (1997) 'The Politics of the EU Single Market for Investment Services: Negotiating the Investment Services and Capital Adequacy Directives', in G. Underhill (ed.) *The New World Order in International Finance*, Houndmills: MacMillan.
Buck, T. (2006) 'EU to unveil financial services shake-up', *Financial Times*, 6 February 2006.
Buck, T. (2007) 'Rating agencies hit by subprime probe', *Financial Times*, 16 August 2007.
Buck, T. and Cohen, N. (2006) 'EU bourses agree to cut trading costs', *Financial Times*, 1 November 2006.
Bundesaufsichtsamt für den Wertpapierhandel (1997) *Jahresbericht 1996*, Frankfurt am Main: BAWe.
Burn, G. (1999) 'The state, the City and the Euromarkets', *Review of International Political Economy*, 6(2): 225–61.
Busch, M. (2001) *Trade Warriors: States, Firms, and Strategic-Trade Policy in High-Technology Competition*, Cambridge: Cambridge University Press.
Bush, J. (1990) 'Mop-up of the 1980s mess under way', *Financial Times*, 25 June 1990.
Cabral, I., Dierick, F. and Vesala, J. (2002) *Banking Integration in the Euro Area*, ECB Occasional Paper No. 6, ECB, December 2002, Frankfurt.
Cafruny, A. and Ryner, M. (2007) 'Monetary Union and the Transatlantic and Social Dimensions of Europe's Crisis', *New Political Economy*, 12(2): 141–65.
Campbell, K. (1990) 'Bundesbank in first move to update issue practices', *Financial Times*, 10 July 1990.
Campbell, K. and Hargreaves, D. (1990) 'Frankfurt fights to regain bunds', *Financial Times*, 26 November 1990.
Carr, J. (1985a) 'Bundesbank presses for greater deregulation', *Financial Times*, 10 April 1985.
Carr, J. (1985b) 'Bundesbank to allow issue of D-Mark CDs', *Financial Times*, 20 December 1985.
Carr, J. (1985c) 'Challenge on several fronts', *Financial Times*, 13 May 1985.
Carr, J. (1985d) 'Germans see no profit in novelty', *Financial Times*, 2 August 1985.
Carr, J. (1986) 'Foreign Banks Drawn Into German Bonds Net', *Financial Times*, 14 July 1986.
Casey, J.-P. and Lannoo, K. (2005) *Europe's Hidden Capital Markets. Evolution, Architecture and Regulation of the European Bond Market*, Centre for European Policy Studies, Brussels.
Cecchini, P. (1988) *1992: the European Challenge: the Benefits of a Single Market*, Aldershot: Wildwood House.
Cerny, P. (1989) 'The 'Little Big Bang' in Paris: financial market deregulation in a *dirigiste* system', *European Journal of Political Research*, 17(2): 169–92.
Cerny, P. (1990) *The Changing Architecture of Politics: Structure, Agency, and the Future of the State*, London: Sage.
Cerny, P. (1994) 'The Infrastructure of the Infrastructure? Toward "Embedded Financial

Orthodoxy" in the International Political Economy', in R. Palan and B. Gills (eds) *Transcending the State-global Divide: A Neostructuralist Agenda in International Relations*, Boulder: Lynne Rienner.
Cerny, P. (1995) 'Globalization and the Changing Logic of Collective Action', *International Organization*, 49(4): 595–625.
Cerny, P. (1997) 'International Finance and the Erosion of Capitalist Diversity', in C. Crouch and W. Streek (eds) *Political Economy of Modern Capitalism: Mapping Convergence and Diversity*, London: Sage.
Cerny, P. (2000) 'Political Agency in a Globalizing World: Towards a Structurational Approach', *European Journal of International Relations*, 6(4): 435–63.
Cerny, P. (2006) 'Restructuring the state in a globalizing world: capital accumulation, tangled hierarchies and the search for a new spatio-temporal fix', *Review of International Political Economy*, 13(4): 679–95.
Chavagneux, C. (2001) 'Economics and politics: some bad reasons for a divorce', *Review of International Political Economy*, 8(4): 608–32.
Christiansen, T. and Jørgensen, E. (1999) *The Amsterdam Process: A Structurationist Perspective on EU Treaty Reform*, European Integration online Papers (EIoP) 3(1).
Clarke, M. (2000) *Regulation. The Social Control of Business between Law and Politics*, Houndmills: MacMillan.
Clift, B. (2004) 'Debating the Restructuring of French Capitalism and Anglo-Saxon Institutional Investors: Trojan Horses or Sleeping Partners?', *French Politics*, 2(3): 333–46.
Coen, D. (1998) 'The European Business Interest and the Nation State: Large-firm Lobbying in the European Union and Member States', *Journal of Public Policy*, 18(1): 75–100.
Coen, D. (2007) 'Empirical and theoretical studies in EU lobbying', *Journal of European Public Policy*, 14(3): 333–45.
Cohen, N. and Gangahar, A. (2007) 'Mifid ushers in a new era of trading', *Financial Times*, 23 May 2007.
Coleman, W. (1994) 'Banking, interest intermediation and political power: A framework for comparative analysis', *European Journal of Political Research*, 26: 31–58.
Coleman, W. (1996) *Financial Services, Globalization, and Domestic Policy Change*, Basingstoke: MacMillan.
Coleman, W. (1997) 'The French State, Dirigisme, and the Changing Global Financial Environment', in G. Underhill (ed.) *The New World Order in International Finance*, Houndmills: MacMillan.
Coleman, W. (2001) 'Governing French banking: regulatory reform and the Crédit Lyonnais fiasco', in M. Bovens, P., T Hart and G. Peters (eds) *Success and Failure in Public Governance: a Comparative Analysis*, Cheltenham: Edward Elgar.
Colvill, L. (1995) 'A test of nerves', *Euromoney*, (October 1995): 59–61.
Commission des Operations de Bourse (1999) *Facts & Figures 1999*, Paris: COB.
Committee of European Securities Regulators (2004) *Which supervisory tools for the EU securities markets? (Himalaya Report)*, Preliminary report, October 2004, Paris.
Committee of European Securities Regulators (2006a) *CESR Mediation Mechanism Feedback Statement and Protocol*, August 2006, Paris.
Committee of European Securities Regulators (2006b) *Protocol on Mediation Mechanism of the Committee of European Securities Regulators*, August 2006, Paris.
Committee of Wise Men (2001) *Final Report of the Committee of Wise Men on the Regulation of European Securities Markets*, 15 February 2001, Brussels.
Commodities and Futures Trading Commission (2005) *The U.S. Commodity Futures Trading Commission and the Committee of European Securities Regulators Met to Facilitate Transatlantic Derivatives Business and to Appoint Task Force to Develop Further Efforts*, Press release 5049-05, 14 February 2005, Chicago.
Corporation of London (2005) *The Competitive Position of London as a Global Financial Centre*, November 2005, London.
Corrigan, T. (1990) 'Home is where the market is', *Financial Times*, 29 November 1990.
Corrigan, T. (1992) 'SEC and regulators deadlocked over capital requirements', *Financial Times*, 30 October 1992.
Cowles, M. G. (1995) 'Setting the Agenda for a New Europe: The ERT and EC 1992', *Journal of Common Market Studies*, 33(4): 501–26.
Cowles, M. G. (2001) 'The Transatlantic Business Dialogue and Domestic Business-Government

Relations', in M. G. Cowles, J. Caporaso and T. Risse (eds) *Transforming Europe: Europeanization and Domestic Change*, Ithaca: Cornell University Press.
Cowles, M. G., Caporaso, J. and Risse, T. (eds) (2001). *Transforming Europe: Europeanization and Domestic Change*, Ithaca: Cornell University Press.
Cox, P., Simpson, H. and Jones, L. (2005) *The Future of Clearing and Settlement in Europe*, City Research Series No. 7, Corporation of London, December 2005, London.
Cox, R. (1996) *Approaches to World Order*, Cambridge: Cambridge University Press.
Crooks, E. and Norman, P. (2000) 'France retreats on EU finance regulation', *Financial Times*, 12 July 2000.
Crouch, C. and Farrell, H. (2004) 'Breaking the Path of Institutional Development? Alternatives to the New Determinism', *Rationality and Society*, 16(1): 5–43.
Crouch, C. and Streek, W. (eds) (1997). *Political Economy of Modern Capitalism: Mapping Convergence and Diversity*, London: Sage.
Culpepper, P. (2006) 'Capitalism, Coordination, and Economic Change: The French Political Economy since 1985', in P. Culpepper, P. Hall and B. Palier (eds) *Changing France: The Politics that Markets Make*, London: Palgrave MacMillan.
Cybo-Ottone, A., di Noia, C. and Murgia, M. (2000) 'Recent Development in the Structure of Securities Markets', *Brookings-Wharton Papers on Financial Services*, 3: 223–82.
Danthine, J.-P., Giavazzi, F. and von Thadden, E.-L. (2000) *European Financial Markets after EMU: A First Assessment*, NBER Working Paper 8044, National Bureau of Economic Research, Washington.
Davies, J. (1985) 'West Germans open bond sector to foreign managers', *Financial Times*, 13 April 1985.
Davison, C. (2001) 'Euro awaits single financial market', *Euromoney*, 392: 76–82.
Dawkins, W. (1991a) 'Block trading review on the way', *Financial Times*, 9 September 1991.
Dawkins, W. (1991b) 'Bourse regulators back plan for reforms', *Financial Times*, 10 July 1991.
de Haan, L. and Prast, H. (1999) *Betekenis Europese kapitaalmarkt voor de financiering van bedrijven*, Onderzoeksrapport WO&E nr. 596, De Nederlandse Bank, Amsterdam.
de Jonquieres, G. (1988) 'The City Of London Wakes Up To The Realities Of 1992', *Financial Times*, 1 March 1988.
de Larosière, J. and Lebègue, D. (2001) 'More pragmatism, please', *Financial Times*, 21 March 2001.
de Vries, J., Vroom, W. and de Graaf, T. (eds) (1999). *Wereldwijd bankieren. ABN AMRO 1824–1999*, Amsterdam: ABN AMRO Bank.
Deeg, R. (2001) *Institutional Change and the Uses and Limits of Path Dependency: The Case of German Finance*, Discussion Paper 01/6, MPIfG, Cologne.
Dehousse, R. (2003) 'Comitology: who watches the watchmen?' *Journal of European Public Policy*, 10(5): 798–813.
Demarigny, F. (1998) 'A European Directive for Regulated Markets? A French Reaction', in G. Ferrarini (ed.) *European Securities Markets. The Investment Services Directive and Beyond*, London: Kluwer International Law.
Dinan, D. (1999) *Ever Closer Union*, Houndmills: MacMillan.
Dixit, A. and Nalebuff, B. (1993) *Thinking Strategically. The Competitive Edge in Business, Politics, and Everyday Life*, New York: W.W. Norton.
Duménil, G. and Lévy, D. (2005) 'Costs and Benefits of Neoliberalism: A Class Analysis', in G. Epstein (ed.) *Financialization and the World Economy*, Cheltenham: Edward Elgar.
Echikson, W. (2001). 'European Regulation Today is Totally Outdated', *Business Week*, 3 January 2001.
ECOFIN (1998) *Conclusions of ECOFIN*, Luxembourg.
ECOFIN (2000) *Regulation of European Securities Markets. Terms of Reference for the Committee of Wise Men*, ECOFIN, 17 July 2000, Brussels.
ECOFIN (2007) *Council Conclusions on Clearing and Settlement*, Luxembourg.
Egan, M. (2001) *Constructing a European Market: Standards, Regulation and Governance*, Oxford: Oxford University Press.
Eichengreen, B. (1998) *Globalizing Capital. A History of the International Monetary System*, Princeton: Princeton University Press.
Eising, R. (2007) 'The access of business interests to EU institutions: towards élite pluralism?' *Journal of European Public Policy*, 14(3): 384–403.

Esty, D. and Geradin, D. (eds) (2001). *Regulatory Competition and Economic Integration*, Oxford: Oxford University Press.
Euromoney (1992) 'When is a bank not a bank? When it's a trading book', April 1992.
European Banker (1994a) 'Banks profit from the Single Market', 1 August 1994.
European Banker (1994b) 'Banks rely on universal structures', *Euromoney*, 1 August 1994.
European Banker (1995a) 'At what cost a French operation?', 1 March 1995.
European Banker (1995b) 'Building faith in Frankfurt', 1 July 1995.
European Banker (1995c) 'On the acquisition trail', 1 May 1995.
European Banker (1996a) 'Changes in German market', 1 January 1996.
European Banker (1996b) 'Laws and logic', 1 February 1996.
European Banker(1996c) 'New chances, new costs', 1 January 1996.
European Banker (1998) 'Major fallout from new LonFurt alliance', 1 August 1998.
European Banking Industry Committee (2004) *Launch of EBIC: A Coordinated Voice for European Banks*, 19 January 2004, Brussels.
European Commission (1985a) *Completing the Internal Market*, Brussels.
European Commission (1985b) *Time Table for Completing the Internal Market by 1992 (Annex to White Paper)*, European Commission, Brussels.
European Commission (1988a) 'Creating a European Financial Area', *European Economy*, 36.
European Commission (1988b) 'Services case-studies. Financial services', *European Economy*, 35: 86–94.
European Commission (1998) *Financial Services: Building a Framework for Action*, 28 October 1998, Brussels.
European Commission (1999a) *Financial Services Action Plan Forum Group on the ISD Green Paper: Issues Paper for the First Meeting of the Group*, October 1999, Brussels.
European Commission (1999b) *Financial Services Policy Group – third meeting*, Press release, European Commission, 26 March 1999, Brussels.
European Commission (1999c) *Financial Services: Implementing the Framework for Financial Markets: Action Plan*, Brussels.
European Commission (1999d) *First meeting of the Financial Services Policy Group*, Press release, European Commission, 28 January 1999, Brussels.
European Commission (2000) *Non-Paper. Preparing the Review of the Investment Services Directive: Key Issues*, June 2000, Brussels.
European Commission (2001) *Commission Decisions establishing the European Securities Committee and the Committee of European Securities Regulators – Frequently Asked Questions*, Press release, 6 June 2001, Brussels.
European Commission (2002) *Financial markets: Commission welcomes Parliament's agreement on Lamfalussy proposals for reform*, Press release, 5 February 2002, Brussels.
European Commission (2003) *Tracking EU Financial Integration*, Brussels.
European Commission (2005a) *Annex III to the White Paper on Financial Services Policy (2005–2010): Resumé of Contributions received from Market Participants on the Green Paper on Financial Services Policy (2005–2010)*, Brussels.
European Commission (2005b) *Financial Integration Monitor. 2005 Update. Annex to background document*, Brussels.
European Commission (2005c) *White Paper Financial Services Policy 2005–2010*, December 2005, Brussels.
European Commission (2006a) *European Securities Markets Expert Group (ESME). [List of members]*, June 2006, Brussels.
European Commission (2006b) *European Securities Markets Expert Group (ESME): Terms of Reference*, June 2006, Brussels.
European Commission (2007a) *FSAP Evaluation. Part I: Process and implementation*, January 2007, Brussels.
European Commission (2007b) *Single Market in Financial Services Progress Report 2006*, Brussels.
European Commission (2008) *Single Euro Payments Area (SEPA): Commission publishes major cost-benefit study*, Press release MEMO/08/25, 28 January 2008, Brussels.
European Council (1998a) *Presidency Conclusions Cardiff European Council*, 15–16 June 1998.
European Council (1998b) *Presidency Conclusions Vienna European Council*, 11–12 December 1998.
European Council (1999) *Presidency Conclusions Cologne European Council*, 3–4 June 1999.
European Council (2000) *Presidency Conclusions Lisbon European Council*, 23–24 March 2000.

European Council (2001) *Presidency Conclusions Stockholm European Council*, 23–24 March 2001.
European Financial Services Round Table (2004) *Towards a lead supervisor for cross border financial institutions in the European Union*, June 2004, Brussels.
European Parliament Committee on Constitutional Affairs (2001) *Report on the implementation of financial services legislation (von Wogau report)*, Doc A5-0011/2002, European Parliament, 23 January 2002, Brussels.
European Savings Banks Group (1998) *The European Savings Banks Group contribution to the European Commission's Framework for Action to improve the Single Market in financial services*, 12 August 1998, Brussels.
Eurostat (2001) *Special Feature on Banking*, Office for Official Publications of the European Communities, Luxembourg.
Evans, G. (1992) 'Bundesbank clings to power', *Euromoney*, April 1992: 55–7.
Federal Trust (2001a) *European Capital Markets Regulation*, 8 February 2001, London.
Federal Trust (2001b) *Reaction to The Wise Men's Final Report*, 13 March 2001, London.
Federation of European Securities Commissions (2000) *Implementation of Article 11 of the ISD: Categorisation of Investors for the Purpose of Conduct of Business Rules*, FESCO, Paris.
Federation of European Securities Exchanges (2000) *Report and Recommendations on European Regulatory Structures*, Press release, 21 September 2000, Brussels.
Feld, W. (1970) 'Political Aspects of Transnational Business Collaboration in the Common Market', *International Organization*, 24(4): 209–38.
FESE, FOA, ISDA, IPMA, ISMA, LIBA, SSDA and EBF (2003) *Joint Response to the Inter-Institutional Monitoring Group First Interim Report*, 7 July 2003.
Fidler, S. (1987) 'Deregulate or risk being left behind', *Financial Times*, 21 October 1987.
Filipovic, M. (1997) *Governments, Banks and Global Capital*, Aldershot: Ashgate.
Financial Regulation Report (1994a) 'CSFB obtains special membership of the Amsterdam Stock Exchange', September 1994.
Financial Regulation Report (1994b) 'Deutsche Bank Spa takes on the Italian Banks', October 1994.
Financial Regulation Report (1994c) 'Rules relaxed for US banks', May 2006.
Financial Regulation Report (1995a) 'Implementation of the ISD', July 1995.
Financial Regulation Report (1995b) 'Proposed Securities Committee to be responsible for CAD and ISD issues', September 1995.
Financial Regulation Report (1995c) 'Securities Committee to be established', September 1995.
Financial Regulation Report (1996a) 'EASDAQ to launch in September', June 1996.
Financial Regulation Report (1996b) 'The ISD in action: liberalization like this, who needs protectionism?', March 1996.
Financial Regulation Report (1996c) 'ISD law approved', July 1996.
Financial Regulation Report (1996d) 'Proposal for a Securities Committee responsible for CAD and ISD issues', July 1996.
Financial Regulation Report (1996e) 'Proposal for a Securities Committee responsible for CAD and ISD issues [1]', May 1996.
Financial Regulation Report (1997) 'Proposed Securities Committee to be responsible for CAD and ISD issues', May 1997.
Financial Regulation Report (1998a) 'Implementation of the ISD: Germany', January 1998.
Financial Regulation Report (1998b) 'Bundestag adopts major financial regulations', March 1998.
Financial Regulation Report (1998c) 'Securities committee still stuck', March 1998.
Financial Services Authority (1999) *The FSA announces view on regulation in Europe*, 19 April 1999, London.
Financial Services Authority (2009) *The Turner Review. A regulatory response to the banking crisis*, March 2009, London.
Fisher, A. (1988) 'Bond Future For German Options Exchange', *Financial Times*, 27 July 1988.
Fisher, A. and Cohen, N. (1994) 'A convergence of cultures: Deutsche Bank's merger plans', *Financial Times*, 29 October 1994.
Flier, B. (2003) *Strategic Renewel of European Financial Incumbents: Coevolution of Environmental Selection, Institutional Effects, and Managerial Intentionality*, Rotterdam: Erasmus University.

Fligstein, N. (2001) *The Architecture of Markets: An Economic Sociology of Twenty-First-Century Capitalist Societies*, Princeton: Princeton University Press.

Fligstein, N. and Mara-Drita, I. (1996) 'How to Make a Market: Reflections on the Attempt to Create a Single Market in the European Union', *American Journal of Sociology*, 102(1): 1–33.

Franke, G. (2000) 'Deutsche Finanzmarktregulierung nach dem Zweiten Weltkrieg zwischen Risikoschutz und Wettbewerbssicherung', *Bankhistorisches Archiv*, Beiheft 39: 66–87.

Frieden, J. (1991) ‚Invested Interests: The Politics of National Economic Policies in a World of Global Finance', *International Organization*, 45(4): 425–52.

Froud, J., Johal, S., Leaver, A. and Williams, K. (2006) *Financialization and Strategy. Narrative and Numbers*, London: Routledge.

Gadinis, S. (2008) 'The Politics of Competition in International Financial Regulation', Harvard International Law Journal, 49(2): 447–507. Gamble, A. (2009) *The Spectre at the Feast. Capitalist Crisis and the Politics of Recession*, Houndmills: Palgrave MacMillan.

Gapper, J. (1996) 'Survey of European Stock Exchanges', *Financial Times*, 16 February 1996.

Gardener, E. and Molyneux, P. (1990) *Changes in Western European Banking*, London: Unwin Hyman.

Gardener, E., Molyneux, P. and Moore, B. (2001) 'The impact of the single market programme on EU banking', *The Service Industries Journal*, 21(2): 47–70.

Garrett, G. (1992) 'International Cooperation and Institutional Choice: The European Community's Internal Market', *International Organization*, 46(2): 533–60.

Garrett, G. (1998) 'Global Markets and National Politics: Collision Course or Virtuous Circle?' *International Organization*, 52(4): 787–824.

George, A. and Bennett, A. (2005) *Case Studies and Theory Development in the Social Sciences*, Cambridge, MA: MIT Press.

Gertler, M. (1988) 'Financial Structure and Aggregate Economic Activity: An Overview', *Journal of Money, Credit and Banking*, 20(3, Part II): 559–88.

Giddens, A. (1984) *The Constitution of Society: Outline of the Theory of Structuration*, Cambridge: Polity Press.

Gill, S. and Law, D. (1989) 'Global Hegemony and the Structural Power of Capital', *International Studies Quarterly*, 33(4): 475–99.

Gjersem, C. (2003) *Financial Market Integration in the Euro Area*, Economics Department Working Paper No. 368, OECD, Paris.

Glyn, A. (2006) *Capitalism Unleashed. Finance, Globalization and Welfare*, Oxford: Oxford University Press.

Goldberg, L., Hanweck, G., Keenan, M. and Young, A. (1991) 'Economies of scale and scope in the securities industry', *Journal of Banking & Finance*, 15: 91–107.

Goldberg, L., Kambhu, J., Mahoney, J., Radecki, L. and Sarkar, A. (2002) 'Securities Trading and Settlement in Europe: Issues and Outlook', *Current Issues in Economics and Finance*, 8(4): 1–6.

Goldstein, D. (1995) 'Uncertainty, Competition, and Speculative Finance in the Eighties', *Journal of Economic Issues*, XXIX(3): 719–46.

Goodhart, C., Hartmann, P., Llewellyn, D. and Rojas-Suarez, L. (1998) *Financial Regulation: Why, How, and Where Now?*, London: Routledge.

Gottwald, J.-C. (2005) *Die politische Gestaltung des europäischen Finanzmarktes*, unpublished habilitation manuscript, Universität Trier, Trier.

Graham, G. (1987a) ‚Matif seeks wider foreign membership', *Financial Times*, 27 January 1987.

Graham, G.(1987b) ‚French bourse flourishes after years of evolution', *Financial Times*, 11 March 1987.

Graham, G. (1987c) 'A late run for the winning post', *Financial Times*, 7 April 1987.

Graham, G. (1987d) 'Asking hard questions', *Financial Times*, 2 December 1987.

Graham, G. (1988a) 'After the scandal, the real trouble starts', *Financial Times*, 4 July 1988.

Graham, G. (1988b) 'Major reforms under way', *Financial Times*, 29 September 1988.

Graham, G. (1989a) 'Reform marred by contradiction and confusion', *Financial Times*, 3 July 1989.

Graham, G. (1989b) 'Taste for regulation revived', *Financial Times*, 2 November 1989.

Graham, G. (1990) 'Tuffier collapse highlights decline in commission rates', *Financial Times*, 22 October 1990.

Grant, Jeremy (2007) 'Transatlantic harmony is in the air'. *Financial Times*. London: 26 September, p. 13.
Greenwood, J. (2003) *Interest representation in the European Union*, New York: Palgrave MacMillan.
Grilli, V. (1989) 'Financial Markets and 1992', *Brooking Papers on Economic Activity*,(2): 301–24.
Groom, B. and Norman, P. (2001) 'Single market for EU financial services', *Financial Times*, 23 March 2001.
Grossman, E. (2004) 'Bringing politics back in: rethinking the role of economic interest groups in European integration', *Journal of European Public Policy*, 11(4): 637–54.
Group of Ten (2001) *Report on Consolidation in the Financial Sector*, Basle: BIS.
Haas, E. (1958) *The Uniting of Europe: Political, Economic and Social Forces, 1950–1957*, London: Stevens & Sons.
Haas, P. (1992) 'Introduction: Epistemic Communities and International Policy Coordination', *International Organization*, 46(1): 1–35.
Haggard, S., Lee, C. and Maxfield, S. (eds) (1993). *The Politics of Finance in Developing Countries*, Ithaca: Cornell University Press.
Haggard, S. and Simmons, B. (1987) 'Theories of International Regimes', *International Organization*, 41(3): 491–517.
Hall, P. (1993) 'Policy paradigms, social learning and the state: the case of economic policy making in Britain', *Comparative Politics*, 25: 275–96.
Hall, P. and Soskice, D. (2001a) 'An Introduction of Varieties of Capitalism', in P. Hall and D. Soskice (eds) *Varieties of Capitalism: The Institutional Foundations of Comparative Economic Advantage*, Oxford: Oxford University Press.
Hall, P. and Soskice, D. (eds) (2001b). *Varieties of Capitalism: The Institutional Foundations of Comparative Advantage*, Oxford: Oxford University Press.
Hall, P. and Taylor, R. (1996) 'Political Science and the Three New Institutionalisms', *Political Studies*, 44(4): 936–57.
Hancher, L. and Moran, M. (1989) 'Organizing Regulatory Space', in L. Hancher and M. Moran (eds) *Capitalism, Culture, and Economic Regulation*, Oxford: Clarendon Press.
Handelsblatt (1990) 'Finanzplatz Deutschland. Brainstorming in Bonn', *Handelsblatt*, 1 February 1990.
Handelsblatt (1998) 'Megafusion im Umfang von 136 Milliarden Dollar in den USA', *Handelsblatt*, 7 April 1998.
Handelsblatt (1999) 'Letzter Appell der Santer-Kommission', *Handelsblatt*, 12 May 1999.
Hardy, D. (2006) *Regulatory Capture in Banking*, Washington.
Harverson, P. and Campbell, K. (1990) 'Wall St yields to Deutsche Bank', *Financial Times*, 20 December 1990.
Hasenclever, A., Mayer, P. and Rittberger, V. (1997) *Theories of International Regimes*, Cambridge: Cambridge University Press.
Hay, C. and Rosamond, B. (2002) 'Globalization, European integration and the discursive construction of economic imperatives', *Journal of European Public Policy*, 9(2): 147–67.
Helleiner, E. (1994) *States and the Reemergence of Global Finance: From Bretton Woods to the 1990s*, Ithaca: Cornell University Press.
Henwood, D. (1997) *Wall Street*, London: Verso.
Herring, R. and Litan, R. (1995) *Financial Regulation in the Global Economy*, Washington DC: The Brookings Institution.
Hertig, G. (2001) 'Regulatory Competition for EU Financial Services', in D. Esty and D. Geradin (eds) *Regulatory Competition and Economic Integration*, Oxford: Oxford University Press.
High-Level Group on Financial Supervision in the EU (2009) *Report [De Larosière Report]*, 25 February 2009, Brussels.
Hillman, A. and Hitt, M. (1999) 'Corporate Political Strategy Formulation: A Model of Approach, Participation, and Strategy Decisions', *The Academy of Management Review*, 24(4): 825–42.
HM Treasury, Financial Services Authority and Bank of England (2003) *The EU Financial Services Action Plan: A Guide*, London.
Hobson, J. and Ramesh, M. (2002) 'Globalisation makes of States what States make of it:

Between Agency and Structure and the State/Globalisation Debate', *New Political Economy*, 7(1): 5–22.
Hoffmann, S. (1966) 'Obstinate or Obsolete? The Fate of the Nation-State and the Case of Western Europe', *Daedalus*, 95(3): 862–915.
Holland, C., Lockett, G. and Blackman, I. (1998) 'Global strategies to overcome the spiral of decline in universal bank markets', *Journal of Strategic Information Systems*, 7: 217–32.
Hooghe, L. and Marks, G. (2001) *Multi-level governance and European Integration*, Lanham: Rowman & Littlefield.
Hutton, R. (1989). Speech given at the FT European Banking Conference, 15 May 1989, *Financial Times*.
Ibanez, D. M. and Molyneux, P. (2002) 'Financial Restructuring in European Banking and Foreign Expansion', *Latin American Business Review*, 3(4): 19–57.
Icard, A. and Drumetz, F. (1994) 'Développement de Marchés de Titres et Financement de l'Economie Française', *Bulletin de la Banque de France*, 6: 83–106.
Ikenberry, J. (1988) 'Conclusion: an institutional approach to American foreign economic policy', *International Organization*, 42(1): 219–43.
Inter-Institutional Monitoring Group (2003) *First Interim Report Monitoring the Process for Regulating Securities Markets in Europe (The Lamfalussy Process)*, Inter-Instititutional Monitoring Group, Brussels.
International Monetary Fund (2009) *Global Financial Stability Report*, Washington DC.
Ipsen, E. (1995) '2 U.K. firms that would be giants', *International Herald Tribune*, 28 August 1995.
Jabko, N. (2006) *Playing the Market. A Political Strategy for Uniting Europe, 1985–2005*, Ithaca: Cornell University Press.
Jachtenfuchs, M. (2001) 'The Governance Approach to European Integration', *Journal of Common Market Studies*, 39(2): 245–64.
Jackson, H. and Pan, E. (2001) 'Regulatory Competition in International Securities Markets: Evidence from Europe in 1999–Part I', *Business Lawyer*, 56: 653.
Jayasuriya, K. (2001) 'Globalization and the changing architecture of the state: the regulatory state and the politics of negative co-ordination', *Journal of European Public Policy*, 8(1): 101–23.
Jenkins, P. (2004). 'Investment banks: Sad tale of those who followed Deutsche', *Financial Times*, 8 December 2004.
Jervis, R. (1997) *System effects: complexity in political and social life*, Princeton: Princeton University Press.
Joerges, C. and Neyer, J. (1997) 'From Intergovernmental Bargaining to Deliberative Political Process: The Constitutionalization of Comitology', *European Law Journal*, 3(3): 273–99.
Josselin, D. (1997) *Money Politics in the New Europe. Britain, France, and the Single Financial Market*, Basingstoke: MacMillan.
Jupille, J. and Caporaso, J. (1999) 'Institutionalism and the European Union: Beyond International Relations and Comparative Politics', *Annual Review of Political Science*, 2: 429–44.
Kapstein, E. (1992) 'Between power and purpose: central bankers and the politics of regulatory convergence', *International Organization*, 46(1): 265–87.
Keohane, R. (1988) 'International Institutions: Two Approaches', *International Studies Quarterly*, 32(4): 379–96.
Keohane, R. and Hoffman, S. (1991) 'Institutional Change in Europe in the 1980s', in R. Keohane and S. Hoffman (eds) *The New European Community: Decision-making and Institutional Change*, Boulder: Westview Press.
Keohane, R. and Milner, H. (eds) (1996). *Internationalization and Domestic Politics*, Cambridge: Cambridge University Press.
Kohler-Koch, B. and Eising, R. (eds) (1999). *The Transformation of Governance in the European Union*, London: Routledge.
Krasner, S. (ed.) (1983). *International Regimes*, Ithaca: Cornell University Press.
Krasner, S. (1984) 'Approaches to the State: Alternative Conceptions and Historical Dynamics', *Comparative Politics*, 16(2): 223–46.
Krätke, M. and Underhill, G. (2006) 'Political Economy: the Revival of an "Interdiscipline"', in R. Stubbs and G. Underhill (eds) *Political Economy and the Changing Global Order*, Toronto: Oxford University Press.

Kraus, J. (1994) 'France's Banque Paribas sets sights on building its U.S. merchant bank', *The American Banker*, 11 January 1994.
Krippner, G. (2005) 'The financialization of the American economy', *Socio-Economic Review*, 3(2): 173–208.
Kroszner, R. and Strahan, P. (1999) 'What drives deregulation? Economics and politics of the relaxation of bank branching restrictions', *Quarterly Journal of Economics*, 114(4): 1437–67.
Kroszner, R. and Strahan, P. (2000) *Obstacles to Optimal Policy: The Interplay of Politics and Economics in Shaping Bank Supervision and Regulation Reforms*, NBER working paper 7582, Cambridge MA.
Krugman, P. (ed.) (1986). *Strategic Trade Policy and the New International Economics*, Cambridge MA: MIT Press.
Lalone, N. (2005) 'An Awkward Partner: Explaining France's Troubled Relationship to the Single Market in Financial Services', *French Politics*, 3: 211–33.
Lane, C. (2000) 'Globalization and the German model of capitalism – erosion or survival?', *British Journal of Sociology*, 51(2): 207–34.
Lascelles, D. (1988a) 'City lobby group aims to regain influence', *Financial Times*, 14 May 1988.
Lascelles, D. (1988b) 'Question mark hangs over future importance of City in single market', *Financial Times*, 4 July 1988.
Laurence, H. (2001) *Money Rules: The New Politics of Finance in Britain and Japan*, Ithaca: Cornell University Press.
Lazer, D. (2001) 'Regulatory interdependence and international governance', *Journal of European Public Policy*, 8(3): 474–92.
Lee, P. (1992) 'Securities houses face capital clampdown', *Euromoney*, April 1992.
Lee, R. (1998) *What is an Exchange? The Automation, Management and Regulation of Financial Markets*, Oxford: Oxford University Press.
Lee, R. (2002) 'The Future of Securities Exchanges', *Brookings-Wharton Papers on Financial Services*, 5: 1–33.
Lehmann, P.-J. (1997) *Histoire de la Bourse de Paris*, Paris: Presses universitaires de France.
Les Echos (1999) 'Les entreprises françaises sont favourable à la bourse pan-européenne, mais pas a n'importe quel prix', 20 July 1999.
Leyshon, A. and Thrift, N. (1992) 'In the wake of money: the City of London and the accumulation of value', in L. Budd and S. Whimster (eds) *Global Finance and Urban Living: The Case of London*, London: Routledge.
Lindberg, L. (1963) *The Political Dynamics of European Economic Integration*, Stanford: Stanford University Press.
Lindblom, C. (1977) *Politics and Markets. The World's Political Economic Systems*, New York: Basic Books.
Loriaux, M. (1991) *France after Hegemony: International Change and Financial Reform*, Ithaca: Cornell University Press.
Lütz, S. (2000) *From Managed to Market Capitalism? German Finance in Transition*, Köln: Max-Planck-Institut für Gesellschaftforschung.
Lütz, S. (2002) *Der Staat und die Globalisierung von Finanzmärkten*, Frankfurt am Main: Campus.
Lütz, S. (2003a) *Convergence within National Diversity: A Comparative Perspective on the Regulatory State in Finance*, MPIfG Discussion Paper 03/7, Cologne.
Lütz, S. (2003b) 'Finanzmarktregulierung: Globalisierung und der regulative Umbau des "Modell Deutschland"', in R. Czada, S. Lütz and S. Mette (eds) *Regulative Politik: Zähmung von Markt und Technik*, Opladen: Leske + Budrich.
Mahoney, P. (2002) ‚Information Technology and the Organization of Securities Markets', *Brookings-Wharton Papers on Financial Services*, 5: 345–50.
Marks, G., Hooghe, L. and Blank, K. (1996) 'European Integration from the 1980s: State-centric v. Multi-level Governance', *Journal of Common Market Studies*, 34(3): 341–78.
Mattli, W. (1999) *The Logic of Regional Integration*, Cambridge: Cambridge University Press.
Mattli, W. and Büthe, T. (2003) 'Setting International Standards: Technological Rationality or Primacy of Power?', *World Politics*, 56: 1–42.
McCahery, J. (1997) 'Market Integration and Particularistic Interests: The Dynamics of Insider Trading Regulation in the US and Europe', in G. Underhill (ed.) *The New World Order in International Finance*, Houndmills: MacMillan.

McCahery, J. and Geradin, D. (2004) 'Regulatory co-opetition: transcending the regulatory competition debate', in D. Levi-Faur and J. Jordana (eds) *The Politics of Regulation*, Aldershot: Edward Elgar.

McClelland, C. (1997) 'Die Deutsche Bank investiert in ihr Nordamerika-Geschäft', *Handelsblatt*, 29 October 1997.

McKeen-Edwards, H., Porter, T. and Roberge, I. (2004) 'Politics or Markets? The Determinants of Cross-Border Financial Integration in the NAFTA and the EU', *New Political Economy*, 9(3): 325–40.

McKenzie, G. and Khalidi, M. (1996) 'The globalization of banking and financial markets: the challenge for European regulators', *Journal of European Public Policy*, 3(4): 629–46.

McKinsey (2007) *Sustaining New York's and the US' Global Financial Services Leadership*, Report commissioned by New York senator Charles Schumer and New York mayor Michael Bloomberg, January 2007, New York.

McNamara, K. (2002) 'Rational Fictions: Central Bank Independence and the Social Logic of Delegation', *West European Politics*, 25(1): 47–76.

Mijs, W. and Caparrós Puebla, A. (2002) 'Making the Single Market in Financial Services a Reality', in R. Pedler (ed.) *European Union Lobbying: Changes in the Arena*, Houndmills: Palgrave MacMillan.

Milbourn, T., Boot, A. and Thakor, A. (1999) 'Megamergers and expanded scope: Theories of bank size and activity diversity', *Journal of Banking & Finance*, 23: 195–214.

Milner, H. (1988) *Resisting Protectionism: global industries and the politics of international trade*, Princeton: Princeton University Press.

Milner, H. and Keohane, R. (1996) 'Internationalization and Domestic Politics: An Introduction', in R. Keohane and H. Milner (eds) *Internationalization and Domestic Politics*, Cambridge: Cambridge University Press.

Milner, H. and Yoffie, D. (1989) 'Between free trade and protectionism: strategic trade policy and a theory of corporate trade demands', *International Organization*, 43(2): 239–72.

Milonakis, D. and Fine, B. (2008) *From Political Economy to Economics. Method, the Social and the Historical in the Evolution of Economic Theory*, London: Routledge.

Mitchell, T. (2002) *Rule of Experts: Egypt, Techno-Politics, Modernity*, Berkeley: University of California Press.

Moir, C. (1997) 'Barriers go up in Europe', *Financial Times*, 28 February 1997.

Moran, M. (1984a) *The Politics of Banking*, London: MacMillan.

Moran, M. (1984b) 'Politics, Banks and Markets: An Anglo-American Comparison', *Political Studies*, 32(2): 173–89.

Moran, M. (1991) *The Politics of the Financial Services Revolution*, Houndmills: MacMillan.

Moravcsik, A. (1991) 'Negotiating the Single European Act: national interests and conventional statecraft in the European Community', *International Organization*, 45(1): 19–56.

Moravcsik, A. (1993) 'Preferences and Power in the European Community: A Liberal Intergovernmentalist Approach', *Journal of Common Market Studies*, 31(4): 473–524.

Moravcsik, A. (1997) 'Taking Preferences Seriously: A Liberal Theory of International Politics', *International Organization*, 51(4): 513–53.

Moravcsik, A. (1998) *The Choice for Europe: Social purpose and State Power from Messina to Maastricht*, Ithaca: Cornell University Press.

Morgan, G. and Kubo, I. (2005) 'Beyond path dependency? Constructing new models for institutional change: the case of capital markets in Japan', *Socio-Economic Review*, 3: 55–82.

Morin, F. (2000) 'A transformation in the French model of shareholding and management', *Economy and Society*, 29(1): 36–53.

Morris, C. (2008) *The Trillion Dollar Meltdown. Easy Money, High Rollers, and the Great Credit Crash*, New York: Public Affairs.

Mosley, L. (2003) *Global Capital and National Governments*, Cambridge: Cambridge University Press.

Mügge, D. (2006) 'Private-Public Puzzles. Inter-firm competition and transnational private regulation', *New Political Economy*, 11(2): 177–200.

Mügge, D. (forthcoming 2010) 'Limits of Legitimacy and the Primacy of Politics in Financial Governance', *Review of International Political Economy*.

Mügge, D. (forthcoming 2011) 'The European presence in global financial governance: a principal-agent perspective', *Journal of European Public Policy*.

Mügge, D. and Stellinga, B. (forthcoming 2010) 'Absent alternatives and insider interests in post-crisis financial reform', *der moderne staat*.
Neyer, J. (2003) 'Discourse and Order in the EU: A Deliberative Approach to Multi-Level Governance', *Journal of Common Market Studies*, 41(4): 687–706.
Nicoll, S. (1993) 'Years of change: securities markets in Europe 1972–92', *European Business Journal*, 5(1): 23–30.
Niemann, A. (2006) *Explaining Decisions in the European Union*, Cambridge: Cambridge University Press.
Nordlinger, E. (1981) *On the Autonomy of the Democratic State*, Cambridge MA: Harvard University Press.
Norman, P. (2000a) 'European SEC plan spurned', *Financial Times*, 16 September 2000.
Norman, P. (2000b) 'Powerful financial services reform body urged', *Financial Times*, 10 November 2000.
Norman, P. (2001a) 'Lamfalussy securities plan hits opposition', *Financial Times*, 28 February 2001.
Norman, P. (2001b) 'Ministers urged to back Lamfalussy report', *Financial Times*, 21 March 2001.
Nugent, N. (1995) 'The leadership capacity of the European Commission', *Journal of European Public Policy*, 2(4): 602–23.
Oatley, T and Nabors, R. (1998) 'Redistributive Cooperation: Market Failure, Wealth Transfers, and the Basle Accord', *International Organization*, 51(1): 35–54.
Observer (1994) 'Trading places', *Financial Times*, 19 April 1994.
OECD (2000) 'Cross-Border Trade in Financial Services: Economics and Regulation', *OECD Financial Market Trends*, 75(March): 23–60.
Olson, M. (1965) *The Logic of Collective Action: Public Goods and the Theory of Groups*, Cambridge MA: Harvard University Press.
Osborn, A. (2000) 'UK fights plans for regulator: Brown to oppose European body', *The Guardian*, 17 July 2000.
Overbeck, H. and D'Alessio, N. (1997) 'The End of the German Model? Developmental Tendencies in the German Banking Industry', in G. Morgan and D. Knights (eds) *Regulation and Deregulation in European Financial Services*, London: MacMillan.
Pagano, M. and Steil, B. (1996) 'Equity Trading I: The Evolution of European Trading Systems', in B. Steil (ed.) *The European Equity Markets: The State of the Union and an Agenda for the Millennium*, London: Royal Institute of International Affairs.
Partnoy, F. (2002) *Infectious Greed: How Deceit and Risk Corrupted the Financial Markets*, New York: Times Books.
Pauly, L. (1988) *Opening Financial Markets: Banking Politics on the Pacific Rim*, Ithaca: Cornell University Press.
Pauly, L. (1995) 'Capital Mobility, State Autonomy and Political Legitimacy', *International Affairs*, 48(2): 369–88.
Peters, G. and Pierre, J. (2001) 'Developments in intergovernmental relations: towards multi-level governance', *Policy & Politics*, 29(2): 131–35.
Pierre, J. and Peters, G. (2002) *Governance, Politics and the State*, New York: St. Martin's Press.
Pierson, P. (1996) 'The Path to European Integration: A Historical Institutionalist Analysis', *Comparative Political Studies*, 29(2): 123–63.
Pierson, P. (2000a) 'Increasing returns, path dependence, and the study of politics', *American Political Science Review*, 94(2): 251–67.
Pierson, P. (2000b) 'The Limits of Design: Explaining Institutional Origins and Change', *Governance*, 13(4): 475–99.
Pollack, M. (1997) 'Delegation, agency and agenda setting in the European Community', *International Organization*, 51(1): 99–134.
Pollack, M. (1998) 'The Engines of Integration? Supranational Autonomy and Influence in the European Union', in W. Sandholtz and A. Stone Sweet (eds) *European Integration and Supranational Governance*, Oxford: Oxford University Press.
Pollack, M. (2004) 'The New Institutionalisms and European Integration', in A. Wiener and T. Diez (eds) *European Integration Theory*, Oxford: Oxford University Press.
Porter, T. (1993) *States, Markets and Regimes in Global Finance*, New York: St. Martin's Press.
Porter, T. (2005) *Globalization and Finance*, Cambridge: Polity Press.
Posner, E. (2009a) 'Making Rules for Global Finance: Transatlantic Regulatory Cooperation at

the Turn of the Millennium', *International Organization*, 63(4): 665–99.
Posner, E. (2009b) *The Origins of Europe's New Stock Markets*, Cambridge MA, Harvard University Press.
Prada, M. (2000) *Integration and Regulation of the European Financial Market*, Speech at Eurofi conference, 15 September 2000, Paris.
Private Banker International (1996) 'Bull on the rampage', May 1996.
Puchala, D. (1972) 'Of Blind Men, Elephants and International Integration', *Journal of Common Market Studies*, 10(3): 267–84.
Putnam, R. (1988) 'Diplomacy and domestic politics: the logic of two-level games', *International Organization*, 42(3): 427–60.
Quaglia, L. (2008) 'Setting the pace? Private financial interests and European financial market integration', *British Journal of Politics and International Relations*, 10(1): 46–64.
Quinn, D. (1997) 'The Correlates of Change in International Financial Regulation', *American Political Science Review*, 91(3): 531–51.
Quinn, D. and Inclan, C. (1997) 'The Origins of Financial Openness: A Study of Current and Capital Account Liberalization', *American Journal of Political Science*, 41: 771–813.
Radice, H. (2000) 'Globalization and national capitalisms: theorizing convergence and differentiation', *Review of International Political Economy*, 7(4): 719–42.
Rajan, R. and Zingales, L. (2003) *Banks and Markets: The Changing Character of European Finance*, NBER working paper 9595, Cambridge MA.
Randzio-Plath, C. (2001) *Letter to Frits Bolkestein*, 2 May 2001, Brussels.
Rawsthorn, A. (1992) 'French try to recapture lost trade in securities', *Financial Times*, 7 February 1992.
Rhinard, M. (2002) 'The Democratic Legitimacy of the European Union Committee System', *Governance*, 15(2): 185–210.
Rhodes, R. (1997) *Understanding Governance*, Buckingham: Open University Press.
Ricol, R. (2008) *Report to the President of the French Republic on the Financial Crisis*, September 2008, Paris.
Riley, B. (1985) 'Weighing up the Eurobond market', *Financial Times*, 10 July 1985.
Riley, B. (1989) 'City wants uniform EC market controls', *Financial Times*, 28 June 1989.
Risse-Kappen, T. (1996) 'Exploring the Nature of the Beast: International Relations Theory and Comparative Policy Analysis Meet the European Union', *Journal of Common Market Studies*, 34(1): 53–80.
Risse, T. (2000) '"Let's argue!": Communicative action in world politics', *International Organization*, 54(1): 1–39.
Risse, T. (2004) 'Social Constructivism and European Integration', in A. Wiener and T. Diez (eds) *European Integration Theory*, Oxford: Oxford University Press.
Risse, T. (2005) 'Neofunctionalism, European identity, and the puzzles of European integration', *Journal of European Public Policy*, 12(2): 291–309.
Rosamond, B. (2000) *Theories of European Integration*, Basingstoke: Palgrave MacMillan.
Ruggie, J. (1982) 'International Regimes, Transactions, and Changes: Embedded Liberalism in the Postwar Economic Order', *International Organization*, 36(2): 379–415.
Ruggie, J. (1993) 'Territoriality and Beyond: Problematizing Modernity in International Relations', *International Organization*, 47(1): 139–74.
Sabatier, P. (1988) 'An Advocacy Coalition Framework of Policy Change and the Role of Policy-Oriented Learning Therein', *Policy Sciences*, 21: 129–68.
Sabatier, P. and Jenkins-Smith, H. (1999) 'The Advocacy Coalition Framework: An Assessment', in P. Sabatier (ed.) *Theories of the Policy Process*, Boulder: Westview Press.
Sandholtz, W. (1993) 'Choosing Union: Monetary Politics and Maastricht', *International Organization*, 47(1): 1–39.
Sandholtz, W. and Stone Sweet, A. (eds) (1998). *European Integration and Supranational Governance*, Oxford: Oxford University Press.
Sandholtz, W. and Zysman, J. (1989) '1992: Recasting the European Bargain', *World Politics*, 42(1): 95–128.
Santos, J. and Tsatsaronis, K. (2003) *The cost of barriers to entry: evidence from the market for corporate euro bond underwriting*, BIS Working Paper No. 134, BIS, September 2003, Basle.
Sapir, A. (2004) *An Agenda for a Growing Europe: The Sapir Report*, Oxford: Oxford University Press.

Saunderson, A. (1992) 'Financial powerhouse starts to take shape', *Euromoney*, Dec 1992: 74–7.
Sauvé, P. and Gillespie, J. (2000) 'Financial Services and the GATS 2000 Round', *Brookings-Wharton Papers on Financial Services*, 3: 423–65.
Scharpf, F. (1997a) *Games Real Actors Play: Actor-Centered Institutionalism in Policy Research*, Boulder: Westview Press.
Scharpf, F. (1997b) 'Introduction: the problem-solving capacity of multi-level governance', *Journal of European Public Policy*, 4(4): 520–38.
Scharpf, F. (1999) *Governing in Europe: Effective and Democratic?*, Oxford: Oxford University Press.
Scharpf, F. (2001) 'Notes toward a Theory of Multilevel Governing in Europe', *Scandinavian Political Studies*, 24(1): 1–26.
Schich, S. and Kikuchi, A. (2003) 'European Banking and Stock Market Integration', *OECD Financial Market Trends*, 84: 99–117.
Schmalz-Bruns, R. (1999) 'Deliberativer Supranationalialismus: Demokratisches Regieren jenseits des Nationalstaats', *Zeitschrift für Internationale Beziehungen*, 6(2): 185–244.
Schmidt, V. (1996) *From State to Market? The Transformation of French Business and Government*, Cambridge: Cambridge University Press.
Schmidt, V. (2002) *The Futures of European Capitalism*, Oxford: Oxford University Press.
Schmidt, V. (2003) 'French capitalism transformed, yet still a third variety of capitalism', *Economy and Society*, 32(4): 526–54.
Schmidt, V. (2004) 'The European Union: Democratic Legitimacy in a Regional State?' *Journal of Common Market Studies*, 42(5): 975–97.
Schmitter, P. (1969) 'Three Neo-Functional Hypotheses about International Integration', *International Organization*, 23(1): 161–66.
Schmitter, P. (1970) 'A Revised Theory of Regional Integration', *International Organization*, 24(4): 836–68.
Schmitter, P. (1979) 'Still the Century of Corporatism?' *The Review of Politics*, 36(1): 85–131.
Schmitter, P. (2005) 'Ernst B. Haas and the legacy of neofunctionalism', *Journal of European Public Policy*, 12(2): 255–72.
Schmitter, P. and Streeck, W. (1981) *The Organization of Business Interests: Studying the Associative Action of Business in Advanced Societies*, WZB Discussion Paper, IIM/LPM 81–13, Berlin.
Schwartz, H. (2009) *Subprime Nation*, Ithaca: Cornell University Press.
Schwartz, R. (1996) 'Equity Trading II: Integration, Fragmentation, and the Quality of Markets', in B. Steil (ed.) *The European Equity Markets: The State of the Union and an Agenda for the Millennium*, London: Royal Institute of International Affairs.
Seabrooke, L. (2006) *The Social Sources of Financial Power. Domestic legitimacy and international financial orders*. Ithaca: Cornell University Press.
Securities Expert Group (2004) *Financial Services Action Plan: Progress and Prospects*, May 2004, Brussels.
Shaffer, B. (1995) 'Firm-level Responses to Government Regulation: Theoretical and Research Approaches', *Journal of Management*, 21(3): 495–514.
Shirreff, D. (1997) 'Naughty Germans', *Euromoney*,(336): 56.
Shirreff, D. (1999) 'Disgrace at the heart of Europe', *Euromoney*, October 1999: 75–8.
Simmons, B. (2001) 'The International Politics of Harmonization: The Case of Capital Market Regulation', *International Organization*, 55(3): 589–620.
Simmons, B. and Elkins, Z. (2004) 'The Globalization of Liberalization: Policy Diffusion in the International Political Economy', *American Political Science Review*, 98(1): 171–89.
Simonian, H. (1987) 'Frankfurt studies the options game', *Financial Times*, 10 June 1987.
Simonian, H. (1988a) 'Not Shattered, only Shaken', *Financial Times*, 13 July 1988.
Simonian, H. (1988b) 'Swiss Influence Plan For New Exchange', *Financial Times*, 13 July 1988.
Simonian, H. (1989a) 'Abolition Of Withholding Tax Agreed In Bonn', *Financial Times*, 26 April 1989.
Simonian, H. (1989b) 'Bundesbank in IOSCO row', *Financial Times*, 26 September 1989.
Simonian, H. (1989c) 'Deutsche Bank boss vilifies SE practices', *Financial Times*, 2 November 1989.
Singer, D. (2004) 'Capital Rules: The Domestic Politics of International Regulatory Harmonization', *International Organization*, 58(3): 531–65.
Skocpol, T. (1985) 'Bringing the State Back In: Strategies of Analysis in Current Research', in P. Evans, D. Rueschemeyer and T. Skocpol (eds) *Bringing the State Back In*, Cambridge:

Cambridge University Press.
Slager, A. (2004) *Banking across Borders*, Rotterdam: Erasmus Research Institute of Management.
Smith, A. (1937 [1776]) *An Enquiry into the Nature and Causes of the Wealth of Nations*, New York: Modern Library.
Smith, R. and Walter, I. (2003) *Global Banking*, Oxford: Oxford University Press.
Sobel, A. (1994) *Domestic Choices, International Markets: Dismantling National Barriers and Liberalizing Securities Markets*, Ann Arbor: University of Michigan Press.
Sobel, A. (1999) *State Institutions, Private Incentives, Global Capital*, Ann Arbor: University of Michigan Press.
Soros, G. (2008) *The New Paradigm for Financial Markets. The Credit Crisis of 2008 and What it Means*, New York: Public Affairs.
Steil, B. (1993) *Competition, Integration and Regulation in EC Capital Markets*, Royal Institute of International Affairs, London.
Steil, B. (1998) *Regional Financial Market Integration: Learning from the European Experience*, Royal Institute of International Affairs, London.
Steil, B. (2002) 'Changes in the Ownership and Governance of Securities Exchanges: Causes and Consequences', *Brookings-Wharton Papers on Financial Services*, 5: 61–82.
Stigler, G. (1971) 'The Theory of Economic Regulation', *Bell Journal of Economics*, 2(1): 113–21.
Stone Sweet, A. and Sandholtz, W. (1998) 'Integration, Supranational Governance, and the Institutionalization of the European Polity', in W. Sandholtz and A. Stone Sweet (eds) *European Integration and Supranational Governance*, Oxford: Oxford University Press.
Story, J. (1997) 'Globalisation, the European Union and German Financial Reform: The Political Economy of "Finanzplatz Deutschland"', in G. Underhill (ed.) *The New World Order in International Finance*, Houndmills: MacMillan.
Story, J. and Walter, I. (1997) *The Political Economy of Financial Integration in Europe: The Battle of the Systems*, Cambridge MA: MIT Press.
Strange, S. (1994 [1988]) *States and Markets*, London: Pinter.
Strange, S. (1996) *The Retreat of the State*, Cambridge: Cambridge University Press.
Strange, S. (1998) *Mad Money*, Manchester: Manchester University Press.
Streeck, W. and Schmitter, P. (1991) 'From National Corporatism to Transnational Pluralism: Organized Interests in the Single European Market', *Politics and Society*, 19(2): 133–64.
Swank, D. (2002) *Global Capital, Political Institutions, and Policy Change in Developed Welfare States*, Cambridge: Cambridge University Press.
Tett, G. (2007) 'Dark pools attract investors', *Financial Times*, 9 February 2007.
The Banker (1988a) 'Can London really compete?', November 1988.
The Banker (1988b) 'French tentacles', November 1988.
The Banker (1991) 'Europe: Many a slip...', December 1991.
The Banker (2004) 'Rating Agencies – EU's Plan to Regulate is Fiercely Opposed', December 2004.
The Economist (1988) 'The barriers within', 9 July 1988.
The Economist (1999) 'No SEC's, please, we're European', 19 August 1999.
The Economist (2000) 'Europe's regulatory muddles', 8 June 2000.
The Giovannini Group (2001) *Cross-Border Clearing and Settlement Arrangements in the European Union (Giovannini Report)*, November 2001, Brussels.
Thompson, P. (1997) 'The Pyrrhic Victory of Gentlemanly Capitalism: The Financial Elite of the City of London, 1945–90', *Journal of Contemporary History*, 32(3): 283–304.
Thomson, R. (1987) 'Merchant banks shake up', *The Times*, 18 December 1987.
Tiebout, C. (1956) 'A Pure Theory of Local Expenditures', *Journal of Political Economy*, 64(5): 416–24.
Trachtman, J. (2001) 'Regulatory Competition and Regulatory Jurisdiction in International Securities Regulation', in D. Esty and D. Geradin (eds) *Regulatory Competition and Economic Integration*, Oxford: Oxford University Press.
True, J., Jones, B. and Baumgartner, F. (1999) 'Punctuated Equilibrium Theory: Explaining Stability and Change in American Policy Making', in P. Sabatier (ed.) *Theories of the Policy Process*, Boulder: Westview Press.

Tsoukalis, L. (1997) *The New European Economy Revisited*, Oxford: Oxford University Press.
Underhill, G. (1993) 'Negotiating financial openness: the Uruguay round and trade in financial services', in P. Cerny (ed.) *Finance and World Politics: Markets, Regimes and States in the Post-hegemonic Era*, Aldershot: Edward Elgar.
Underhill, G. (1997) 'The Making of the European Financial Area: Global Market Integration and the EU Single Market for Financial Services', in G. Underhill (ed.) *The New World Order in International Finance*, Basingstoke: MacMillan.
Underhill, G. (1998) *Industrial Crisis and the Open Economy: Politics, Global Trade and the Textile Industry in the Advanced Economies*, Houndmills: MacMillan.
Underhill, G. (2000) 'State, market, and global political economy: genealogy of an (inter-?) discipline', *International Affairs*, 76(4): 805–24.
Underhill, G. (2001) *States, Markets, and Governance*, Amsterdam: Vossiuspers.
Underhill, G. (2003) 'States, markets and governance for emerging market economies: private interests, the public good and the legitimacy of the development process', *International Affairs*, 79(4): 755–81.
Underhill, G. (2006) 'Conceptualizing the Changing Global Order', in R. Stubbs and G. Underhill (eds) *Political Economy and the Changing Global Order*, Oxford: Oxford University Press.
Underhill, G. (2007) *Markets, Institutions, and Transaction Costs: the Endogeneity of Governance*, Working paper 25, ESRC World Economy and Finance research programme, London.
Underhill, G. and Zhang, X. (2005) 'The Changing State-Market Condominium in East Asia: Rethinking the Political Underpinnings of Development', *New Political Economy*, 10(1): 1–24.
Urry, M. (1985) 'New advisory body for issuers seeks to add order to the market', *Financial Times*, 19 February 1985.
Usher, J. (2000) *The Law of Money and Financial Services in the European Community*, Oxford: Oxford University Press.
van Apeldoorn, B. (2002) *Transnational Capitalism and the Struggle over European Integration*, London: Routledge.
van Schendelen, R. (2006) *Machiavelli in Brussels. The Art of Lobbying the EU*, Amsterdam: Amsterdam University Press.
Viermetz, K. (2006) 'No need to tinker with the integrated clearing model', *Financial Times*, 13 April 2006.
Vietor, R. (1987) 'Regulation-Defined Financial Markets: Fragmentation and Integration in Financial Services', in S. L. I. Hayes (ed.) *Wall Street and Regulation*, Boston: Harvard Business School Press.
Vitols, S. (2003) 'From Banks to Markets: The Political Economy of Liberalization of the German and Japanese Financial Systems', in K. Yamamura and W. Streeck (eds) *The End of Diversity? Prospects for German and Japanese Capitalism*, Ithaca: Cornell University Press.
Vitols, S. (2004) *Changes in Germany's Bank-Based Financial System: A Varieties of Capitalism Perspective*, Discussion Paper SP II 2004–04, Wissenschaftszentrum Berlin für Sozialforschung, Berlin.
Vittas, D. (ed.) (1992). *Financial Regulation. Changing the Rules of the Game*, Washington DC: The World Bank.
Vogel, D. (1995) *Trading Up. Consumer and Environmental Regulation in a Global Economy*, Cambridge MA: Harvard University Press.
Vogel, S. (1996) *Freer Markets, More Rules: Regulatory Reform in Advanced Industrial Countries*, Ithaca: Cornell University Press.
Walker, D. (2001) 'Europe's capital market has chance for prompt progress', *Financial Times*, 23 March 2001.
Wall Street Journal (1990) 'Bundesbank to Let Banks Underwrite Non-Mark Debt', *Wall Street Journal*, 8 January 1990.
Waller, D. (1990) 'Warburg wins soft-commission clearance', *Financial Times*, 16 August 1990.
Walter, I. (1988) *Global Competition in Financial Services*, Cambridge MA: American Enterprise Institute/Ballinger.
Walter, I. and Smith, R. (1989) *Investment Banking in Europe. Restructuring for the 1990s*, Cambridge MA: Basil Blackwell.

Walter, I. and Smith, R. (2000) *High Finance in the Euro-Zone: Competing in the New European Capital Market*, Harlow: Pearson Education.
Walter, N. (1989) 'Implications of EC Financial Integration', *Business Economics*, 24(4): 18–23.
Waters, R. (1989a) 'German action threatens capital adequacy accord', *Financial Times*, 21 September 1989.
Waters, R. (1989b) 'Germans back down on capital plans', *Financial Times*, 22 September 1989.
Waters, R. (1990) 'Drexel's fall may spur the talking-shop', *Financial Times*, 2 July 1990.
Waters, R. (1991a) 'Securities firms look across borders', *Financial Times*, 7 January 1991.
Waters, R. (1991b) 'BT share issue prepares ground for stabilisation', *Financial Times*, 14 November 1991.
Waters, R. (1992a) 'Capital questions for EC investment', *Financial Times*, 22 May 1992.
Waters, R. (1992b) 'International draft rules on capital delayed', *Financial Times*, 12 August 1992.
Waters, R. (1992c) 'Securities industry capital rules move closer', *Financial Times*, 30 January 1992.
Waters, R. (1992d) 'Securities regulators close to capital rules', *Financial Times*, 27 January 1992.
Waters, R. (1993) 'IOSCO drops common capital rules plan', *Financial Times*, 11 February 1993.
Waters, R. and Kellaway, L. (1990) 'Europe's investors seek a Cad with sense of fair play', *Financial Times*, 9 February 1990.
Weber, K. and Hallerberg, M. (2001) 'Explaining variation in institutional integration in the European Union: why firms may prefer European solutions', *Journal of European Public Policy*, 8(2): 171–91.
Weiss, L. (ed.) (2003). *States in the Global Economy: Bringing Domestic Institutions back in*, Cambridge: Cambridge University Press.
Wendt, A. (1987) 'The Agent-Structure Problem in International Relations Theory', *International Organization*, 41(3): 335–70.
Wessels, W. (1998) 'Comitology: fusion in action. Politico-administrative trends in the EU system', *Journal of European Public Policy*, 5(2): 209–34.
Wiener, A. and Diez, T. (eds) (2004). *European Integration Theory*, Oxford: Oxford University Press.
Williamson, J. and Mahar, M. (1998) *A Survey of Financial Liberalization*, Princeton: Princeton University, Department of Economics.
Woll, C. (2008) *Firm Interests. How Governments Shape Business Lobbying on Global Trade*, Ithaca: Cornell University Press.
Wolman, C. (1986) 'Eurosecurities Fraud "Ignored"', *Financial Times*, 14 July 1986.
Wood, D. (2005) *Governing Global Banking. The Basel Committee and the Politics of Financial Globalisation*, Aldershot: Ashgate.
World Trade Organization (1997) *Opening Markets in Financial Services and the Role of the GATS*, Geneva.
Yamamura, K. and Streeck, W. (eds) (2003). *The End of Diversity? Prospects for German and Japanese Capitalism*, Ithaca: Cornell University Press.
Young, A. and Wallace, H. (2000) 'The Single Market', in H. Wallace and W. Wallace (eds) *Policy Making in the European Union*, Oxford: Oxford University Press.
Zito, A. (2001) 'Epistemic Communities, European Union governance and the Public Voice', *Science and Public Policy*, 28(6): 465–76.
Zysman, J. (1983) *Governments, Markets, and Growth*, Ithaca: Cornell University Press.

LIST OF INTERVIEWS

Interview number	Date	Place	Affiliation/background of respondent
211105.a	21 November 2005	The Hague	Stock exchange official
211105.b	21 November 2005	Brussels	European investment bank
221105	22 November 2005	Brussels	European trade association
231105	23 November 2005	Brussels	European investment bank
011205	1 December 2005	Brussels	National representative office to the EU
021205.a	2 December 2005	Brussels	Brussels lobbyist
021205.b	2 December 2005	Brussels	European trade association
061205	6 December 2005	Brussels	European trade association
071205.a	7 December 2005	Brussels	Member of the European Parliament
071205.b	7 December 2005	Brussels	National representative office to the EU
91205	9 December 2005	Brussels	European Commission official
141205	14 December 2005	Brussels	European Commission official
120106.a	12 January 2006	Brussels	National representative office to the EU
120106.b	12 January 2006	Brussels	Member of the European Parliament
220206	22 February 2006	London	European trade association
270206	27 February 2006	London	Global trade association
130306	13 March 2006	London	Stock exchange official
140306	14 March 2006	London	British trade association
160306.a	16 March 2006	London	Regulatory authority
160306.b	16 March 2006	London	European investment bank
210306	21 March 2006	London	Former FESCO assistant
230306.a	23 March 2006	London	Former member 'Lamfalussy Committee'
230306.b	23 March 2006	London	British trade association
300306	30 March 2006	London	European trade association

Interview number	Date	Place	Affiliation/background of respondent
030406	3 April 2006	London	Former European Commission official
050406	5 April 2006	London	US investment bank
070406	7 April 2006	London	US investment bank
020506	2 May 2006	Bonn	Regulatory authority
030506	3 May 2006	Frankfurt	Regulatory authority
160506.a	16 May 2006	Paris	European investment bank
160506.b	16 May 2006	Paris	CESR representative
180506.a	18 May 2006	Paris	European investment bank
180506.b	18 May 2006	Paris	French trade association
190506	19 May 2006	Paris	Regulatory authority
220506	22 May 2006	Berlin	German trade association
240506.a	24 May 2006	Berlin	German government
240506.b	24 May 2006	Berlin	Former stock exchange official
240506.c	24 May 2006	Berlin	Stock exchange official
131206	13 December 2006	Brussels	European Commission official

index

Abbott, K. 27
Abdelal, R. 19
Abell, P. 72
Abiad, A. 146
ABN AMRO 1, 73, 78, 79, 90, 97, 98, 99, 102, 103, 105, 117, 127, 153
Adler, E. 4
Akerlof, G. 20
Alex Brown 78
Allen, F. 23, 35
Amable, B. 23
American Securities Industry & Financial Markets Association 148
Amsterdam Stock Exchange 33, 90, 117
Amsterdam Treaty 132
Andrews, D. 18
Arbeitskreis der deutschen Wertpapierbörsen 39
Ashall, P. 62, 63
Asmussen, J. 99
Augar, P. 1, 19, 45, 48, 58, 78, 80, 101, 133

Bach, D. 5, 59, 148
banks, European 144, 148-9
　institutional power of 23
　internationalisation of 80-8
　　interest margins and 81-5
　investment 71, 74-8, 133, 136, 137
　　CESR involvement 129-30
　market concentration and 72-3, 77
　2007 global crisis and 146
　privatisation of 41
　public trust of 150
　strategy formulation of 26, 70, 72, 94
　　identification of 70
　see also capital market regulation; names of individual banks; under individual countries
Bank of England 45, 47, 96, 101
Bank of New York 139

Bankers Trust 79
Banque de France 138
Barclays Bank 47, 52, 73, 80, 86, 96, 98-9, 117
Barnett, M. 8, 23
Basle Capital Accord 57
Basle Committee on Banking Supervision (BCBS) 57, 59, 65
Belaisch, A. 77, 81
Belgium, financial system of 34, 63
　lobbyists 98
Berger, A. 81, 83, 84
Berger, S. 18
Bergström, C. F. 103, 116
Bhagwati, J. 71 n.24
Bieling, H.-J. 17, 93
'Big Bang' (1986) 42, 46, 47, 48, 49, 52, 58, 80
Bindemann, K. 33, 58, 85, 107
Bishop, G. 103
BNP (Banque National de Paris, later BNP Paribas) 42, 79, 129, 139, 140, 141
Bolkestein, F. 119
Boot. A. 83, 84
Borsa Italiana 90, 135, 136
Bouwen, P. 101
Brady, S. 37, 78, 97
Braithwaite, J. 6, 24, 88, 134
Bream, R. 79, 86
Bretton Woods 29, 41
Breuer, R. 89, 91, 112, 114
British Bankers Association (BBA) 46, 101, 118
British Merchant Banking and Securities Houses Association (BMBA) 48, 63, 101, 102
Brittan, L. 62
Brown, P. 2, 51, 59, 62
Brown-Humes, C. 118
Burn, G. 47, 58
Busch, M. 27
Bush, J. 60
Büthe, T. 27

Cabral, I. 73, 84, *156*
Cafruny, A. 17
Caisse des Depots et Consignations 40 n.4

Caisses d'Epargne 41
Campbell, K. 37, 38
Caparrós Peuble, A. 99, 101, 103, 111, 119, 127
capital adequacy 60-1, 65
Capital Adequacy Directive (CAD) 51, 52, 59, 60, 62, 64, 65-6, 68, 110, 127
  'trading book' and 66
capital market regulation 34, 139, 143, 151
  clearing and settlement (C&S) 139
  post-trade services 139
  see also Lamfalussy process
capital mobility 5-6, 18, 19, 41, 57, 146
Capital Movements Directive 56
capitalism, 'managed' 35
capture theory see 'regulatory capture'
Casey, J.-P. 73, 84, 85
Cecchini, P. 55
Cecchini Report 55, 67
central counterparties (CCPs) 139
central securities depositories (CSDs) 139
Cerny, P. 10, 13, 19, 23, 24, 29, 31, 40, 144, 146
Chavagneux, C. 13
Christiansen, T. 13
Citibank 97, 98, 99
Citigroup 139
Clarke, M. 6, 24
Clearstream 139, 140
Clift, B. 75, 137
Club-Med 57
Coen, D. 15
Coleman, W. 23, 24, 35, 40, 41, 42, 43, 44, 80
collateralised debt obligations 84
Colvill, L. 32, 86
Commerzbank 38, 79
Commission des Operations de Bourse (COB) 43, 110-11
Committee of European Banking Supervisors (CEBS) 129
Committee of European Securities Regulators (CESR) 109, 117, 119, 121-3, 129-31, 141, 148, 150
  Himalaya report (2004) 122
  mediation mechanism of 122
Committee of Wise Men 2001 113, 114, 115, 116, 118
  'comitology-plus' approach of 116
competition politics, market governance and 7, 8, 13, 25-30, 51, 52, 60, 123, 139, 142, 146-7
  structuration in 69
conduct-of-business-rules (CBRs) 62, 97
Conseil de Bourses de Valeur (CBV) 43
coordinated market economies 137
corporate bonds 77, 84, 85
Cowles, M. G. 27, 54, 126
Cox, P. 139
Cox, R. 10
Crédit Agricole 143
Crédit Commercial de France (CCF) 44
Crédit Lyonnais 40 n.4, 79, 80
credit rating agencies 131, 142, 151
Credit Suisse 80, 147
Credit Suisse First Boston (CSFB) 80, 90
Crooks, E. 115
Crouch, C. 22, 23, 29, 113
Culpepper, P. 137
custody services 139
Cybo-Ottone, A. 20, 91

D'Alessio, N. 36
Danthine, J.-P. 77, 81
Davies, H. 38, 113, 115
Dawkins, W. 44
de Haan, L. 81
de Larosière, J.
de Vries, J. 78
Deeg, R. 22, 23, 36, 75
Dehousse, R. 116, 121
Delors, J, 40 n.4, 102
Demarigny, F. 86, 131
derivatives trading 38, 73 n.28, 75, 84, 91, 101, 107, 127, 148, 149
Deutsche Bank 37, 38, 62 n.18, 52, 63, 73, 78, 79, 80, 81, 89, 91, 97, 98, 99, 105, 112, 117, 147
Deutsche Börse 75, 87, 91, 135-6, 139, 140
Deutsche Girozentrale 38
Deutsche Terminbörse (DTB) 38

Diez, T. 3, 13
Dinan, D. 14, 54
dot com crash 149
Drahos, P. 6, 24, 88, 134
Dresdner Bank 38, 79
Duménil, G. 74
Duvall, R. 8, 23

EASDAQ 91
Echikson, W. 115
ECOFIN 66, 105, 108, 114, 115, 141
economies of scale 20, 54, 55, 83
Egan, M. 52, 55, 57
Eichengreen, B. 29
Eising, R. 14, 101
Elkins, Z. 5
employment 9, 21, 33, 34, 46, 54, 151, 152
  UK and 33, 46
encadrement du credit 41
engrenage 123
equity markets 33, 69, 89
  acquisitions of listed companies 33
Esty, D. 18
euro 88, 107
Eurobond 48, 77
Euroclear 139-40
EuroFi 100
Euromarkets 35, 45, 47, 48
Euronext 90, 91, 122, 135, 139, 140, 147
European Association of Co-operative Banks 100
European Banking Federation (EBF) 98, 99, 101, 102, 118, 127, 128, 137, 138
European Banking Industry Committee (EBIC) 129
European Central Bank 40 n.4, 107, 114
European Commission 51, 53, 101, 136
  advisory groups to 131
  clearing and settlement issues and 140
  comitology procedures 119
  financial structures 1991 32
  Forum Groups 108, 134, 140
  lobbying in 130-2
  Market Abuse Directive (2001) 119
  Prospectus Directive (2001) 119, 128
  single market, role in 53-4, 104, 126, 145
  transparency issues- pre and post trade 135, 136, 137, 138
European Council 93, 105
  Cologne Council (1999) 105, 106
  Lisbon Council (2000) 108
  Stockholm Council (2001) 118
  Vienna Council (1998) 105
European Court of Justice (ECJ) 117
European Integration 3, 4, 7, 13-14, 17, 54, 59, 67, 142, 145
European Parliament 116, 118, 119-20, 129, 130, 137
  'inter-group' on financial services 119
  MEP's and lobbying 132
  role of 132
  'sunset-clause' 120
European Parliamentary Financial Services Forum (EPFSF) 119
European Payment Council 129
European Round Table of Industrialists (ERT) 54
European Savings Bank Group 100
European Securities Committee (ESC) 109, 116-17, 120-1, 150
European Securities Forum (ESF) 129, 140-1
European Securities Market Expert Group (ESME) 131
European Union, capital market governance
  debt issues 84
  foreign equity turnover 33, 34
  global imbalances and 148
  High-Level Group on Financial Supervision 148
  insider politics and 150
  internet and technological changes 143
  market integration 143
    business strategies of firms 70, 143
    financial liberalisation and 146
    measurement of 71
  pan-European regulator initiative 114
  Single European Payments Area 101
  single market project 52-6, 94, 145, 151

mutual recognition and 94
regulatory harmonisation and 94, 105, 130
state-market condominiums 49
structuration and 143-4
supranationalisation and 3, 7, 8, 13, 16, 18, 29, 69, 92, 121, 123, 126, 132, 141, 145, 149, 150, 151-3
'competition politics' and 7, 8, 13
financial crisis of 2007 141
normative implications of 151
supervisory fragmentation 151
US-EU Coalition for Financial Regulation (2007) 148
European Venture Capital Association 54
Evans, G. 37

Fabius, L. 114-15
Farrell, H. 22, 29, 113
FBF 101
Federal Bond Consortium 37
Federation of European Securities Commissions (FESCO) 107, 110-11, 117, 127
as an epistemic community 111
Federation of European Securities Exchanges (FESE) 114, 117, 123, 135, 136
Feld, W. 4, 15
Filipovic, M. 46, 48, 61, 62, 63, 64, 101
Financial Services Action Plan (FSAP) 93, 103, 104, 105-9, 111-12, 113
Financial Services Authority (FSA) 113-14, 121, 148, 150
Financial Services Policy Group (FSPG) 105, 108
Financial Services Strategy Review Group (FSSRG)103
First Banking Coordination Directive (1977) 53
Fisher, A. 38, 53, 78
Flier, B. 26
Fligstein, N. 10, 26, 30, 39, 54, 69, 91, 101, 144, 147
floating rate notes 36
France, financial system of 32, 76, 137, 144
agents de change 40, 42
banking industry in 40-3, 79-80, 82, 100, 133, 137, 138, 140, 141
ISD's and 86
sociétés de bourse 43
state-led capitalism in 40-4
stock markets 75, 133, 140
Trésor, the 40, 42, 138, 140
Franke, G. 36
Frankfurt stock exchange 35, 89, 91
Frieden, J. 29
Froud, J. 26, 70

G20 summit (2009) 150
Gadanis, S. 30
Gale, D. 23, 35
Gamble, A. 148
Gapper, J. 91
Gardener, E. 32, 34, 47 n.8
Garrett, G. 17, 18
George, A. 11
Geradin, D. 18
Germany, financial system of 32, 76, 78-9, 86-7, 137, 144
banking and 78-9, 82, 133, 140
ISD implementation in 86
Bundesaufsichtsamt für den Wertpapierhandel (BaWe) 87
Bundesverband der Deutschen Banken 101
Bundesbank 35-7, 38, 61
Certificates of Deposit (CDs) 36-7
monetary policy of 35-40
capital gains tax 36
Deutschland AG 36
Hausbanks 35
industrial policy 35
'managed capitalism' in 35-40
see also Deutsche Bank
Gertler, M. 20
Giddens, A. 7, 13
Gill, S. 18
Gillespie, J. 5
Giovanni Group, The 139
Gjersem, C. 71 n,23
globalisation, market 11, 29, 49, 146
capital mobility and 18, 146
EU effect on 3
Glyn, A. 3, 23, 137

Goldberg, L. 83, 139
Goldman Sachs 73, 79, 86, 98, 99, 117, 149
Goldstein, L. 20
Goodhart, C. 6, 20
Gottwald, J.-C. vi, 16, 93, 94, 103, 104, 105
Greenwood, J. 15
Grilli, V. 35, 56
Groom, B. 118
Grossman, E. 15

Haas, E. 4, 13, 14, 121, 145
Haas, P. 23, 111
Haggard, S. 14
Hall, P. 10, 23, 40, 137
Hancher, L. 24
Hardy, D. 26
Hasenclever, A. 3, 14, 19
Hausbanks 35
Hay, C. 16, 23
hedge funds 142
Helleiner, E. 19, 47
historical institutionalism 22
Hitt, M. 26
Hobson, J. 13
Hoffman, S. 3, 13, 120
Holland, C. 20
Hong Kong 74, 79

Inclan, C. 5
Indosuez 79
ING 52, 97
intergovernmentalism, liberal 14, 67, 145
International Capital Market Association (ICMA) 101
International Organisation of Securities Commissions (IOSCO) 59, 60, 61, 62, 64, 65, 107
International Primary Market Association (IPMA) 48, 128
International Swaps and Derivatives Association (ISDA) 101, 127
Investment Services Directive (ISD) 51, 52, 62-5, 66-7, 85, 86, 93, 96-7, 110, 125, 134
  Article 11 96, 111
  'concentration principle' and 63
  home country supervision and 63
  implementation, critique of 97
  mutual recognition approach and 66
  reform of 106-9
  remote access to securities exchanges and 85, 89
  'single passports' 67
issuers 84, 98
Italy 57, 63, 67, 73
  banking 78, 80
  non-government securities 32
  SIMS law 86
  stock exchanges in 90, 135, 140
  see also Borsa Italiana

Jabko, N. 93, 98, 103, 110, 133, 134
Jachtenfuchs, M. 14
Jackson, H. 19
Japan 32, 54, 59, 146
  capital markets in 21, 146
  European 37, 78
Jayasuriya, K. 23, 35, 152
Jenkins, P. 79, 84
Jenkins-Smith, H. 24
Jervis, R. 16, 29
Joerges, C. 15
Jørgensen, E. 13
Josselin, D. 24
JP Morgan 139
Jupille, J. 16

Kapstein, E. 60, 111
Keohane, R. 3, 5, 14, 18, 20
Kikuchi, A. 90
Kleinwort Benson 79
Kohler-Koch, B. 14
Krasner, S. 3, 10, 14, 16, 19, 22, 29, 109, 144
Krätke, M. 13
Kraus, J. 79
Krippner, G. 151
Kroszner, R. 22, 25
Krugman, P. 27

Lalone, N. 23, 100, 140
Lamfalussy, A. 114
Lamfalussy process 109, 113-20, 122, 125, 129, 131, 133, 141, 143
  'Aerosol clause' 118

prudential supervision and 115
Landesbanken 79, 143
Lane, C. 23
Lannoo, K. 73, 84, 85
Lascelles, D. 47, 48
Laurence, H. 7, 18-19, 20, 33
Lazer, D. 18
LCH.Clearnet 139
Lebègue, D. 40 n.4, 118,
Lee, P. 59, 62, 64, 65
Lee, R. 6, 20, 88, 89, 91, 134, 135
Lehman Brothers 60
Lehmann, P.-J. 43
Lévy, D. 74
Leyshon, A. 55-6
liberalisation, financial 18-19, 146
Lindberg, L. 13
Lindblom, C. 144
lobbying, business 3, 9, 12, 15, 19, 22, 46, 80, 98-103, 105, 107, 111, 123, 125, 126-32, 135, 145
  Brussels offices 126-32
  Europeanisation of 129
  industry ties, formalisation of and 129
  MEP's and 132
London International Financial Futures and Options Exchange (LIFFE) 38, 135
London Investment Banking Association (LIBA) 48, 101, 102, 117, 127, 138, 145
London Stock Exchange (LSE) 35, 45, 46, 74, 133, 136, 139
  Deutsche Börse and 91
  Parkinson-Goodison agreement and 46
Loriaux, M. 41
Lütz, S. 38

Maastrict Treaty 51
McCahery, J. 66
McClelland, C. 78-9
McKeen-Edwards, H. 93
McKenzie, G. 16
McNamara, K. 16
Mahar, M. 5, 18, 35, 57, 87
Mara-Drita, I. 26, 54
Marché á Terme International d'Instruments Financiers (MATIF) 38, 42, 91
market functioning and efficiency 134, 146-7
  competition politics approach and 25-30, 146-7
Market in Financial Instruments Directive (MiFID) 93, 125, 128, 129, 133, 135, 136, 138, 141
  clearing and settlement issues and 140
  internalisation issue and 128, 134-5
  Lamfalussy process and 133
Mattli, W. 27, 94, 109, 147
merchant banks 45, 78, 80, 83
Merrill Lynch 73, 79, 85, 99, 112
Milbourn, T. 26, 83
Mijs, W. 99, 101, 103, 107, 111, 119, 127
Milner, H. 27
Mitterand, F. 40
Mody, A. 146
Mogg, J. 97, 99, 103, 104, 105, 108
  Mogg Commission 97, 108
Moir, C. 142
Molyneux, P. 32, 34, 47 n.8, 78
Monti, M. 104, 111
Moran, M. 46
Moravcsik, A. 14, 27, 52, 54, 67, 93, 145
Morgan, G, 23
Morgan Grenfell 78, 81, 159
Morgan Stanley 73, 79, 98, 99, 112, 117, 149
Morin, F. 75, 137
Morris, C. 148
Mosley. L. 18
Mügge, D. 20, 48, 142, 147, 150, 151, 152

Nabors, R. 19, 60
Nalebuff, B. 69
NASDAQ 17, 90, 91, 108, 147
neofunctionalism 14, 17, 18, 121, 123, 145
Netherlands, The, financial system of 77
  banking system 78
  stock market 33, 73, 77, 90, 97-8
  see also ABN AMRO; Amsterdam

Stock Exchange
Newman, A. 5, 59, 148
Neyer, J. 15, 17
Nicoll, S. 53, 58
Niemann, A. v, 4, 13, 14, 16, 17, 121, 123
Nordlinger, E. 16, 109
Norman, P. 115, 116, 118, 119
Nugent, N. 145

Oatley, T. 19, 60
Olson, M. 21
Osborn, A. 115
Overbeck, H. 36
Own Funds Directive 57

Padoa-Schioppa, T. 110-11
Pagano, M. 89, 90, 91
Paribas 41, 42, 79
    see also BNP Paribas
Paris Bourse 42
Partnoy, F. 20, 48, 81, 84
Pauly, L. 5, 18
Peters, G. 14, 22
Pierre, J. 14, 22
Pierson, P. 4, 16, 22, 93
Pollack, M. 14, 16, 93, 119, 145
Porter, T.
Posner, E. 5, 16, 17, 91, 93, 108, 148
Prada, M. 115
Prast, H. 81
privatisations 41, 42, 49, 75
Prodi, R. 136
Puchala, D. 25
Putnam, R. 2, 14

Quinn, D. 5, 146

Radice, H. 23
Randzio-Plath, C. 119
Rawsthorn, A. 44
regional integration theory 3, 4, 14, 147, 149
regulation, financial market 5, 23, 25, 44, 47
    capital 68, 122, 145
'regulatory capture' 20-1, 144
'regulatory competition' 7, 19, 43, 52
Rhinard, M. 121

Rhodes, R. 24
Ricol, R. 148
Riley, B. 48, 63
Risse, T. 15, 16, 123
Risse-Kappen, T. 14
Rosamond, B. 3, 13, 16, 23
Ruggie, J. 29, 71
Ryner, M. 17

Sabatier, P. 24, 39
Sandholtz, W. 14, 17, 18, 27, 52, 54, 94, 109
Santer, J. 108
    Commission 102, 108
Santos, J. 73
Sapir, A. 108
Saunderson, A. 39
Sauvé, P. 5
Scharpf, F. 3, 14, 16, 17, 27, 109, 123
Schich, S. 90
Schmalz-Bruns, R. 15
Schmidt, V. 3, 15, 23, 35, 40, 44, 100, 137, 152
Schmitter, P. 4, 13, 15, 16, 17, 23, 94, 109, 126
Schwartz, H. 89, 148
Seabrooke, L. 152
SEAQ International 43-4, 58, 63, 66, 89
Second Banking Coordinating Directive (2BCD) 51, 52, 56, 57, 58
Securities and Exchange Commission (SEC) 65, 147-8
securities exchanges 88, 91, 125
    cross-border European 91
    see also Federation of European Securities Exchanges (FESE)
S. G. Warburg 47, 48, 80, 156
Shaffer, B. 26
'shareholder value' 75, 83
Shirreff, D. 86, 87, 97, 98, 103, 104, 105, 108
Simmons, B. 5, 14, 19, 147
Simonian, H. 37, 38, 61, 62 n.18
Singer, D. 5, 19
Single European Payments Area (SEPA) 128
Skocpol, T. 22, 40 109, 144
Slager, A. 77, 78, 79, 82

Smith, A. iv, 25, 143, 144, 153
Smith, R. 20, 31, 32, 33, 34, 69, 73, 75, 83
Snidal, D. 27
Sobel, A. 7, 20, 21, 22, 25, 33, 42, 45, 46
Société Générale 41, 79
Solvency Ratio Directive 57
Soros, G. 150
Soskice, D. 10, 23, 40, 137
sovereign debtors 85
'state-market condominium' 10, 29, 49-50, 64, 144
State Street 141
Steil, B. 2, 33, 51, 62, 67, 89, 90, 91, 134
Stellinga, B. v. 142, 151
Stigler, G. 6, 7, 21, 22, 24, 26
stock exchanges 34
  'alternative trading systems' (ATS) 89
  clearing and settlement services (C&S) 139-40
  demutualisation of 88, 134, 146
  1990's market boom 74
  2007 global finance crisis 146
  see also names of individual exchanges e.g., London Stock Exchange (LSE)
Stone Sweet, A. 14, 17, 18, 94, 109
Story, J. 36, 39, 42, 51, 53, 57, 62, 66, 80, 115, 137
Strahan, P. 22, 26
Strange, S. 13, 31
strategic potential 83
strategies, business 26, 69, 70, 88, 149
Streeck, W. 23, 126
Streek, W. 23
structuration, market 10, 27-8, 30, 83, 85, 126, 143
  open-endedness of 30
  regulatory reforms and 85-8
supranational integration, theories of 145, 147
Swank, D. 18
Swiss Options and Futures Exchange (SOFFEX) 38
Switzerland 33, 61, *156*
  banking system 61, 77, 80
  securities market in 32

technological progress, financial markets and 20
Thatcher, M. 44, 58
Thomson, R. 48
Thrift, N. 55, 56
Tiebout, C. 18
Trachtman, J. 19
True, J. 29
Tsatsaronis, K. 73
Tsoukalis, L. 14, 55, 56
Turner, A. 150

UBS 80, 147
Underhill, G. v. 2, 5, 10, 13, 19, 24, 26, 29, 51, 57, 58, 60, 64, 144, 146-7
underwriters 48, 73
United Kingdom, financial system of 32, 76, 144
  Accepting Houses Committee (AHC) 45
  banking system in 80, 87-8, 133, 144
  capital markets 33
  City, the 33, 45, 58, 63, 77, 95-6, 136, 143
    American firms operating in 95-6
  Gower Report 47
  market capitalism in 44-9
  Office of Fair Trading (OFT) 46
  Parkinson-Goodison agreement 46, 48
  Securities and Futures Authority 62
  Securities and Investment Board (SIB) 47, 48, 62
  see also London Stock Exchange (LSE)
United States
  Commodities and Futures Trading Commission 148
  housing market 148
  investment banking and 73, 87, 137
    European operation of 95-6
    'value-added' products and 81
  New York Federal Reserve 37
  New York Stock Exchange 74, 147
  stock markets 73
  Union Bank of Switzerland (UBS) 80
Urry, M. 48

Usher, J. 66

van Apeldoorn, B. 14, 15, 17, 27, 52, 54
van Schendelen, R. 15
Viermetz, K. 140
Vietor, R. 25
Vitols, S. 26, 36, 75, 139
Vittas, D. 6
Vogel, D. 18, 44
Vogel, S. 6, 7, 19, 23, 31, 44, 46, 47, 146

Walker, D. 118
Wallace, H. 53, 54
Wall Street Journal 37
Waller, D. 48
Walter, I. 20, 31, 32, 33, 35, 36, 39, 42, 47, 51, 53, 57, 62, 66, 69, 73, 75, 80, 83, 115, 139, 160
Walter, N. 56
Waters, R. 48, 51, 59, 60, 61, 63, 65
Weber, K. 109
Weiss, L. 14
Wendt, A. 13
Wessels, W. 103
Wicks, N. 115
Wiener, A. 3, 13
Williamson, J. 5, 18, 35, 57, 87
Woll, C. 98
Wolman, C. 48
Wood, D. 57, 58
World Federation of Exchanges 71
World Trade Organisation (WTO) 5, 71 n.25
Wright, D. 102, 115

Young, A. 53, 54

Zentraler Kreditausschuss 39
zero coupon bonds 36
Zito, A. 23
Zysman, J. 23, 27, 35, 45, 52, 53, 54, 144

www.ingramcontent.com/pod-product-compliance
Lightning Source LLC
Chambersburg PA
CBHW071358290426
44108CB00014B/1593